Flowers That Kill

Flowers That Kill

COMMUNICATIVE OPACITY
IN POLITICAL SPACES

Emiko Ohnuki-Tierney

STANFORD UNIVERSITY PRESS
STANFORD, CALIFORNIA

Stanford University Press
Stanford, California

Printed in the United States of America on acid-free, archival-
quality paper

Library of Congress Cataloging-in-Publication Data

Ohnuki-Tierney, Emiko, author.
  Flowers that kill : communicative opacity in political spaces /
Emiko Ohnuki-Tierney.
      pages cm
  Includes bibliographical references and index.
  ISBN 978-0-8047-9410-7 (cloth : alk. paper)--
  ISBN 978-0-8047-9589-0 (pbk. : alk. paper)
  1. Symbolism in politics--Japan--History. 2. Symbolism in
politics--Europe--History. 3. Symbolism in communication--
Japan--History. 4. Symbolism in communication--Europe--
History. 5. Flowers--Symbolic aspects--Japan--History.
6. Flowers--Symbolic aspects--Europe--History. I. Title.
  JC347.J3O35 2015
  320.9401'4--dc23

                          2015011809

  ISBN 978-0-8047-9594-4 (electronic)

Typeset by Bruce Lundquist in 11/14 Adobe Garamond Pro

In memory of my parents,
Ohnuki Kōzaburō and Ohnuki Taka

Contents

Illustrations

Color plates follow page 46

Acknowledgments

This book has been in the making for a long time—for, in fact, my entire career as an anthropologist, from the days of my study of the Sakhalin Ainu and their hunting-gathering life to the most recent foray into World War II. This is a thorough reconceptualization of my previous ethnographic and historical work, in light of what I have learned, often slowly, from the changing emphases in anthropology and history. All along I have received insights, criticisms, suggestions, and warm encouragement from a great number of colleagues in various countries, whose generosity does not cease to amaze me.

This book, the result of such a long-term project, would not have been written if it were not for the generous support of the William F. Vilas Trust Fund of the University of Wisconsin, Madison, for which I would like to extend my deepest appreciation. My interest in communicative opacity started way back, when I was working on the Japanese monkey performance, during which different actors were reading different meanings of the monkey. I was overwhelmed by a most generous remark from Edmund Leach, who was a discussant at an American Ethnological Society meeting. In fact he was the first to articulate the concept of communicative opacity, or failure of communication, in his study of the *gumsa* and *gumlao* systems of the Kachins in highland Burma. Keith Basso, James Fernandez, Stanley Jeyaraja Tambiah, Terry Turner, Victor Turner, Valerio Valeri, and many others all extended warm encouragement to my fledging efforts, as did Clifford Geertz, who pushed me to engage in comparative work while I was at the Institute for Advanced Study at Princeton for a year at his invitation. I have been fortunate to receive encouragement and inspiration from scholars of different persuasions. Sidney Mintz has always been willing to share his professional "capital" as was Eric Wolf, who sent me postcards when he traveled, in one of them declaring his priority being tai chi over the American Anthropological Association meetings. Since the time we spent a year together at the Center for Advanced Study in Behavioral Sciences at Stanford, Peter Stansky has become my regular sounding board, and so has Henry Rosovsky, whose wisdom I have sought over many years since my year at Harvard. An appointment as Distinguished Chair of Modern Culture at the Kluge Center of the Library of Congress by Dr. James H. Billington, the Librarian, enabled me to have access to that treasure-house of books and archival material. His work on a long-term Russian cultural history, with the symbolism of the axe and the icon, became an inspiration for my own long-term cultural history, as did his explication of the limits of rational enlightenment. Even now, his discussion of synesthesia in the sung liturgy of the Eastern Church, together with his powerful baritone voice—with which he sang, only too briefly, a piece from *Boris Godunov*, his favorite—resonates. The work by Natalie Zemon Davis alerted me to the antiestablishment message carried by flowers, and roses, in particular, which led me to an understanding of the rose as the logo of the Socialist International. H. Mack Horton offered me crucial information and suggestions from his vast and meticulous knowledge of ancient Japanese culture and history. Special thanks are due Stanley Payne for suggesting an extraordinary title for the book, *Flowers That Kill*. Renée Fox and Jan Vansina have been advisers/critics of the direction I have taken in my work.

In the United Kingdom, Tim Ingold offered invaluable comments on my work, first as the editor of the *Journal of the Royal Anthropological Institute*, then with his invitation to be a Lord Simon Professor at the University of Manchester. I will not forget a kind invitation to give a lecture in the Social Anthropology Department, Cambridge University, arranged by Ernst Gellner, with whom I had the pleasure of feeding ducks together after our breakfast at his house. During my stay at idyllic Bellagio, I forged a lifelong collegiality with Sergio Bertelli, whose work opened my eyes to the medieval European "king's body."

My fortunate encounters with French scholars began when Professors Marc Augé and Francis Zimmermann welcomed me to the École des Hautes Études en Sciences Sociales several times. Pierre Bourdieu at the Collège de France listened intently to my plan for research in its inchoate state, which resulted in *Kamikaze, Cherry Blossoms, and Nationalisms*, the predecessor of this book. The central theme of this book is indebted to his *méconnaissance*. Most recently, L'Institut d'Études Advançées–Paris became my headquarters, with a most memorable stay in 2014 after it moved to l'Hôtel de Lauzun, a paradise for scholars. I was ecstatic to be in this beautiful seventeenth-century mansion where Charles Baudelaire, one of the most influential figures in my work, resided, leaving behind colorful legends. I thank the directors, Professor Alain Schnapp and Professor Gretty Mirdal, and Dr. Simon Luck. My delivery of two lectures in January 2014 at the Collège de France, arranged by Philippe Descola, helped me finalize Chapters One and Four of this book. Dr. Jean-Luc Lory, anthropologist and director at Maison Suger of the Fondation Maison des Sciences de l'Homme, always welcomed me and provided a scholarly environment I could rely on. My stays in France over all these years were made most enjoyable by the sustained friendship and collegiality of Marie-Thérèse Cerf, whose formidable knowledge of and voracious appetite for art and intellectual endeavors have been most stimulating.

In Japan, I am indebted to a large number of scholars and institutions. Let me first thank Prince Mikasa-no-miya Takahito Shinnō, a younger brother of Emperor Shōwa. He not only listened to my talk on rice in Japanese culture at the Japanese Academy of Science but also took me to Sutoraipuhausu Museum to watch a performance of *In the Forest, Under Cherries in Full Bloom* by Sakaguchi Ango. It gave me a flash of insight into the connection between cherry blossoms and madness, a vital element of the polyseme of the flower. For a number of dimensions of this book, I am profoundly grateful to Professors Irokawa Daikichi, Kasaya Kazuhiko, Kuramoto Kazuhiro, Miyake Hitoshi, Miyata Noboru, and Amino Yoshihiko, and to Professor Inoki Takenori, who extended to me a special invitation as director's guest at the International Research Center for Japanese Studies, where I learned from many experts in Japanese history.

Given the importance of publishing in one's academic career, I was unbelievably fortunate that two young editors found my work worthy of publication at a very early stage of my career: in the United States, Walter Lippincott, when he was a young editor at Cambridge University Press and eventually director of Princeton University Press; and in Japan, Ōtsuka Nobukazu, a young editor at Iwanami Publishing who became its director. The books they published formed the basis of this book. Without their open-minded generosity (I did not belong to any "power" group), I would not have been able to pursue my writing, which has become the central obsession in my life.

At an early stage of the preparation for this project, I received invaluable help from the following scholars who were then graduate students and now are successful academics: Professor Suzuki Keiko of Ritsumeikan University, Professor Erika Robb Larkins at the University of Oklahoma, and Professor Tajima Atsushi at the State University of New York, Geneseo. I thank Nancy McClements and Andy Spencer at the University of Wisconsin Memorial Library for their expert help. I should like to extend my deep appreciation for excellent editorial help from Leslie Kriesel, a co-sufferer during all these years when the manuscript went through many revisions. The two anonymous reviewers for the press offered exceptionally constructive critiques that were most helpful in the final revision.

The book publishing business is always very exhausting. I could not be more thankful for the support of Michelle Lipinski at Stanford University Press, who is generous, brilliant, and professional—a superb acquisitions editor indeed—and who made this process so much more pleasant than usual for me. Richard Gunde, a scholar of Chinese culture, did a superb job in editing the manuscript, with his scholarly insight coming through in his comments and suggestions.

While I was growing up in Japan, "girls" were all to be wise mothers and good wives. I am indebted to two of my teachers in my early school days for encouraging me to be otherwise. Mr. Fujita Akira at Kōnan Elementary School took us to see a film on Madame Curie, who inspired me so much that I told him that I would like to be a Mme Curie. Rather than laughing at me, he suggested that we begin a chemistry experiment every day after school to discover a way to produce artificial potato starch. Mr. Ishimura Iwao at Kōnan Girls' High School introduced us to Ralph Waldo Emerson's "Hitch your wagon to a star"—a motto taught to young men at higher schools and one that appears in the diary of Sasaki Hachirō, *tokkōtai* pilot. I have failed to follow the teaching in the motto but Mr. Ishimura's encouragement of my studies was invaluable at the school where sewing, cooking, child-rearing, and morality were required courses, with English and mathematics optional. We keep in touch via email.

The unconditional love of my parents shaped my life, providing me with a sense of security and warmth always available when I needed it. My father, Ohnuki Kōzaburō, fluent in five languages, taught me to appreciate every individual regardless of class or "racial/ethnic" background. Despite occasional questioning by the Japanese police, he remained friends with some of the local foreigners in Kobe, and helped them during the war, including two Americans from Guam who saved him during the 1923 Great Kantō Earthquake and were captured by the Japanese military and imprisoned in Kobe. My mother, Ohnuki Taka, made quilted clothes for them to survive the Kobe winter, which was much colder than in Guam. In this childhood environment, my sense of the Japanese and Japan was as a part of the world. My mother, raised in a wealthy household where she never cooked or cleaned, became a "tigress" during the war. During an air raid, when I was nearly shot at, my mother risked her life to find me. When wartime conditions became severe and food grew increasingly scarce, she managed to feed us, even swallowing her pride by begging from her former servants who had returned to their farms. Toward the end of the war, the pupils in our small elementary school were moved to a Zen temple in the mountains on the orders of the government so that the adults would be free to fight the fires caused by the continuous aerial bombardment. Despite the long and arduous trip, my mother came every weekend, carrying a huge backpack full of food; the school could feed us only a handful of beans and literally a few grains of rice in a bowl of hot water—we chanted a sutra we invented to express how hungry we were.

Much later in life and after my college years in Tokyo, I came to the United States, not realizing that I would not be there to take care of my parents in their advanced age, when they needed me most. I will always remember them with profound love and respect.

I must also thank Alan Ohnuki Tierney, a historian at heart, whose sustained thoughtfulness has provided me with the very best environment for concentration on research and writing at home. R. Kenji Tierney has been the very best colleague one can wish for and his vast knowledge has always stimulated me and broadened my vista. I thank them deeply.

A Note to the Reader

Following the Japanese practice, the family name is written first, followed by the given name.

Flowers That Kill

Introduction

*Opacity, Misrecognition, and Other Complexities
of Symbolic Communication*

Even Marxist student soldiers who were forced to become pilots for the special attack force (kamikaze) were utterly unaware that the single pink cherry
blossom painted on the side of the airplane for their final flight represented,
not the celebration of life, but their own life sacrificed for a country they
deemed to have been corrupted by its imperial ambitions, militarism, capitalism, and egotism. When Hitler's propaganda machinery foregrounded the
Führer receiving roses from women and children, he was portrayed as the
benevolent father to all Germans without a hint of the utterly destructive
power he wielded. By leading people to their own deaths and those of countless others, these flowers did, after all, kill, albeit indirectly and in somewhat
different ways.

The explanation for this phenomenon lies in our unawareness of communicative opacity, which can lead people to unknowingly cooperate
in their own subjugation and/or march to their own destruction in war,
a denouement that people realize when it is too late, as happened to the
Japanese. Even in ordinary circumstances, communicative opacity plays an
important yet often highly subtle role when marginalized social groups are
not represented in a symbol of the collective self and yet are unaware of
this, being co-opted by the symbolic meaning and power of the dominant
group within society.[1] This book represents my effort to seek possible factors
that contribute to communicative opacity and to point out the urgency of
considering communicative opacity an important political issue—including
when people's lives are on the line.

Communication is of fundamental importance not only for the survival of a social group but also for the daily interactions among social animals, especially humans. Communication is the bedrock of any society and is synonymous with culture (Hall ([1966] 1969; Leach 1976).

Although its difficulties and complexities have been a central and perennial interest of scholars of many disciplines, a major assumption has been that human communication is possible if only we try hard enough. A detailed discussion of Enlightenment rationality and political rationality is beyond the scope of this book, but let me choose just one representative scholar—Jürgen Habermas, who advocated "communicative rationality," which enables "coordination" among individuals with different goals: "Language is a medium of communication that serves understanding, whereas actors, in coming to an understanding with one another so as to coordinate their actions, pursue their own particular aims" (Habermas 1984: 101). His communicative action takes place when "*all* participants harmonize their individual plans of action with one another and thus pursue their illocutionary aims *without reservation*" (Habermas 1984: 294, italics in the original). In his view, language and the illocutionary act, in particular, lead to "Reason and the Rationalization of Society"—the subtitle of volume one of *The Theory of Communicative Action* (1984). His model and those who follow political rationality in general do not leave room for communicative opacity.

Without altogether negating the importance of communication and language, this book aims to explore *communicative opacity*—an absence of communication or mutual understanding due to individuals in a given social/historical context drawing different meanings from the same symbol, or, more often, due to an absence of articulation in their minds of the meaning they are drawing. This leads to the unawareness of the absence of communication among the social actors involved.

Let me elaborate on the two examples presented at the beginning of this chapter: two historical developments that show how cherry blossoms and roses had undergone significant and yet imperceptible transformations under authoritarian regimes. Although cherry blossoms (Chapter One) stood for life, women's reproductive power, agrarian productive power, and other sunny meanings, one of this flower's symbolic meanings—pathos over the brevity of life—was transformed into a military dictum: "Thou shalt fall like beautiful cherry petals after a short life for the emperor-cum-Japan." It became the Japanese state's major trope of propaganda during its quest for imperial power, which began at the end of the nineteenth century.[2] The motto had been intensively and extensively used during the Russo-Japanese War and the two Sino-Japanese wars, culminating in the Second World War, at the very end of which the *tokkōtai* (kamikaze operation) was instituted. None of the pilots was aware that a pink cherry blossom, painted on the side of each *tokkōtai* plane, represented their sacrificed life. The pilots were to fall, like beautiful cherry petals, in order to protect the beautiful land of cherry blossoms. Although falling petals had long been associated with death, it was not as sacrifice for the emperor-cum-Japan (Ohnuki-Tierney 2002a; 2006a).

Why did Japanese student soldiers fail to notice that the meaning of the flower had changed under the military government? They were cosmopolitan intellectuals who read widely in Latin, German, and French as well as Japanese and Chinese, and were liberals or even radicals (Ohnuki-Tierney 2002a; 2006a). This transformation was hardly recognized by anyone else as well—people at home, soldiers at the front, even scholars of liberal persuasion. Why?

A similar question may be posed about roses, which in many cultures in Europe, the Middle East, and elsewhere traditionally stood for interpersonal love ("Love is like a red red rose") and later came to mean solidarity among workers, as expressed through the emblem of the Socialist International ("Bread and Roses") (Chapter Two). During the authoritarian era in twentieth-century Europe, the flower became ubiquitous in propaganda photos of Lenin, Stalin, and Hitler, all of whom received roses from women and children. Each of these dictators sent countless people to their death. Did the citizens of the USSR and Germany realize how the rose had been co-opted, as it were, by dictators to aestheticize their subjugation of the people?

Although cherry blossoms and roses played significantly different roles, each flower in its specific cultural and political context helped create communicative opacity, which facilitated, subtly and indirectly, political oppression at home, aggression abroad, and the death of millions. They became, as it were, "flowers that kill."

The basic question then is how people, including political leaders, articulate in their minds the meaning(s) of a symbol in a given social/political context. Are they unaware that they do not recognize the opacity of symbolic communication? What are the negative consequences of such unawareness for people involved in critical political spaces? Eric Wolf urged those who study symbols to ask "how ideologies become programs for the deployment of power" (Wolf 1999: 4) and compared the role of ideologies among the Kwakiutl, the Aztecs, and National Socialist Germany. I attempt to address this question by examining the power of important symbols as conveyers of ideology, and its limits.

With this aim, I begin this book with the political roles of quotidian symbols and identify the factors that facilitate communicative opacity. The examples I chose are deliberately not obvious political symbols, such as national flags, monuments, and the like. Instead, my focus is on quotidian objects, such as flowers, rice, and the monkey, which have been brought into political spaces, including deployment in geopolitical conflicts, without the public knowing of their changed role. They look too ordinary to be able to harness political power. Mona Ozouf ([1976] 1994: 232–33) has shown how French revolutionary symbolism, especially the official symbol of the Liberty Tree (*arbre de la liberté*), was derived from the maypole of the folk tradition in many parts of France. The Republican borrowings from popular festivals made revolutionary symbolism "less alien . . . to the popular sensibility." As I have noted above, roses—a traditional symbol of interpersonal love—were deployed by the propaganda machinery of twentieth-century dictators, especially Stalin and Hitler. But, the flower is too quotidian to be threatening to people, who did not realize the profound change in its meaning and function.

Culture: *A* Potential *Source of Communication*

Communicative opacity derives in part from culture, whose complexity and multiplicity have been long debated. While some anthropologists consider culture separate from society, economics, and polity, I concur with Chabal and Daloz (2006: 21), who view culture as "one of the key fundaments of social life, the matrix within which . . . political action takes place," just as Sahlins (1976: 207) sees "no material logic apart from the practical interest" that is "symbolically constituted." Pace Geertz (1973), it is a system of meanings, but not primarily values, that offers ways for the individual to comprehend his/her environment using one's senses, mind, and affect (Ohnuki-Tierney 1981b). However, it is not a private property. Rather, it is the primary means by which individuals within a group *communicate*, a *capability* shared by the members of a social group. "Culture as communication," however, offers only the *possibility*, rather than a guarantee, of understanding.

PARADIGMATIC PLURALITY OF CULTURE

Multiplicity, plurality, heterogeneity, and other concepts have often been recognized in the social sciences as key constituents of plurality within society— groups based on gender, age, ethnicity, or some other characteristic. Rarely has the paradigmatic plurality of culture been emphasized when it contributes to the complexity and richness of the cultural repertoire but also increases the possibility of communicative opacity. Almost always more than one basic paradigm coexists, at times with equal force, but at other times a dominant paradigm is underscored by the presence of others. By "paradigm" I mean the basic model or patterns of thought or *Weltanschauung* (worldview) of a people.

For example, in the literary field, Charles Baudelaire (1821–1867), in his well-known essay *Peintre de la vie moderne* (The Painter of Modern Life) clearly defined the term *moderne* (modernity) for the first time: "By 'modernity' I mean the ephemeral, the fugitive, the contingent, the half of art whose other half is the eternal and the immutable" (Baudelaire [1855] 2001: 12). Baudelaire's modernity was a new paradigm that emerged at the time, and assumed dominance along with another that was stable and noncontingent. Likewise, Stéphane Mallarmé (1842–1898) called attention to the notion of fragments— different fonts, readings by many voices, the polymorphous rhythms of free verse, as in his 1895 poem, "Un coup de dés jamais n'abolira le hazard" (Mallarmé 1945: 457–77). In visual art, Édouard Manet (1832–1883) helped launch modernism. The pointillism of Georges Seurat (1859–1891) succeeded in fragmenting pure color, while the cubists fractured pure form. Artists such as these were indeed predecessors of postmodernism, as acknowledged by both Jean-François Lyotard ([1979] 1989: 79) and Fredric Jameson ([1991] 1993: 59).

However, the new paradigm did not replace the old altogether. Claude Lévi-Strauss (1908–2009), who introduced the structural linguistics of the Prague school to anthropology, was roughly contemporaneous with Mikhail Bakhtin (1895–1975), who foregrounded the stylistic plurality in literatures through polyphony and dialogism,[3] just as Ernest Meissonier (1815–1891) remained an ardent pursuer of the realist tradition in genre painting. Structuralism and Marxism, among others, continued to be important analytical tools for Pierre Bourdieu (1930–2002), whose central concern was the structural reproduction of power inequality. According to Marc Augé ([1992] 1995: 79), with *surmodernité* we witness the emergence of "non-place" (*non-lieux*)—impersonal space—without the complete erasing of "place," with its personal connections to the individual's space. He argues that the two constitute "palimpsests." When a new paradigm emerges, it interacts with the previous ones and may eventually become dominant.

Paradigmatic plurality plays out in "culture as historical process." Culture as a historical process is always in motion (Moore 1986)—becoming, reproducing itself even when disintegrating. It transforms itself at the core in a constant ebb and flow, with local-transnational interactions as the engine of historical change.

Culture is never static or singular, even at its basic paradigmatic level. Even the meanings of quotidian symbols, such as Japanese cherry blossoms and European roses, pulsate in the vertigoes of geopolitics. If this continuous interpenetration of the local and the transnational/global is what constitutes culture, it is a logical contradiction to propose that a culture is a "hybrid"—an idea predicated upon the notion of a pure culture, two of which could meet and combine to produce a hybrid (Ohnuki-Tierney 1995; 2001; 2006b).

WHAT IS SHARED: THE FIELD OF MEANING

"Sharedness" has been a perennial issue in anthropological debates on culture. Clifford Geertz (1973: 12) pointed out that "culture is public because meaning is"; by "public" he means "intersubjective" (1980: 135). If culture consists of polysemic symbols and plural paradigms, and it is historically contingent, there is ample room for communicative opacity to arise in social discourse. I propose that what is "public," "shared," or "collective" is not a particular signification in a given context of communication, but *the field of meaning*, that is, all the culturally recognized meanings of a given symbol, which are vast in the case of polysemic symbols. A particular signification in a given context is often *not* shared among social actors and yet communicative opacity is rarely recognized. "Communication" goes on because they share the field of meaning of a symbol, not because they share the same signification. What is shared is communicative *capability*, which represents merely a potential for communication.

AGENCY

Insofar as it clarifies my approach to communicative opacity, let me briefly discuss several important points concerning the dialectic between the individual and his/her culture/society, which Anthony Giddens (1979) referred to as the central problem in modern social theory ever since the influential work by Marcel Mauss (1938). Few would disagree that the individual is socially localized—a point highlighted by Bourdieu (1990: 13), for whom "*generative capacities* of disposition" are a "socially constituted disposition" (italics in the original). De Certeau ([1975] 1988: 59) likewise emphasizes the inseparability of ideas and their "social localizations." Socially located individuals and their culture/society are not separate entities or antitheses.

At the individual level, the individual's action and thoughts must be distinguished. Most telling is a well-known passage from an ode by the Roman poet Horace (Quintus Horatius Flaccus, 65 BCE–8 BCE) ([23 BCE] 1999: 162):

> Sweet and proper it is to die for your country,
> But Death would just as soon come after him
> Who runs away; Death gets him by the backs
> Of his fleeting knees and jumps him from behind.[4]

I have detailed the thoughts of the student soldiers who were forced to fly to their death on a one-way mission as *tokkōtai* pilots—most of them were far from embracing the patriotism of that time. Roman soldiers as well as Japanese pilots performed patriotic acts without embracing patriotism in their mind.

What is at stake in the anthropological discussion of this perennial problem are the *changes* in the structure of society/culture and how they are brought about by the actions of individuals. "Culture through time" is never a process of self-reproduction. Culture does not move through time as if it were an objectified entity walking on its own feet. Instead, it moves because of the actions of individual *actors*, some of whom become historical *agents*. Every member of a social group is a social actor, but not everyone becomes a social agent with access to power, nor does everyone with power wield it in a way that influences the course of history. Sidney Mintz (1985: 158), critical of Geertz, points out the impotence of the "web of signification" most individuals spin: such webs are "exceedingly small. . . . For the most part they reside within other webs of immense scale, surpassing single lives in time and space."

The vision of a Napoleon or other powerful leaders in "heroic histories" as agents wielding power singlehandedly is far from reality. From Abraham Lincoln to Martin Luther King, Jr., and Barack Obama, their accomplishments involved a great number of other individuals and historical developments (Ohnuki-Tierney, ed., 1990a). In this book, when I refer to the state as an agent of change, I specify no individuals, since a large number participate in the process of historical change. It is important to discard the notion that a single individual "makes history." The plurality of historical agents—layers and series of individual agents—is what makes history move, reproducing itself while transforming itself.

Furthermore, social actors do not always have a goal in mind. Bourdieu's notion of "symbolic violence" is strikingly insightful. It is the *unconscious* exercise of "power which manages to impose meanings and to impose them as legitimate by concealing the power relations which are the basis of its force" (Bourdieu and Passeron 1977: 4). Those with power do not have to consciously strive to maintain it, since they have a feel for the game, the "judgment of taste." "Taste" in art, music, household furnishings, etc., is "the supreme manifestation of . . . discernment" and is critical in producing "distinction"—i.e., the structure of domination (Bourdieu [1979] 1984: 11; for art, see Bourdieu and Darbel [1969] 1990).

Be it linguistic, or class/economic/political, the structure of power inequality is seldom articulated in the minds of the people, as Marx so clearly articulated in his concept of "commodity fetishism," where the value of commodities is seen as *natural* by people who are not aware of "all the magic and necromancy that surrounds the products of labour as long as they take the form of commodities" (Marx [1867] 1992: 80–81).

Important to note also is the distinction between the actions and intentions of individuals, on the one hand, and their impact, if any, on culture or society, on the other. Individuals can protest or try to subvert, but their actions must bear the fruit of changes in society and culture, the assessment of which, however, is complex. Karl Marx famously cautioned, "Men make their own history, but they do not make it just as they please" (Marx and Engels [1852] 1989: 320). One should not dismiss "surface oscillations" and wait for the geological *longue durée* (Braudel [1958] 1980), but historical change cannot be fully assessed at the time when actions take place. In the United States, for example, there were many riots, demonstrations, and the like in the latter half of the twentieth century, but only a handful, such as the series of nonviolent protest marches of the African American civil rights movement and the Vietnam War protests, led to lasting changes in American society and culture.

"Culture as historical process" is an enormously complex dialectic: the individual plays a significant role in preventing the perfect self-reproduction of his or her culture, and yet the power of individuals over the course of history is severely circumscribed and indirect. Our scholarly interest in individual thoughts, feelings, and actions is in how they relate to the collectivity (culture/society) and thus take part in historical processes (see Moore 1987). Understanding the constraints on their power by culture and society is not incompatible with recognizing the power of individuals as agents.

Unawareness of Communicative Opacity: Scholarly Tradition

The complexity of discursive communication has been pointed out by thinkers from Aristotle on. In 1884 Gustave Flaubert lamented the impotence of human speech with a well-known cracked kettle (*un chaudron fêlé*) metaphor. Rodolphe in *Madame Bovary* is exasperated by a hollow and repeated conversation with Emma: "human speech is like a cracked kettle on which we strum out tunes to make a bear dance, when we would move the stars to pity" (Flaubert 1884: 212; English translation, Flaubert [1950] 1968: 203). In anthropology, social scientist Edmund Leach pointed out in 1954 how different individuals draw different meanings from the same symbols and actions:

> And just as two readers of a poem may agree about its quality and yet derive from it totally different meanings, so, in the context of ritual action, two individuals or groups of individuals may accept the validity of a set of ritual actions without agreeing at all as to what is expressed in those actions. (Leach [1954] 1965: 86)

Likewise, Sidney Mintz stated: "People's agreeing on what something *is* is not the same as their agreeing on what it *means*" (Mintz 1985: 158).

By far the most articulate in pointing out our *unawareness* of the *absence* of communication is Baudelaire, who was also one of the first, if not the first, to point out that the ground was shaking with the emergence of significant paradigmatic instability with the rise of modernité. In *Mon coeur mis à nu*, posthumously published in 1869, Baudelaire explains:

> Le monde ne marche que par le malentendu.
>   C'est par le malentendu universel que tout
> le monde s'accorde.
>   Car si, par malheur, on se comprenait, on
> ne pourrait jamais s'accorder.
>
> (Baudelaire [1869] 1949: 98)

The world gets by because of misunderstanding. / Universal misunderstanding enables people to agree with each other. / For if, by misfortune, people understood each other, they would never come to agreement.

Baudelaire did not explain how *malentendu* takes place. The term has been used sometimes to mean misunderstanding and other times the absence of communication, seldom with an examination of how it actually happens.

A most systematic analysis of communicative opacity was advanced by Pierre Bourdieu, who, from the late 1960s on, developed his notion of *méconnaissance* (1991: 153), the "institutionalized circle of collective misrecognition" in which the habitus of the dominant class trickles down (1991: 170; Bourdieu and Wacquant 1992: 168). During this process, underclass individuals unconsciously volunteer to support the domination of the upper-class habitus, which they perceive as "legitimate" and "natural." Crucial in his theoretical formulation are: 1) the invisibility of symbolic power; 2) a unitary system of beliefs and values embraced by both those who benefit from the exercise and those who participate in their own subjugation; 3) the non-dependence of symbolic power upon the individual's illocutionary power in a given social context (Bourdieu 1991: 23, 113, 118, 170, 209).[5]

Communicative Opacity: Analytical Framework of This Book

Building on the insights of Baudelaire, Bourdieu, and others, I foreground the importance of recognizing the unawareness of communicative opacity and attempt to identify specific factors responsible for the phenomenon. My interest in communicative opacity is not confined to analyses of power inequality in class structure in a given society, an almost exclusive concern of Bourdieu, but includes broader political spaces, such as wars and societies under dictatorship.

POLYSEME

One of the major factors contributing to communicative opacity is the nature of polyseme. For any major polysemic symbol, there is a vast semantic *field* consisting of a large number of meanings. Victor Turner, with his performative approach to culture and his proposition of multivocality, opened up the way to understanding how "a dominant symbol has a 'fan' or 'spectrum' of referents" (Turner 1967: 50), each of which has "complexity of association, ambiguity, open-endedness" (Turner 1975: 155). Nevertheless, he located in multivocality the basis for communication and social integration (Turner 1967: 30). Building on his insight but taking an opposite direction, I propose that *polysemy* is the basis for communicative opacity, rather than a foundation facilitating the functional integration of a symbolic system or society.

Although the meanings of a symbol are often thought of in isolation, I propose that every meaning is always defined in relation to other meanings of a given symbol. That is, rather than being discrete entities, each in a pigeonhole, meanings are embedded in social relationships and life processes. The concept of "women" is necessarily predicated by men, just as life is a stage of a process leading to death. The normative structure of society or a symbolic system is underscored by its subversion of the anti-self and the anti-structure. What are seemingly "contradictory" or "opposite" are in fact the two ends of the same pole. An important implication of this understanding is that when symbolic representation shifts its weight and foregrounds, for example, death instead of life, the shift looks *natural*, and people fail to realize the magnitude of the shift. Thus, the relational and processual nature of each of a large number of meanings of a polysemic symbol is a potential source for communicative opacity.

To show how this works, I focus first on Japanese cherry blossoms (Chapter One) and European roses (Chapter Two). The symbolism of cherry blossoms in Japanese culture has been rich and complex, with a vast set of often seemingly contradictory meanings: men and warriors who were said to be "men among men"; young women, representing life and their reproductive capacity vital for the continuation of society; and geisha, nonreproductive women situated outside normative society. The flower also represents destabilization of the social persona—madness, that is, the loss of social identity, thought to occur under full bloom, and the assumption of another social persona by donning a mask during the ritual of cherry blossom viewing. In addition, it represents the processes of life, death, and rebirth—each stage of the life cycle. Above all, it symbolizes love: intense human relationships and the bedrock of human sociality. In addition, cherry blossoms have stood for the collective identity of the Japanese as a whole as well as of virtually every social group within Japanese society—neighborhood associations, schools, companies, etc. On the other hand, the ritual of cherry blossom viewing has always provided space for the challenge of gender reversal and other oppositions to societal norms.

Although it is indeed daunting to select a commensurate major symbol not only in Europe but also in the Middle East and elsewhere, I introduce the symbolism of the rose (Chapter Two) since it is, like cherry blossoms, a polysemic symbol of enormous complexity. The rose has been assigned an important symbolic space in Christianity, with, for example, the red rose symbolizing the sacrifice by Christ and the white rose representing the purity of the Virgin Mary. The rose also shares the representation of opposites—love and its loss, life and death, for example—as represented by the flower and the thorn. Uncannily, like cherry blossoms, it represents madness—the loss of a socially localized self—as exemplified by Ophelia in *Hamlet*.

Both flowers are involved in power inequality. While the adoration and viewing of cherry blossoms were shared by all Japanese—each social group doing so in a separate space—the warlords of yesterday seized the occasion to display their political power. For ancient political leaders like Nero and Cleopatra, roses were a symbol of political power and wealth, and the craze over roses institutionalized the massive labor—exacted from peasants at the sacrifice of raising food crops—to produce them. On the other hand, the viewing of cherry blossoms has been a space for slapsticks, transvestites, and other elements that defy societal norms. Roses also share an antiestablishment stance, but their role has been far more institutionalized. They became the symbol of antiestablishment sentiment in medieval May Day celebrations. May Day celebrated the spring, but it also served as a venue to express villagers' opposition to the local government. This meaning was adopted by the Socialist International. With the genesis of the labor movement in Russia, the red rose became its logo and that of most socialist parties in the world. In Germany, students at Munich University who opposed the Nazi regime called themselves the "White Rose," expressing the purity of their political convictions, since in German culture the white rose represents purity.

Cherry blossoms were not overtly involved in violence and conflicts, as were roses, for example in the War of the Roses between the houses of Lancaster and York. Yet, cherry blossoms became the symbol of political nationalism and, moreover, the emblem of the ultraright in the 1930s, unlike European roses.

This embeddedness in layers of multi-referentiality and interreferentiality of a polysemic symbol creates a multitude of interrelated concepts. Thesis is embedded in antithesis. However, the dynamics of a polysemic symbol do not lie in the static fact of having many meanings, but in the symbol's role *in practice*, that is, when in a given social context social actors draw different interpretations from a vast set of interlocking and multilayered meanings, which constitute the semantic field for polysemy. Changes in the semantic field may result from fluctuations in geopolitics. Sometimes all the meanings are present simultaneously, but more often they constitute a palimpsest, with some meanings, such as cherry blossoms as a symbol for agrarian productivity, no longer dominant but nonetheless present. Likewise, the rose had represented both egalitarianism and anti-structuralism ever since medieval times. It is this characteristic that Lenin (posthumously), Stalin, Hitler, and the Socialist International deployed for their own purposes.

Neither the Japanese under the military government nor the Germans under the Nazis consciously recognized the fundamental shift in meaning, precisely because the field of meaning of these dominant symbols is so rich, complex, and vast. A Soviet worker who saw the rose as a symbol of solidarity did not see the same flower given to Stalin as a symbol of subjugation, just as Japanese soldiers did not perceive cherry blossoms as a symbol of sacrificial "victims"—themselves. To advance the *pro rege et patria mori* ideology, under the Japanese military state the flower's semantic field was stretched—falling petals as fallen soldiers and new blossoms as their metamorphosed souls. Since the end of the nineteenth century the state had advocated sacrifice for Japan. Many Japanese during this period felt an urgent need to protect their country against Western colonialism; the notion of self-sacrifice loomed large, and cherry blossoms representing the aesthetic of sacrifice for causes larger than oneself seemed natural. Specific individuals did not make a conscious decision to change the meaning of the flower. Even the state did not systematically orchestrate the change. Furthermore, the shift was not recognized by the people, because cherry blossoms had always stood for a set of life forces while simultaneously symbolizing the opposite. Communicative opacity facilitated the imperceptible transformation of the flower of love into a weapon of mass destruction.[6]

If polysemy is a factor in communicative opacity, symbols of collective self-identity offer a different path to communicative opacity through partial representation of the referent. As an example, I use rice in Japan: "rice as self." Since the collective self always emerges when people are pressed to define themselves vis-à-vis a specific other in a given historical context, there is strong pressure for "United we stand"—people united as a single homogeneous social group. The selection of a symbol is seldom questioned nor do people articulate in their minds the meaning of a particular symbol. A danger of symbolic representation of the collective self is that it totalizes the referent, that is, the people. The symbolic representation of "rice as self" excludes all non-agrarian peoples in Japan, whom the dominant agrarian group has turned into the "internal other" (Ohnuki-Tierney 1998). Yet those excluded have not been aware of their own exclusion and even subscribe to the cosmology based on rice agriculture. For example, the four seasons of the year based on the stages of the growth of the rice plant have become the seasons for all Japanese, including those involved in fishing, lumbering, trade, and other non-agrarian occupations. In real-time politics, such exclusion can have tragic consequences. Under imperial nationalism (see Althusser 1971: 137) or nationalizing the masses (Mosse 1975), they are made to fight for the state, political control of which is held by the domi-nant group. Suddenly they are made into soldiers of Imperial Japan.

If the totalizing metaphor of "rice as self" hides that "the self" excludes the members of non-agrarian social groups, the polysemy of the monkey symbolism underscores the other side of the coin (see Chapter Three). The polysemy includes the sacred messenger, scapegoats, and clowns whose metaphysical laughter at received wisdom—mockery of social stratification, of the sanctity of Japan's imperialism, and of the Japanese as a whole—conceals the real-life marginalization of the social group, stigmatized because of the culturally defined impurity which characterized their occupations of handling animals. A kaleidoscopic array of meanings leads to communica-tive opacity in the delivery of meanings.

THE AESTHETIC

Whether Japanese cherry blossoms, European roses, or other markers of collective self-identity, symbols are often assigned aesthetic qualities. If polysemy creates space for communicative opacity, the aesthetic has even stronger potential for doing so by transforming, for example, the ugly—killing and violence—into the sublimity of sacrifice for the state and other causes greater than oneself. The process of transformation naturalizes *all* to be sublime, whether the symbol is polysemic or has only one meaning, as with the case of Japanese rice, since the beauty of the symbol must be trans-lated into the sublimity of the self. The assignment of sublimity is a subtle and yet spectacularly effective means of disarming people when any regime attempts to drive them toward its own purposes, such as fighting for it.

My interest is in the aesthetic of quotidian objects perceived by ordinary people, rather than aesthetic traditions established as a system by scholars, which I refer to as "aesthetics."[7] In Western scholarship on the aesthetic, art as well as literary representations have been seen as representing the human endeavor to imitate nature and capture the truth of "reality" (Auerbach [1946] 1974: 14, 554–57), which Plato ([1935] 2000: esp. 429–33) saw as a failed attempt. In this tradition, art is defined by "beauty," the standards for which are assumed to be universal. Although the idea of *la beauté du quotidian* emerged during the seventeenth century in Holland, the decisive watershed took place in the 1930s when Martin Heidegger, Leon Trotsky, Walter Benjamin, Bertolt Brecht, and others brought down high art, and de-classicized and de-sanctified the work of art (see Chamberlain 2014). The trilogy of Art, Truth, and Beauty along with the German idealist culture that upheld the ideal of beautiful semblance, *schöner Schein*, for the preceding 150 years gave way to this new anti-auratic view of art. Hashish-loving Baudelaire's praise of the beauty of the red lipstick of Parisian prostitutes, was, in fact, his defiance of high art (see also Eagleton [1983] 2001).

My interest is not only in locating the quotidian aesthetic but in understanding its role in political spaces. Although Kant's aesthetic judgment has been severely criticized (see Eagleton [1990] 1991: 87–90), as a heuristic device, I find most useful his distinction between the beautiful and the sublime,[8] as well as the transference and countertransference between them. According to Kant, "The Beautiful in nature is connected with the form of the object, which consists in having [definite] boundaries. The Sublime . . . is to be found in a formless object" and thus "does not reside in anything of nature, but *only in our mind*" (1790 [2000]: 129, emphasis added; see also 1790 [2000]: 101–2; 1793 [2001]: 306–8). Elsewhere, he emphasizes that it is incorrect to call any object of nature sublime, but correct to call many objects of nature beautiful (1790 [2000]: 103). "The *beautiful* is that which pleases universally without [requiring] a concept" (1790 [2000]: 67).

I use the "beautiful" to refer to the sensory perception of an object's aesthetic *without* moral, religious, political, or other dimensions, and the "sublime" to refer to the aesthetic attached to a concept, be it moral, religious, political, etc. I have chosen political symbols to explore the complexities of the quotidian aesthetic as they play out in symbolic practice.

Like most anthropologists, I hold that the aesthetic is culturally construed. Furthermore, I do not assume the beautiful in nature and the sublime as concept are universal. In the first place, "art" has not been a separate category of mental and physical activities for many peoples past and present, but the aesthetic is part of their daily lives, such as carvings on a wooden eating bowl. For the Ainu, a hunting-gathering people of southern Sakhalin, Hokkaidō, and the Kuriles, every object and being of the universe that is related to deities (*kamui*) is *pirika*, sublime. A bear is *pirika* because it is a deity, rather than because it is magnificent in terms of sensory perception. In other words, sublimity—*pirika*—is the only aesthetic value for the Ainu; they recognize no concept of "beauty in/of nature." Flowers receive no cultural space; only leaves, roots, and any other parts of the plant that are useful as food or medicine are each given a distinct lexeme (Ohnuki-Tierney 1974: 31). In this respect, the Ainu are far from unique. Goody begins his encyclopedic *The Culture of Flowers* with the chapter "No Flowers in Africa?" and shows how, unlike in the Middle East and Europe, in Africa flowers are not culturally recognized (Goody 1993: 1–27).

Nonetheless, the Kantian distinction takes on critical significance for an understanding of how beauty serves to naturalize the sublimity of symbols in political spaces. For example, rice—the plant and the grain—has long been considered beautiful in Japanese culture (Chapter Four). In ancient Japan it was the abode of deities. It was also believed that the Mountain Deity descended to a rice paddy on a cherry petal. Do we conclude that rice was *not* "naturally" beautiful, but the sublimity of the deity was transferred to the plant, which then became beautiful because of its importance in the political economy of the dominant group in Japanese society? Indeed, state protection of rice agriculture dates all the way back to the seventh century, suggesting that the state had a strong hand in constructing sublimity, which was then transferred to the plant, making it "beautiful."

Another example of the relationship between beauty and sublimity in political space is the flowery wars of the Aztecs. The ruling-class Aztecs engaged in "flowery wars" (*xochiyaoyotl*) against enemy states such as Tlaxcala, Cholula, and Huexotzinco (Durán 1964: 348). These were ritual wars "allegedly . . . for combat training and securing captives for religious sacrifices," although sacrificial victims were taken in ordinary wars as well (Durán 1964: 348; Hassig 1988: 10). Mario Erdheim (1972: 47–50) argues that the beauty of flowers symbolized prestige and fame, the most important and recurring themes in flowery wars. Metaphors of flowers included "dancing flowers" for warriors; "flower water" as warriors' blood; "flowers of the heart" for enemies captured for sacrifice; and "flowery death," after which warriors became hummingbirds or butterflies, sucking nectar from the choicest blossoms. Praised in songs, these warriors gained prestige at death.[9] Was the "beauty" of flowers transformed into the sublimity of Aztec warfare and sacrifice for the state? Or was self-sacrifice considered sublime, which made flowers beautiful?

These examples help us understand an important question explored in this book: How is sublimity assigned to concepts, including patriotism and nationalism, and how is the beautiful summoned to duty in this process? The sublimity of symbols of cultural nationalism is often represented by "beautiful" beings of nature. However, innocent cultural nationalism can easily be turned into dangerous political nationalism orchestrated by the state, as its aesthetic masks the reality of war and violence and leads people to rush to their own destruction, as witnessed in many authoritarian states, past and present (Ohnuki-Tierney 2002a: 248–51).

The fluidity facilitated by the transference/countertransference process leads to another, perhaps more fundamental nature of the aesthetic—its polyvalence, having more than one value. In Western art, there has been a long debate over the relationship between the beautiful and the ugly (see Eco, ed., 2005).[10] Kant pointed out that the ugly had to be portrayed as "beautiful": "Beautiful art shows its superiority in this, that it describes as beautiful things which may be in nature ugly or displeasing. The Furies, diseases, the devastations of war, etc., may [even regarded as calamitous] be described as very beautiful, as they are represented in a picture" ([1790] 2000: 194–95). With the advent of modernity, however, artists confronted the inherent doubling of the beautiful and the ugly. Baudelaire identified François Rabelais (1483 [?]–1553) as "the great French master of the gro-tesque" ([1855] 2001: 159; see also Bakhtin [1965] 1984) and pointed out how "this indefinable element of beauty" in art was intended to represent "proper ugliness" ([1855] 2001: 147). Baudelaire's major thesis was *les fleurs du mal*, which served as the title of his well-known collection of poems. For him, as expressed in his poem "Hymn to Beauty," beauty embodied "heaven's depths or hell's infinity," "crime and courtesy." And murder, beauty's cameo, dances amorously on its "proud abdomen" (Baudelaire [1857] [1869] 1991: 53–55).

The symbols I have chosen as examples in this book clearly demonstrate an important dimension of symbolism: polysemic symbols are also polyva-lent in aesthetic references. The polysemy of cherry blossoms includes life, death, men, women, and various other meanings, while carrying various aesthetic values—vigor, sorrow, pathos, gaiety, etc. The aesthetic of sunny cherry blossoms representing life's vigor is necessarily different from the aesthetic of pathos represented by falling or fallen cherry blossoms, just as the aesthetic of cherry blossoms as geisha is starkly different from the aes-thetic of cherry blossoms as warriors. Likewise, roses, with their meanings of life, death, the power of the establishment and anti-power, etc., lead to various aesthetic values.

If polyseme consists of meanings that represent different stages of the same process or identities of social relationships, the aesthetic is necessarily polyvalent, representing different valences. Anthropology has not developed a sufficient vocabulary to identify a wide range of the aesthetic, let alone interpretive tools to understand its various valences. Most important, the transference and countertransference between the "beautiful" and the "sublime" must be further explored, especially in political spaces.

Theoretical issues of the quotidian aesthetic are explored further in Chapter Four, where I examine the aesthetic of purity and impurity in practice—that is, how these qualities are assigned to domestic rice and foreign rice in Japanese culture, which translates into the purity of the self and impurity of internal and external others. There has been a long tradition of scholarship in anthropology on the aesthetic values of purity and impurity, beginning with Robertson Smith ([1889] 1972) and Arnold van Gennep ([1908] 1961). Their argument has centered on the premise that impurity is assigned to structural anomalies in the classificatory schema of people—objects or beings that do not fit in the classificatory system—and that impurity generates religious/symbolic power.

Structural analysis *in the abstract* without a grounding in sociopolitical contexts brutally sanitizes symbolic interpretations (Ohnuki-Tierney 1981a: 119–31). Examining the long-term historical process of the dialectic between the symbolism of rice and political economy shows that the aesthetic of purity and impurity assigned to rice, representing the dominant self and its internal and external others, arose from the necessity to maintain and enhance the purity of the self of the dominant group amid geopolitical change. This was accomplished by assigning impurity to the scapegoats of society; it did not emerge out of structural anomaly. Recall also how impurity was used by the Nazis to justify the Holocaust, just as the dominant agrarian group in Japan used it to discriminate against Japan's minorities. In fact, impurity has been a stock excuse for discrimination against minorities by the dominant social group in many societies. The dominant group can easily construe ex post facto how "anomalous" they are: they just don't fit with "us."

ZERO SIGNIFIER

Although I have presented polysemes with objectified symbols, such as cherry blossoms and roses, the relationship between the signifier and the signified/meaning is far more complex (Ohnuki-Tierney 1993c; 1994a). In

Chapter Six I call attention to the nonmateriality of signifiers and the absence of meaning, which I refer to as the "zero signifier" and "zero meaning," respectively, and a nondirect mode of signification whereby a sign or symbol is not directly linked to its meanings but operates according to a different principle—"the logic of the predicate." This was foregrounded by Nishida Kitarō—the founder of the Kyoto school of philosophy—who contrasted "the logic of the predicate" of the Japanese with the Aristotelian logic of the subject (Nishida 1965a: 124–76; see also Berque 1984: 102).

The absent pronouns in daily discourse offer concrete examples, as I have detailed elsewhere (Ohnuki-Tierney 1993c; 1994a). There is little structural pressure in Japanese to use pronouns. In Japanese sentences subjects are often missing or absent, transitive verbs do not have objects, including pronouns, and word order is quite flexible. Furthermore, Japanese lacks authentic third person pronouns (for details, see Kuno 1973: 17–18). Needless to say, the ellipsis of subjects and objects is not due to a paucity of pronouns. On the contrary, there are more than thirty linguistic forms that serve syntactically as pronouns.[11]

The ellipsis of pronouns is especially conspicuous in the discourse of politeness and deference. In fact the deletion of pronouns—especially the first and second pronouns and their possessive cases—is *obligatory* as a *social* practice. Their deletion must be accompanied by the additions of or changes in inflections, expressing deference or humbleness either toward the subject or the object, in other parts of the discourse, i.e., nouns, verbs, auxiliary verbs, etc., which constitute a sentence and identify the absent subject, the speaker and the addressee, as well as the social relationships between the people involved, indexically in a given social context or defined in the social structure.

In addition, I propose that zero signifiers are situated at the focal arena of culture and society. Therefore, *transgression* in the form of the objectification of zero signifiers constitutes a serious offense, in some cases, blasphemy, against the societal norm, and provides performative power to social actors, as in many religions, as shown below.

Zero signifiers in political spaces: The question of zero signifiers or externalized signifiers takes on critical significance when the symbols are in political spaces (Chapter Seven). Put another way, for an understanding of symbolic representations in political spaces, an important question is whether externalization is a prerequisite for all types of power. It is almost axiomatically acknowledged that visual objectification, such as portraits, monuments, statues, parades, and auditory objectification, such as "the king's speech," are the stuff of politics—the means to maintain and enhance political power. Hitler's face in a thousand poses was imprinted everywhere from postal stamps to innumerable posters. His speeches at Nuremberg and elsewhere, as well as the almost incessant shouts of "Heil Hitler," still ring in our ears, just as does the sound of the goose steps of "his" soldiers, as Jean Gabin famously complained in *La Grande Illusion*. Hitler was not unique in this regard. For Stalin, Mussolini, Mao, and a number of other dictators, the "externalization" of their images and speeches constituted crucial propaganda machinery.

In some religions, an enormous importance is placed on images, for example, in what Meyer and Houtman (2012) call "material religion" (see also Meyer 2008). On the other hand, in institutionalized religions, such as Christianity, Judaism, and Islam, the most sacred is seldom externalized as an image or word, whereas lesser figures are shown as images. For example, in Christianity, God without an image contrasts with Christ and saints, who are visualized. The Supreme Being in Judaism remains without both a name and an image. Islam is well known for its austerity in the use of icons. The Japanese native religion of Shintoism eschewed externalization—no icons were made and no shrines were built, until Shinto was forced to compete with Buddhism, introduced from India via China and Korea, for which temples and statues were of paramount importance.

This vast and complex field becomes even more complicated when we consider that Japanese emperors were visual and auditory zero signifiers— they were not represented in images nor did they deliver speeches. During World War II, the Japanese were told to fight for and die for the emperor, who was nominally the political leader of the country. The Japanese have been portrayed as shouting *banzai* (Eternal Life) or *tennōheika banzai* (Hail the Emperor) as they waved the rising sun on flags and wore a headband with the rising sun on it. But not a single image of the emperor appeared. Not a single speech by him was delivered to the people until his announcement of Japan's surrender. They fought for an invisible and inaudible emperor.

The case of the Japanese emperors raises an important question that cannot be understood within the framework of the binary—objectification or its negation, which presupposes objectification. It derives from Japanese ontology in which the soul is the essence of being whose presence and identity does not rely on any objectified entity, such as an object or a voice (Chapter Six).

Until the Meiji, while warlords had taken over political power, the main role of the emperor, who had been one of the millions of deities in the pantheon, was to preside over rituals concerning the growing of rice. For warlords, who held society's military, political, and economic power, portraits were important for the display of their power. Even after the nature and role of the emperor were redefined in the 1889 imperial constitution of Japan, Emperor Meiji was represented by symbols of the ancient imperial system (the phoenix) and of Japan (Mount Fuji, the rising sun). Instead of a portrait, he was represented by someone else—a convention known as *mitate*, a standard practice in Japanese visual art that uses substitutions and other devices to avoid direct representations. With the progressive militarization of the state and the accelerated development of mass media, the later emperors Taishō and Shōwa became much more visible to the people, but they were never seen or heard to the same degree as European monarchs and dictators.

What was the political rationale behind these contrasting emphases in each country and to what extent did culture play a role in political reasoning? What were the differences between the Germans who fought for a blatantly present Führer versus the Japanese fighting for the zero presence of the emperor? And, what were the differences between Germany and Japan in the way the memory of the war has been dealt with?—another way to understand the differences in modes of representation and their political power.

Although I stress the theoretical dimensions of symbolic communication or its opacity, the symbols I have chosen to examine are those of collective identities that have often been transformed into symbols of cultural nationalism, and often used by the state to promote political nationalism. As detailed in Chapter Five, collective identities continue to be of critical importance as, unfortunately, wars and fighting never seem to stop, be it in Ukraine, the Gaza strip, or elsewhere. Collective identities are also of increasing importance today in the form of ethnic and national identities risen against the tide of globalization. The ethical and political challenges involved in immigration and border crossing in Europe, the United States, Japan, China—in fact, all over the world—also require careful rethinking of collective identities. "Who we are" is always defined in relation to who "they" are, that is, various external groups in different historical contexts. The symbols of the collective self are usually assigned aesthetic dimensions, such as sublimity and purity, in contrast to the ugliness and impurity of the other. "Japanese rice" represents the purity and sublimity of the Japanese, in contrast to the impurity of foreign rice, representing external others (Ohnuki-Tierney 1994a). This leads to a broader examination of various symbols of cultural and political nationalisms in imperial Japan and Nazi Germany, which are introduced in order to compare and contrast the two countries' symbolic representations of the collective self.[12]

The importance of awareness of communicative opacity and its dire consequences to individuals remains even greater as we reflect on the astonishingly long list of post–World War II dictators, with Viktor F. Yanukovych of Ukraine, not to mention Vladimir Putin of Russia and Kim Jong-un of North Korea, among the latest. Or, as discussed in the Afterword, the uses of the symbols related to the *tokkōtai* (kamikaze) operation by ring-wingers in Japan today show how easily symbols and the aesthetic can be manipulated. Indeed, the importance of communicative opacity and its unawareness on the part of individuals is timeless, however unfortunate that may be.

It is imperative to closely examine how symbols work—their relational and processual meanings as well as the roles that the aesthetic plays in this process—and how these characteristics create communicative opacity. The focus on symbols in political spaces helps us understand how communicative opacity misleads people to believe in the aesthetic of the self, thereby facilitating a smooth translation of cultural nationalism into state-mandated political nationalism—a process that can lead people to unknowingly cooperate in wrong causes, such as wars. Being unaware of communicative opacity and the strategic deployment of symbolism for malevolent purposes, we may not even question what exactly "we" means when the call "United we stand" rings loud.

The power of communicative opacity is hidden; it plays upon the unawareness of people who are victimized. But its impact may be serious. This profound power has the capacity to make changes in prevailing conceptual structures, and, in turn, in society and polity over the course of history, often without involving individuals as social agents.

PART I

Sources of Communicative Opacity

Many Meanings, One Meaning, the Aesthetic

Japanese Cherry Blossoms

From the Beauty of Life to the Sublimity of Sacrificial Death

Every spring, cherry blossoms cover the entirety of the Japanese archipelago, appearing first in Okinawa and then all the way to Hokkaidō, presenting a spectacular view. For the Japanese, it is the blossoms, not the fruit or the tree trunks, that are the source of the cherry tree's importance.[1] Cherry blossoms, with their wide range of meaning, are an excellent example of how a polysemic symbol operates in practice and how it contributes to communicative opacity. Its polysemy demonstrates the fundamental nature of meanings, that meanings are *relational*—for example, women in relation to men—and *processual*—life leading to death. Also, the polysemy springs from the multiple structures of the Japanese *Weltanschauung*—the normative structure and the structure leading to an alternative imagination.

In addition, cherry blossom viewing (*hanami*), plays an essential role in establishing the collective identity of every social group within Japan as well as Japan and the Japanese as a whole, as it has been an important ritual/recreation at all levels of society. The historical development of the meanings of this symbol shows how different dominant meanings surfaced in different historical contexts, and that polysemy is not a timeless set of meanings set in stone.

Furthermore, the beauty of cherry blossoms was *naturally* transformed into the sublimity of patriotism as Japan's imperial ambitions heightened its militarism—the beauty of falling petals represented the sublimity of patriotic sacrifice. In this process the aesthetic played a key role in creating communicative opacity whereby the direct transference of the beauty of cherry blossoms to the sublimity of sacrifice was hardly recognized even by those who were to lose their lives.

Polysemy

HUMAN LIFE/REPRODUCTIVITY; AGRARIAN PRODUCTIVITY

Unambiguously, in Japanese culture the dominant meaning of cherry blossoms, seen as pink blossoms against the blue sky, is the celebration of life, youth, and vigor. In Japan's ancient agrarian cosmology, cherry blossoms were thought to be the symbolic equivalent of rice, the most sacred plant. Each spring, the Mountain Deity descends on a cherry blossom petal to rice paddies where he lodges (*yadoru*), becoming the Deity of Rice Paddies (Ta-no-Kami), in order to look after agricultural production. This most powerful of all deities offers his own soul, embodied in grains of rice, to humans, who raise the rice to full maturity under the warm rays of the Sun Goddess and, in the fall, give him in return a gift of a bounty of grains. The term *sakura* (cherry blossoms) is written with two characters: *sa* (the spirit of the deity) and *kura* (the seat);[2] that is, it is the seat for the deity when he descends to the rice paddies. Farmers therefore have traditionally taken the appearance of cherry blossoms as a signal to prepare for planting rice seedlings (Figure 1 and Plate 1).[3] In the fall, after being feted with offerings of food by farmers during the harvest ritual, the deity returns to the mountains (Miyata 1993; Sakurai 1976; Suzuki 1991: 6–9). Some scholars suggest that *sa* in *sakura* (cherry blossoms) has the same root as *sa* in such terms as "to prosper" (*sakaeru*), "to be prosperous" (*sakan*), "good fortune" (*sachi*), and "rice wine" (*sake*), reinforcing the symbolic association of cherry blossoms with the life force (Saitō 1979 [1985]: 45–46; Yamada 1977: 21).

The belief in cherry blossoms as the abode of the deity gave rise to a practice of wearing the blossoms on one's head in order to receive his blessings (Yamada 1977: 116). This appears already in the *Man'yōshū*—the earliest collection of Japanese poems, dating from the eighth century. In one poem, the poet sings of the land of the emperor engulfed in the fragrance of cherry blossoms because men and women are wearing the flowers in their hair (Omodaka [1961] 1983: 39–40). The tradition continued until later periods, evolving into geisha wearing a rice stalk bearing grains.

Of the two major religions of Japan, Shintoism is generally in charge of matters related to life, such as birth celebrations and weddings. Buddhism, introduced to Japan during the sixth century, from India via China and Korea, takes care of most matters related to death, such as funerals and

FIGURE 1. Cherry blossoms as the spring counterpart of rice in the fall with rice paddies below. Artist: Hiroshige. Source: E.B. Van Vleck Collection of Japanese Prints #1980.1108. Courtesy of Chazen Museum of Art, University of Wisconsin, Madison.

so-called ancestor worship. In Buddhism, flowers occupy important symbolic space, including lotus flowers, on which the Buddha sits or stands. The Pure Land denomination, which became popular among both the folk and aristocrats during the late Heian period (794–1185), when the ancien régime was crumbling, portrayed paradise (*gokuraku jōdo*) as resplendent with flowers and birds all through the four seasons and music constantly floating in the air. Flowers are the major motifs of the designs of high-ranking monks' ceremonial robes. The association of flowers with death and the afterworld led to the custom of flowers as an important offering at the ancestral alcove in individual homes or at grave sites. Importantly, however, cherry blossoms are *never* used for these purposes. In earlier times, even though cherry trees grew only in the mountains, cherry blossoms were not symbolically associated in any direct way with the mountains, which were believed to be one of the spaces to which the dead departed (Miyata 1993: 3–4; Roubaud 1970).

THE HEIGHT OF LIFE/LOVE AND LOSS

Besides the celebration of life, another dominant meaning of cherry blossoms throughout history has been the celebration of love—an intense *relationship* between a man and a woman. In the aforementioned *Man'yōshū*, there are fourteen poems in which cherry blossoms appear, all with "sunny meanings," as Edwin Cranston notes: "*aware* [pathos over impermanence]—an important ethos in later history—has no place in these sunny glades" (Cranston 1993: 539).[4]

Although the Chinese aesthetic of plum blossoms was embraced by the elite of the ancient period (250–1185 CE), by the time of the *Kokinwakashū*, a collection of some 1,100 poems compiled in either 905 or 914 CE, cherry blossoms were decisively at the center stage of love and aesthetics. In the *Kokinwakashū*, dubbed the collection of poems of cherry blossoms and love, this most frequent poetic motif symbolizes the beauty of women and the Imperial Palace in Kyoto. The poem by Monk Sosei, often cited to convey the splendor of the capital when the cherry trees are in full bloom, reads: "Seen from a distance / willows and cherry blossoms / all intermingled / the imperial city / in truth a springtime brocade" (Kojima and Arai, eds., 1989: 34; McCullough 1985: 24; Kubota 1960 [1968]: 180).

In *The Tale of Genji* by Murasaki Shikibu (c. 978–1014), cherry blossoms appear more often than any other flower.[5] It is commonly assumed that *The*

Tale of Genji gives pride of place to *monono aware*, the aesthetic of pathos, because the story focuses on the ephemeral beauty of the fleeting world, where nature and humans enjoy but a short life (Field 1987: 211; Morris 1964 [1979]: 207–8). However, cherry blossoms are rarely associated with *aware*. Even in *Genji* they are predominantly "sunny," with blooming cherries representing youth, love, and courtship.

On the other hand, from early on opposite meanings—the loss of the life force, power, wealth, and love—have also been an integral part of the polysemy of cherry blossoms. Already in the eighth-century myth histories, short life as a characteristic of the flower is noted. The short life span of humans is explained as a result of the marriage of the Sun Goddess's grandson to a female deity, called "Blossom on a Tree" (Konoha-no-Sakuya-Bime), identified by some scholars as cherry blossoms. At the time of the marriage, the woman's father warns the grandson that his life will be short like that of the blossoms.[6] Nevertheless, the marriage produces a son, which symbolizes the birth of rice, that is, deities qua emperors, who in turn represent Japan and the Japanese.

There are some instances in *The Tale of Genji* where the ephemeral nature of love and life is symbolized by phenomena of nature, including cherry blossoms.[7] For example, after the death of the Shining Prince and his wife, Murasaki, the world is described as "The cherry blossoms of spring are loved because they bloom so briefly" (Yamagishi, ed., 1962: 222; Seidensticker 1977b: 736). The Heian period was the last hurrah of the ancien régime in Japan (Kitagawa 1990). Aristocrats enjoyed pomp, gaiety, and a lavish lifestyle at the court in Kyoto, but their lives were also ridden with power struggles, as depicted in *The Tale of Genji*. Its central figure, Hikaru Genji, epitomizes "unparalleled glory and unparalleled sorrow" (Field 1987: 215), like the gorgeous blooms, which fall to the ground usually after about two weeks. In other words, cherry blossoms represent both the life force and its loss.

In the early tenth-century *Kokinwakashū*, of the seventy poems with cherry blossoms as their theme, fifty focus on blossoms between their peak and their fall, whereas only twenty are about blossoms from budding to full bloom (Noguchi 1982: 78). Some poems link *falling* cherry petals not only to the impermanence of life but also directly to death.[8] In *Tales of Ise* (*Ise Monogatari*), compiled by an anonymous person most likely before 950 CE, falling cherry blossoms are foregrounded, and they were increasingly linked to pathos over the impermanence of life and of love in Heian high culture; yet they are not directly associated with death itself.[9] Along with the sunny

Tale of Genji, these collections of poems indicate that falling cherry petals symbolized the loss of love, life, power, and wealth.

If men used the metaphor of cherry blossoms for women, women too used the flower in their expressions of love. As records from ancient times show, young women wore a cherry branch with its blossoms on their head and placed it atop a bamboo pole in their yard. During the Edo period (1603–1868) a woman would tie her *kosode*, a type of garment, to a cherry tree as a sign of her willingness to accept her lover (Miyata 1987: 123–24).

These literary pieces tell us that during ancient and medieval times (1185–1603), cherry blossoms stood for the life force, but also its loss, especially after a short period. This symbol denoted the entire process of life and death, but not exclusively death itself.

CELEBRATION OF ALTERNATIVE IMAGINATIONS

The polysemy of cherry blossoms presented so far belongs to the normative world of Japanese culture. The same polysemy, if not even more accentuated, appears in the Japanese depiction of alternative imagination. Every society institutionalizes and often celebrates the forces and ideas that oppose and subvert the norm. Ritualized forms include carnivals, charivaris, and a number of folk festivals, such as May Day (see Chapter Six). In Japan, cherry blossoms, central to the normative social structure and its values, are also the master trope for the celebration of an alternative universe.

During medieval times, the term *kuru'u* meant both "to become insane" and "to dance," and dancing in turn was an act of communicating with the deities (Ohnuki-Tierney 1987: 78–81, 104, 150, 227). Thus, those who "lost their mind" and those who "danced" acquired a special religious power, thereby gaining another identity beyond the one in society. The two major traditions of the performing arts, noh and kabuki, are called *kyōgen kigyo*, meaning "the world of make-believe" (*tsukurimono no sekai*), reminding us of existential instability, posing basic questions about the order of the universe, and offering provocative alternatives for imagination.

The loss of self through madness is another phenomenon associated with cherry blossoms (Watanabe Tamotsu 1989: 181), as expressed in a well-known phrase, "The flower [cherry blossoms] turns people's blood crazy."[10] Expressions of this association are found in some of the best-known plays in the performing arts and literature. For example, in the noh play *Cherry Blossom River* by Ze'ami Motokiyo (1935a), a woman loses her mind when her daughter, named Cherry Blossom Child, sells herself to a merchant in order to help her mother out of dire poverty. The mother goes in search of her child. In a famous scene, the daughter finds her mother, who had lost her mind, scooping cherry petals—that is, her daughter—out of a river, so as not to lose her (Matsuoka 1991: 228–35; Nakanishi 1995: 259–70).

Nullification and destabilization of the socially constructed self through the use of masks is a practice found in many festivals worldwide. The use of masks and masquerade has also been a quintessential feature of cherry blossom viewings among both the elites and the folk, in the past as well as today. A popular form of masquerade is cross-dressing, most often men wearing a wig and a woman's kimono with face painted white and lips red. Slapstick (*chaban*), ubiquitous in cherry blossom viewings, also emphasizes changing identities (Ono 1992: 168–69).

In the noh play, a classical theater form of Japan since medieval times,[11] actors always wear a mask, taking on the identity of the character they represent. The noh theater thus institutionalizes the impermanence of self-identity through this obligatory use of masks. A highly complex system of symbolism characterizes noh and involves cherry blossoms in a number of well-known plays.[12] Stylized cherry blossoms are a major motif on noh robes, fans, and lacquerware containers used on stage.

Kabuki also abounds with plays in which cherry blossoms are associated with madness. In Takeda Izumo's *Branches of Cherry Blossoms Deep in the Mountains Beyond One's Reach* (Gunji et al., eds., 1970: 121–24), Abe-no-Yasuna, a handsome young man, loses his mind upon the death of his love. He movingly dances on the stage under a blooming cherry tree while trying to capture a butterfly, which symbolizes his soul, departing from his body. Cherry blossoms here represent and aestheticize madness.[13]

The institutionalization of an alternative universe is also marked by cherry blossoms. An example is the medieval practice at powerful and wealthy temples where a number of young men, called *chigo*, who stayed for an average of four to five years, underwent a temporary change of gender. During this period the youths applied cosmetics like women and learned flower arrangement and other forms of art to simulate idealized court ladies. In paintings they are often depicted with cherry blossoms, and in literature metaphors of cherry blossoms are used in reference to them (Haruyama 1953: 211; Umezu 1978: 5).

Another example of the institutionalization of an alternative universe, marked by a symbolic equation with cherry blossoms, is geisha and the geisha quarters. Though culturally sanctioned, the institution of geisha, non-reproductive members of society, was outside, or an antithesis to, the society whose continuity depends on women's reproductive capacity. Yet they were celebrated in visual and performing arts and romanticized by the folk. Along Nakanochō, the main street of Yoshiwara, the former geisha quarters in Tokyo, a long, rectangular bamboo-fenced platform is built, filled with dirt, and then planted with cherry trees on February 25 of the lunar calendar each year (Ono 1983: 34–35; Shibundō Henshūbu 1973: 84).[14] Guests are invited to view the cherry blossoms on March 3, the day of the Doll Festival, when families with girls celebrate with a replica of the imperial court in Kyoto, with dolls representing the emperor, empress, and imperial court officials, and with a miniature artificial cherry tree and *tachibana* citrus tree.

Woodblock prints of the Edo period depicting the idealized world of geisha, called *ukiyo-e* and originally derived from Buddhist cosmology, treat the "floating world" as an expression of the ephemerality of life in general. Cherry blossoms began to be associated with the pathos of evanescence during the medieval period, and they were summoned to represent the floating world as well. The aesthetic of these representations has a dual quality—threatening and enticing at the same time (Nishiyama 1985: 11). The effect of duality is produced by depicting blossoms in the dark of night, but always highlighted by the full moon or lanterns from the windows of geisha houses to attract clients. The universe represented by cherry blossoms, then, is full of paradoxes that become a generative power operating at both the individual and the collective level—simultaneously subverting and upholding received wisdom and the normative social structure. These antitheses keep in check the hegemony of the normative world and its grip on the individual.

For ordinary people, woodblock prints offered access to a fantasy world. The mysterious beauty of white cherry blossoms against the dark sky became a favorite motif for masters of woodblock prints (Figure 2). *Flowers at Yoshiwara* (*Yoshiwara no Hanazu*) by Utamaro, dated 1794 or 1795, depicts the glittering gaiety of Nakanochō nightlife, with forty-five colorfully dressed geisha and attendants under cherry trees in bloom highlighted by the glow of the full moon (Narazaki, ed., 1981: 49–50). Another famous print, *Famous Places in the Eastern Capital: Night Cherry Blossoms at Yoshiwara Nakanochō* by Andō Hiroshige (1797–1858), portrays a night scene with lanterns, geisha and their attendants, and fully blooming cherry trees planted on the bamboo-fenced platform (Nihon Ukiyo-e Kyōkai, ed., 1968). The eerie effect of white blossoms in the dark is created by light from the full moon and the

FIGURE 2. Dawn at the pleasure quarters. A man leaving the Yoshiwara geisha quarters, perhaps having overstayed, in violation of the rule that clients could stay only one day and evening. Artist: Hiroshige. Source: E.B. Van Vleck Collection of Japanese Prints #1980.1617. Courtesy of Chazen Museum of Art, University of Wisconsin, Madison.

lanterns, seen through the windows of geisha houses, casting light on the blossoms. The juxtaposition of cherry blossoms aglow in the night with geisha in the geisha quarters adds a threatening sensuality to the image.

Daytime cherry blossoms occupy the opposite space from those at night. They are an important symbol for *maiko*, young apprentices to the geisha. Today in Kyoto, for the famous Dances of the Capitol (*miyako odori*), the debut performance by *maiko*, the main and almost exclusive motif is cherry blossoms. Blossoms are painted over the entire background of the stage; they hang from the ceiling and adorn the *maiko's* hair, and are used in the design on their kimonos. All of these cherry blossoms are depicted against a brightly lit blue spring sky (Figure 3 and Plate 2).

Cherry blossoms are a major stage prop and theme in the kabuki theater, "the vessel of the sunny (*yang*) principle" (*yōno utsuwa*), used to create a sense of beauty and gaiety (Yoshida and Hattori 1991: 219). This popular theater form reached its apogee during the Edo period and has sustained its popularity until today. Cherry blossoms in full bloom are often painted on the back wall of the stage and artificial branches of cherry blossoms are

FIGURE 3. The Dance of the Capitol (*miyako odori*). The debut performance by *maiko* (young apprentices to geisha). Source unknown.

fixtures in the theater, always hung from above across the entire stage. Many well-known scenes take place under artificial blossoming cherry trees on-stage.[15] The geisha quarters, a major theme of the theater, are symbolized almost solely by cherry blossoms—the daytime blossoms representing their gaiety, with the high-ranking geisha (*oiran*) clad in gorgeous multicolored kimono, and the eerie whiteness of cherry blossoms at night representing their sensuality. Dancer-entertainers (*shirabyōshi*) are also popular figures in kabuki, and their dances involve cherry blossom motifs. The association of masculinity with cherry blossoms is conspicuously expressed in the well-known repertoire of kabuki actors. "Falling flower petals" (*rakka*) is a regular stage technique to enhance an actor's performance by having cherry petals fall where he dances. In another standard technique, "flower rains" (*hana-no-ame*), an actor dances carrying an umbrella on which petals fall (Toita and Yoshida 1981: 50, 44, respectively). Many plays are famous for scenes that involve cherry blossoms.[16] In these scenes the flowers represent an unqualified celebration of life (Watanabe Tamotsu 1989: 179).

On the other hand, kabuki, which celebrates sunny cherry blossoms, also has a standard stage motif of a broken branch of blooming cherry as a sign of approaching death.[17] In folk beliefs, cherry trees, especially the drooping cherry (*shidarezakura*), are thought to be a conduit between the dead and the living, between the afterworld and this world (Yanagita 1930 [1982]: 215–16; [1947] 1982a: 225–26).

LIFE UNTO DEATH

The delicate balance between life and death—two meanings represented by the flower—can tip one way or the other, and the two are intimately linked layers in the polysemy of cherry blossoms. An example is the transformation of the flower's meaning from life to death during the military period in Japan. After Japan embarked on its march toward imperialism from the end of the nineteenth century until 1945, the state made a strenuous effort to modernize, industrialize, militarize, and Westernize all at the same time, with great urgency and intensity. During this period the symbolism of the cherry blossom underwent dramatic changes, facilitated by its polysemy.

In the face of encroachment by Western colonialism, which had seized all the other nations in the Far East, the building of a modern military force was the utmost priority. An Imperial Rescript to Soldiers, written by Nishi Amane, was issued in 1882, before the promulgation of the Constitution of

Imperial Japan in 1889. A famous/infamous passage in the rescript states that soldiers' obligation to the country is as heavy as the mountains, but their own lives are as light as feathers. In his 1878 lecture, "The Moral Code of Soldiers" (*Heike Tokkō*), a draft of this rescript (Yui, Fujiwara, and Yoshida, eds., [1996] 1989: 149–62), Nishi advocated that Japan's new soldiers embrace the Japanese spirit, referring to a very well-known poem by Motoori Norinaga in which he equates the Japanese spirit with "mountain cherry blossoms / that bloom fragrantly in the morning sun."[18] In this poem Motoori Norinaga praises cherry blossoms as a celebration of life (e.g., Saitō 1979 [1985]: 54; Toita and Yoshida 1981: 20; Yamada 1977: 117), without any reference to falling cherry petals.[19]

An even more explicit connection between the flower and the Japanese is found in *Bushido: The Soul of Japan*, published in 1899 in English, with a Japanese translation in 1908,[20] by Nitobe Inazō (1862–1933). Like many other Meiji intellectuals, Nitobe was a cosmopolitan liberal, opposed to both militarism and imperialism. Between 1919 and 1926, he worked closely with intellectual leaders such as Albert Einstein, Marie Curie, and Henri Bergson at the League of Nations. Nitobe stripped *bushidō* of its militaristic and antimodern elements and presented it as the most admirable aspect of the Japanese tradition. As seen in the subtitle, he equated *bushidō*, "chivalry" in his translation, with the "Japanese soul" (*tamashii*) and declared: "Chivalry is a flower no less indigenous to the soil of Japan than its emblem, the cherry blossom; nor is it a dried-up specimen of an antique virtue preserved in the herbarium of our history. It is a living object of power and beauty among us" (Nitobe 1899 [1912]: 1).

By "indigenous," Nitobe means that the sources of *bushidō* are to be found in Buddhism, Shintoism, and the doctrines of Confucius and Mencius, although he was a Christian himself. Citing the poem by Motoori Norinaga, he establishes cherry blossoms as a metaphor for the Japanese soul (*Yamato damashii*) (Nitobe 1899 [1912]: 150–53). Thus, like Nishi Amane, he saw cherry blossoms, standing for *bushidō*, as sunny flowers, symbolizing life. However, Nitobe placed *bushidō* in Japan's emperor-centered ideology (Nitobe 1933 [1969]: 330).

The subsequent deployment of the symbolism of cherry blossoms by the state led to a radical shift, with hardly anyone noticing it. The sunny and vigorous flower was transformed into fallen petals to symbolize soldiers' sacrifice of their lives for the emperor/Japan. In this transformative process, the Yasukuni National Shrine played a decisive role (Figure 4 and

FIGURE 4. Yasukuni National Shrine today. Photo by the author.

Plate 3). Originally, the shrine was constructed to console the souls of fallen warriors who had fought on the side of the "restoration"; cherry trees were planted and the shrine was a space for various entertainments, including sumō matches, fireworks, and horse racing in 1877, 1878, and 1881 and an Italian circus in 1871.[21] It was a public park where people strolled, enjoying cherry blossoms, as depicted in an 1893 print by Yōsai Nobukazu (1872–1944) (reproduced in Yasukuni Jinja 1984: n.p.; see Tsubouchi 1900: 55, 57).

Despite its beginnings, the shrine had become the preeminent citadel of military ideology by the time Japanese militarism reached its height in the 1930s. In this process cherry blossoms became thoroughly militarized. As Japan adopted the Western military system, it developed military insignias with cherry buds, leaves, and blossoms (Figure 5).[22] First in 1933 and then every year between 1937 and 1942, sometimes twice a year, the government performed a mass enshrinement ceremony at the Yasukuni Shrine for the souls of fallen soldiers (Earhart 2008: 412) and gave the mothers of fallen soldiers medals with a cherry blossom attached. Between 1933 and 1935, the shrine published a five-volume history, edited by Kamo Momoki, its High Priest, together with the Offices of the Ministry of Army and Navy (Kamo,

FIGURE 5. Cherry blossom motifs in military insignias, 1870–1943. Although Japanese military insignias are numerous and have undergone many transformations, those in the drawings are representative insignias of the Imperial Navy and Imperial Army, both of which used cherry blossoms, leaves, and branches as major motifs. Drawings by the author.

Kaigun Daijin Kanbō, and Rikugun Daijin Kanbō, eds. 1933–1935). The title, *The History of the Loyal Souls at Yasukuni Shrine*, makes evident that the character of the shrine had undergone a basic change. "Falling cherry petals"— such as those emblazoned on the book jackets of each volume—became the emblem of soldiers' sacrifice for the emperor (Figure 6 and Plate 4).[23]

Another expression of the militarization of cherry blossoms is the formation of the ultraright Cherry Blossom Society (Sakura-kai) in 1930 by army officers with the goal of domestic reform and the colonization of Manchuria. They advocated the use of violence, if needed. By 1931, after several unsuccessful attempts at a coup d'état, the society was dissolved (Takahashi [1965] 1969). Even though the Sakura-kai was a short-lived affair, it left a conspicuous presence in the history of Japan's march toward militarization.

Like other authoritarian states, Japan embarked on the inculcation of the young through the nationalization of the school system. In 1873, the government codified that the school year would start in April, since it was the beginning of spring, marked by the blossoming of cherry trees. This was gradually adopted, beginning in 1892 with elementary schools, in 1901 for middle schools, in 1919 for high schools, and only in 1921 for universities. Since then, the beginning of the school year at all levels has been symbolically associated with full-bloom cherry blossoms.[24] The state deployed textbooks and school songs in an effort at what George Mosse (1975) called the "nationalization of the masses." The Ministry of Education issued a new series of textbooks for the national language in 1932 that were used from 1933 to 1940.[25] They were commonly known as *Cherry Blossom Readers* (*Sakura Dokuhon*) and had a color illustration of full-bloom cherry blossoms on the cover and the first page. The series ends with volume 12 for sixth graders, in which ten poems equating mountain cherry blossoms with the Japanese soul (*Yamato damashii*) by well-known Edo period intellectuals are cited. The last poem, by Takazaki Masakaze, expresses how lucky a human being is to be born in the country under the sun (Japan) (Yamazumi 1970: 8–11).

Music underwent a drastic change during the same period, with an almost complete switch to the Western melodic pattern. In the very first music textbook for elementary schools, published in 1881, cherry blossoms appeared as a symbol of cultural nationalism, without reference to militarism. Later, school songs and other songs became increasingly laden with political, nationalistic, and militaristic propaganda. A kindergarten song published in 1887, "The Counting Song" (*Kazo'e Uta*) (Horiuchi and Inoue, eds., [1958] 1995: 28–29), originally an innocent children's song in the Tokyo area during the Edo period, with lyrics by an unknown writer, was altered in the 1887 school song version to include a blatant "die for the emperor" ideology: "Mountain cherry blossoms, mountain cherry blossoms, even when they fall, it is for His Majesty." In 1888 the song for "The Day of Commemoration of the Founding of the Imperial System" (*Kigensetsu*) (Horiuchi and Inoue, eds., [1958] 1995: 30) was composed, following the government's proclamation in 1872 that the emperor Jinmu had acceded to the imperial throne on February 11, 2,600 years earlier. The song, which became compulsory in schools, portrayed the Japanese as joyful and grateful for the emperor, the father of all Japanese, and his reign, even though Jinmu was only a legendary figure.

The symbolic complex "to fall like cherry blossoms for the emperor/country" began to appear frequently in song lyrics from the period just be-

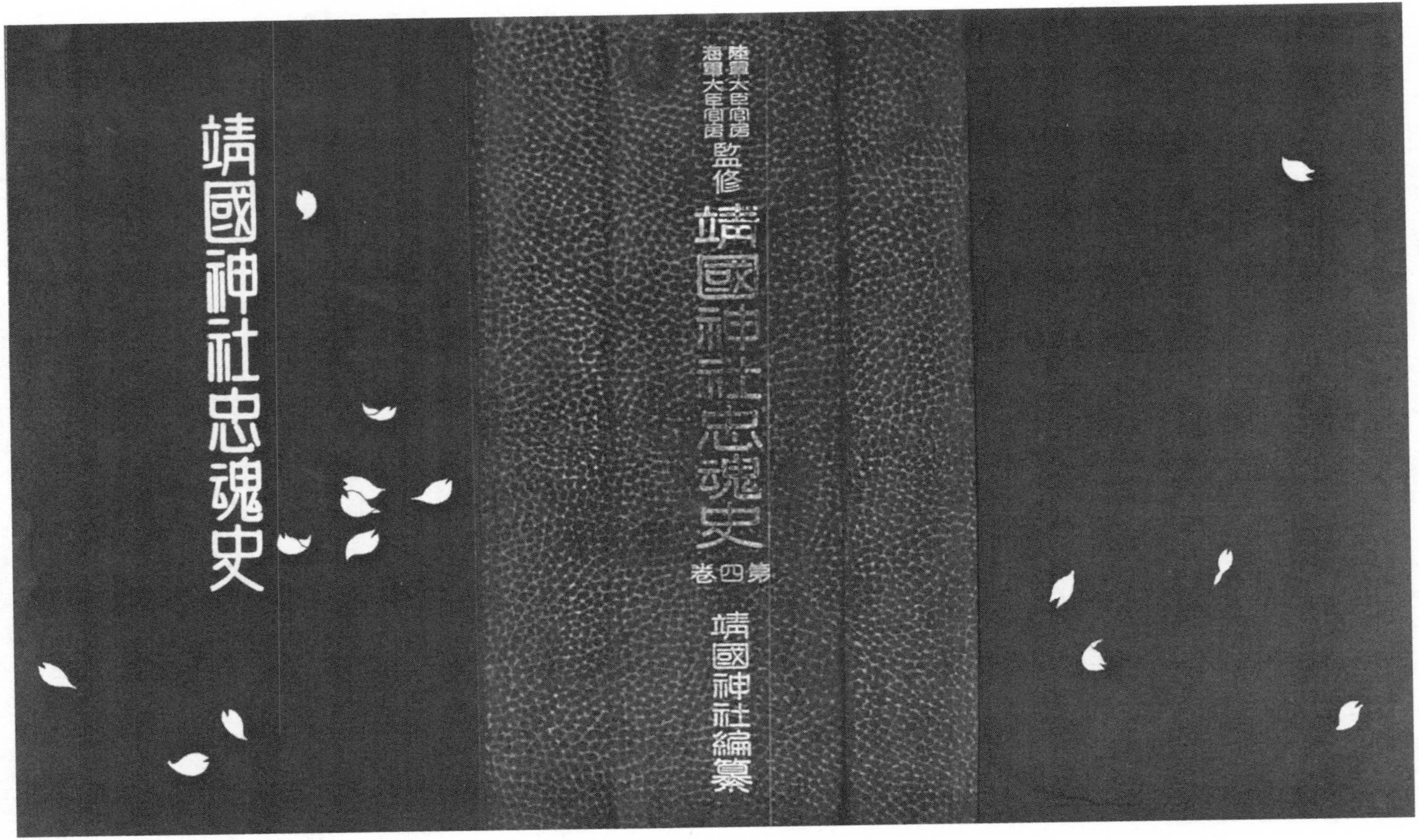
靖國神社忠魂史
陸軍大臣官房
海軍大臣官房 監修
靖國神社忠魂史
第四巻
靖國神社編纂

fore the Sino-Japanese War (1894–1895). In 1894, Sasaki Nobutsuna (1872–1963), a highly regarded scholar of classical poetry, composed a lengthy song entitled "The Song of the Conquest of China" (*Shina Seibatsu no Uta*). It is replete with references to mountain cherry blossoms fragrant in the morning sun and sacrifice of the Japanese for the country/emperor. It proclaims that Japan must help its neighbor (China), which is still not "enlightened," by "conquering" (*seibatsu*) its citizens (Nishizawa 1990: 1987–2106).

Military songs (*gunka*) reached a peak of popularity during the Sino-Japanese War (Sonobe and Yamazumi 1962 [1969]: 64–68) and again during the Russo-Japanese War (1904–1905) (Horiuchi and Inoue, eds., [1958] 1995), although those of the earlier conflict remained the best-known and most popular among the general public. Remarkably, a number of children's songs, based on old children's stories, created around 1900,[26] all shared the basic melodic pattern of military songs (Sonobe 1962 [1980]: 82–83, 88–89). The Western melodic pattern adopted by the Japanese at that time appealed also to young men—the intellectual crème de la crème who attended the elite higher schools and universities and were to become leaders in politics, business, and education. Since they all were housed in dormitories, some of the students composed dormitory songs, which became well-known among the Japanese public. Many of these songs appealed to the students' sense of masculinity and their pride as future leaders, which in turn made fighting for Japan their responsibility and also a virtue (Horiuchi and Inoue, eds., [1958] 1995: 76–77, 104–5).

The state continued to inculcate the people with the idea of falling petals symbolizing loyalty to the emperor throughout the Taishō period (1912–1926), when more liberal and democratic trends were also developing (Duus 1988). This effort culminated in 1937 when Nobutoki Kiyoshi composed a melody with lyrics from a long poem from the *Man'yōshū* by Ōtomo no Yakamochi (716–785), who was in charge of the imperial guards (*sakimori*) in ancient Japan. Although it does not contain references to cherry blos-

---

FIGURE 6 (*opposite*). Falling cherry petals as metamorphoses of fallen soldiers. The illustration shows how the symbolic association between "falling cherry petals" and fallen soldiers who sacrificed their lives for the emperor had been firmly established by the 1930s. Source: cover of Kamo Momoki, Kaigun Daijin Kanbō, and Rikugun Daijin Kanbō, eds., *Yasukuni Jinja Chūkonshi* (History of the Loyal Souls at the Yasukuni Shrine), 1933–1935. Published by Yasukuni Jinja Shamusho; courtesy of Yasukuni Shrine.

soms, it became the de facto national anthem, encouraging soldiers to die for the emperor:

> In the sea, waterlogged corpses,
>> In the mountains, those corpses with grasses growing on them.
>> But my desire to die next to our emperor is unflinching.
> I shall not look back.

(Omodaka [1967] 1984: 86–91, poem 4094)

Nobutoki's song was broadcast on the day Japan entered World War II; it was played to accompany the silent prayer for the Nine War Deities who had perished at Pearl Harbor on December 8 (Japan time), and every time a *tokkōtai* (Special Attack Force; "kamikaze") plane took off toward the end of the war. The Imperial Rule Assistance Association (Taisei Yokusankai) (Kisaka 1996), founded in 1940 by Prime Minister Konoe to mobilize the people for the war effort, declared that this song was next in importance to the national anthem for its "national subject." Indeed, this dirge was broadcasted far more frequently than the national anthem.

With the abolition of regional lords and the wave of "civilization and enlightenment" sweeping through Japan in the early Meiji (1868–1912), castles were seen as useless vestiges of a wicked feudal age, ready to be turned into more useful spaces, such as public parks (Yamada [1941] 1993: 399–401). But, having resurrected the "warrior's way" without the warriors, the state established the symbolic association between cherry blossoms and soldiers qua yesteryear's warriors by systematically planting cherry trees in castle compounds, despite protests by former warriors that pine trees better represented them (Takagi 1999). Wherever a military unit was established, including at castles, cherry trees were planted. Many planted trees after military victories, especially at the end of the Russo-Japanese War. As Sano Tōemon, a third-generation cultivator of cherry trees, recollected, cherry blossoms "marched with the military" (Sano 1998: 95–96). The trees were also planted in the colonies to mark them as belonging to imperial Japan and to give comfort to and encourage Japanese emigrants to continue the Japanese way of life, including the viewing of cherry blossoms (for Manchukuo, see Kawamura 1998: 42–43). For the colonized Koreans, cherry trees planted by the Japanese on their land became a symbol of Japanese colonialism—far from being beautiful or sublime. After World War II they chopped down those at the Kyongbok Palace in Seoul in preparation for the fiftieth anniversary of the liberation from Japanese colonialism.

The symbolism of falling cherry petals reached its height with the *tokkōtai* operation at the very end of World War II (Figure 7). None of the young men in this operation truly volunteered (see Ohnuki-Tierney 2006a). When Japan was surrounded by American aircraft carriers whose sophisticated radar would not allow any Japanese military attacks, Vice-Admiral Ōnishi Takijirō and his right-hand men found the only solution left was to resort to the notion that the Japanese soul was supposed to be able to face death without hesitation. They hoped these soldiers would bring about the miracle of victory, just as when the *shinpū* (God's wind; pronounced also as *kami-kaze*) sank the Mongol fleet in 1281, preventing the Mongols from landing

FIGURE 7. Umezawa Kazuyo, *tokkōtai* pilot, 18 years old, before his final flight. Family photo. Courtesy of Dr. Umezawa Shōzō, his younger brother.

on Japan. The first *tokkōtai* army corps was named *Shinpū*. The pilots wore white headbands emblazoned with the rising sun in red and the two characters for "God's wind" (*shinpū*) in black calligraphy. A single pink cherry blossom in full bloom against a white background was painted on the side of each plane (Ebina 1977: 219) (Figure 8 and Plate 5). Many of the names chosen for the *tokkōtai* corps bore various Japanese words for cherry blossoms (Hattori 1991: 343; Ohnuki-Tierney 2002a: 163–66). In a well-known photo, Chiran High School girls waved cherry branches as the planes took off (Figure 9). It was taken on April 4, 1945, four months before the end of the war, that is, when the American invasion of Okinawa had already begun and the carpet bombing of Tokyo and other cities had been going on for some time. By then most of the Japanese would have been either starving or had been burned to death. Thus, it would be hard to imagine that the photo served any propaganda purpose. Unfortunately, this photo has been used extensively in publications about the *tokkōtai*, without contextualizing it and often inferring that the photo shows how the Japanese were all united in a fight to the death.

FIGURE 8. *Tokkō* plane with a single cherry blossom painted on its side. Housed in the Exhibit Hall of Yasukuni Shrine. Photo by the author.

FIGURE 9. Chiran High School girls waving branches with cherry blossoms at departing *tokkōtai* pilots of the Shinbu Corps, April 1945. Source: *Mainichi Shinbun.* Courtesy of the *Mainichi Shinbun.*

ONE FLOWER/MANY SELVES

Either an individual self or the collective self of a social group is born or redefined as it encounters the other (Ohnuki-Tierney 1998). Cherry blossoms have been a major symbol of collective identity of the Japanese as they encountered different selves throughout history. However, their representation by a single flower as metaphor is misleading, since an enormous array of meanings for different purposes emerged.

Many Selves within Japanese Society: Cherry Blossom Viewing   Perhaps the most conspicuous expression of the Japanese celebration of the flower is the *hanami,* the ritual of cherry blossom viewing, almost always involving drinking, dancing, and other merry-making. Different social classes and regions have developed their own traditions. When the blossoms are in full bloom, the entire archipelago becomes a mosaic of social groups represented by many varieties of *hanami.*[27]

The *hanami* among the folk dates back to the ancient period, as described in an eighth-century record, *Hitachi-no-Kuni Fudoki,* which testifies that it was an already established annual ritual with the exchange of poems and dancing as essential components (Akimoto [713] 1958: 41). In ancient Japan, singing, dancing, and playing music were all religious activities. Even sexual intercourse had a religious meaning. *Hanami* seems to have been an important spring religious ritual during which women and men climbed a mountain—a sacred space—where cherry trees grew in order to feast and drink, while composing poetry, dancing, and making love.

The relationship between the agrarian tradition of *hanami* and *hanami* among religious specialists and aristocrats in Kyoto, the capital as well as the urban center, is unclear, although they shared the agrarian cosmology based on the political economy of rice production. Since the Nara period (646–794), cherry blossom viewing at established shrines and temples has followed another religious ritual, *sakura-e* (cherry blossom meetings), during which monks and priests pray (Sakamoto 1995). The drinking of sake is an important part of these observances; it is an act of commensality between humans and the deity, because the wine made from rice is symbolically the deity's body (Wakamori 1975: 180–81).

In 813 Emperor Saga (r. 809–823) held the first imperial viewing of cherry blossoms, called "the feast of the flowers" (*hana-no-en*), according to *Teiō Hen'nenki* (Kuroita and Kokushi Taikei Henshūkai, eds., 1965b: 183). The aristocratic *hanami* tradition lasted well into the night (Seidensticker 1977a: 150–57; Yamagishi, ed., 1958: 301–14) as the elite composed and read poems and played musical instruments. It epitomized the opulence and high culture at the imperial court, as portrayed in many literary pieces, such as *The Tale of Genji*, and in the visual arts. This tradition, although changing in form and nature over time, continued until the early 1930s (Nihon Hōsō Kyōkai, ed., 1988).

As the so-called ancient imperial system (*kodai ōchō*) came to an end and Japan entered the long period of being governed by warriors (1185–1868) the warlords established their own tradition of *hanami*.[28] Famous is one held by Toyotomi Hideyoshi, the first political leader who not only controlled the entirety of Japan but also attempted to build an empire by conquering Korea and China. On April 20, 1598, he held the ritual at Daigo Temple, known as the *Hanami* at Daigo. His wife, secondary wives, and their servants—altogether 1,300 women—were clad in fabulous kimonos, which they changed twice during the event. Altogether 3,900 kimonos had to be prepared, a task that fell on the Shimazu clan, whose feudal lord was one of the most powerful in Japan. This was obviously a way to

PLATE 1. Cherry blossoms as the spring counterpart of rice in the fall with rice paddies below. Artist: Hiroshige. Source: E.B. Van Vleck Collection of Japanese Prints #1980.1108. Courtesy of Chazen Museum of Art, University of Wisconsin, Madison.

PLATE 2. The Dance of the Capitol (*miyako odori*). The debut performance by *maiko* (young apprentices to geisha). Source unknown.

PLATE 3. Yasukuni National Shrine today. Photo by the author.

PLATE 4. Falling cherry petals as metamorphoses of fallen soldiers. The illustration shows how the symbolic association between "falling cherry petals" and fallen soldiers who sacrificed their lives for the emperor had been firmly established by the 1930s. Source: cover of Kamo Momoki, Kaigun Daijin Kanbō, and Rikugun Daijin Kanbō, eds., *Yasukuni Jinja Chūkonshi* (History of the Loyal Souls at the Yasukuni Shrine), 1933–1935. Published by Yasukuni Jinja Shamusho; courtesy of Yasukuni Shrine.

PLATE 5. *Tokkō* plane with a single cherry blossom painted on its side. Housed in the Exhibit Hall of Yasukuni Shrine. Photo by the author.

PLATE 6 (*right*). Folding screen depicting Edo period scenes of cherry blossom viewing (seventeenth century). Artist unknown. The screen shows that each social group has its own space. Courtesy of Chazen Museum of Art, University of Wisconsin, Madison, John H. Van Vleck Endowment Fund purchase, 1995.44.

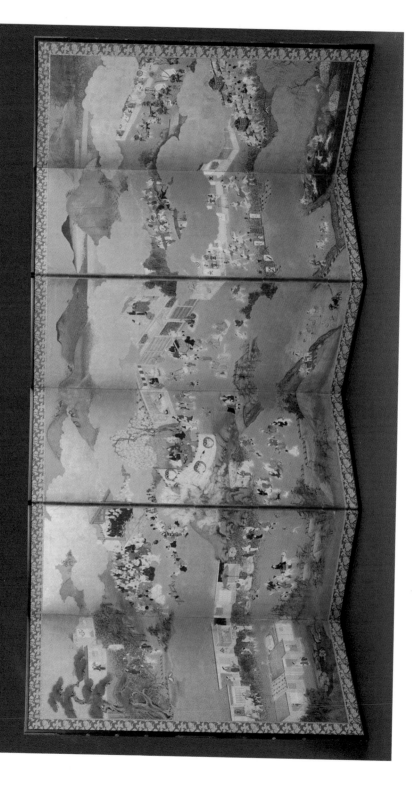

PLATE 7. *The First of May. Long Live the Festival of the Workers of All Countries*, by S. I. Ivanov. The May Day Goddess sprinkles roses, with workers below receiving them. Colored lithograph, 1920. 106×65 cm, BS 427. Russian State Archive.

PLATE 8. The Socialist International logo: a red rose with a clenched fist. Source: www.socialistinternational.org.

PLATE 9. *Thanks to Beloved Stalin for Our Happy Childhood*, by Nina Vatolina. Chrome-lithograph postcard, 1950. Stalinka GR000025. Courtesy of the Russian State Library.

PLATE 10. A Hitler stamp: Hitler receiving a bouquet of flowers from a little girl, 1940. Source: Colin Welch, "Stamps of the Nazi Era," http://research.calvin.edu/german-propaganda-archive/stamps.htm. Courtesy of Colin Welch.

deplete his financial resources and test his allegiance—a tactic Hideyoshi used for other feudal lords as well. The site of the *hanami* was made into a fortress, with twenty-three checkpoints tightly guarded by men with bows, spears, and guns (Shirahata 2012: 203–8). However, Hideyoshi included the regular repertoire of the *hanami*, including the carnivalesque. He himself wore a fake goatee and eyebrows and painted his teeth black (Kumakura 2007: 11), which was the practice of aristocrats (*kuge*) but not of warriors like himself.[29] He ordered all the feudal lords to appear dressed as Portuguese, the only Westerners granted access to Japan after Christianity was forbidden.

For both aristocrats and upper-class warriors, the *hanami* was an occasion to demonstrate their cultural sophistication, since composing and reading poems in praise of cherry blossoms were the most important features of the ritual, along with playing musical instruments and other expressions of refined taste. These lavish *hanami* of the elite were also occasions for the display of political power and wealth.

The *hanami* among common people reached its zenith during the Edo period, when the people of Edo (Tokyo) developed cherry blossom viewing as their major annual event—complete with masquerades and feasting, as well as the composition of poems (Ono 1992; see also Kawasaki 1967: 66–76). Men, women, and even monks enjoying dancing under blossoms is depicted in a number of folding screens and woodblock prints.

Today each and every segment of Japanese society—schools of all levels, neighborhoods, voluntary associations, and every social class—has its tradition of viewing the blossoms. Social stratification remains a salient feature. While major companies, schools, and other institutions have their own *hanami*, public places such as Ueno Park are where some, usually small and less established, companies claim their own space, sending the most junior employee early in the morning to claim a place and wait until early evening, when the rest of the employees come. The CEOs do not join them, but donate money for the purchase of food. These groups enjoy their own *hanami* but do not mix with each other.

The salient and enduring characteristics of *hanami* defy simple labeling and challenge some theoretical propositions about ritual in anthropology. *Hanami* takes place at the only public space in Japan. Yet it is far from the Habermasian public sphere, a discursive space characterized by free discussions among individuals to arrive at a common judgment. *Hanami* is an ephemeral space, lasting only as long as people choose to gather. It is public,

but is characterized by social stratification and reflects the divisions in Japanese society. Although the term *kisengunshū* (crowd of both high and low people) has been applied to describe the crowd (e.g., Shirahata 2000: 218–19), paintings of Edo period *hanami* depict the upper class having their own festivities behind a cloth curtain, bearing a family crest, that demarcates their space (Figure 10 and Plate 6). Aristocrats and the folk did not mingle. Each social group still had their own space and sociality.

Many Selves of the Japanese in the World   From ancient times, the flower stood for the Japanese as a people. Originally, mountain cherries were the only cherry trees that grew in Japan. During later periods the Japanese actively planted them in their yards, along rivers, and in temples, shrines, schoolyards, and geisha quarters—literally all over the country—in order to benefit from the tree's sacred power. In later years cherry trees were thought to have the power to purify water, which led to plantings along the embankments of rivers and aqueducts (Smith and Poster [1986] 1988).

In the *Man'yōshū*, references to cherry blossoms appear in verses by unknown poets and poets from rural Japan, indicating that the beauty of cherry blossoms was embraced by the folk.[30] At that time the elite in the capital at Kyoto adopted the aesthetic of plum blossoms as part of the high civilization of China (Saitō 1977: 41–43; Wakamori 1975: 172–73). In the eighth and ninth centuries, however, the elite gradually turned toward the native aesthetic of cherry blossoms. This was part of an effort among the Japanese, especially the elite, to assert their own identity as distinct from that of the dominant other, i.e., the Chinese, succinctly expressed by the replacement of the plum tree in front of the Imperial Palace with a cherry tree.

When Emperor Kanmu relocated Japan's capital from Nara to Kyoto in 794, a plum tree was planted on the left and a *tachibana* (*Citrus tachibana*) on the right in front of the Imperial Palace.[31] In the mid-ninth century the plum tree was permanently replaced by a cherry tree.[32] The cherry stood for life, while the citrus tree, with its evergreen leaves, stood for eternal life. The image has become familiar even to children through the observation of the Doll Festival on March 3.[33]

FIGURE 10 (*opposite*).   Folding screen depicting Edo period scenes of cherry blossom viewing (seventeenth century). Artist unknown. The screen shows that each social group has its own space. Courtesy of Chazen Museum of Art, University of Wisconsin, Madison, John H. Van Vleck Endowment Fund purchase, 1995.44.

The replacement of a plum tree by a cherry tree in front of the palace was not an isolated act. The ninth century saw significant changes in the attitude of the Japanese elite toward the Chinese, including the discontinuation in 894 of the official envoy to Tang China, which had been started in 630.[34] The Japanese style of painting, called *Yamato-e*, developed during the latter half of the ninth century, was a conscious effort by Japanese artists to develop their own style and break free of the tradition dominated by the Chinese style of painting, *kanga*, in which cherry blossoms did not have a place. Cherry blossoms became an important and frequently used motif in *Yamato-e*. Again they were chosen as a symbol of the Japanese and their art as opposed to Chinese art. The *Yamato-e* tradition focused on depicting the four seasons and the months of the year, each of which is represented by flowers and other features of nature.[35]

The development of the aesthetic of cherry blossoms and the abolition of the envoy to Tang China testify to the development of collective sentiment as a people at the time, at least among the elite. But this development was not so strong that the Japanese abandoned all Chinese influences. Profound admiration for Chinese civilization continued.[36]

In 1590 Edo (Tokyo) became Japan's urban center when Tokugawa Ieyasu, who became the shogun in 1603, occupied the castle there. Regional lords, who were forced to reside in the capital for three years at a time, brought cherry trees from their own region, resulting in 250 to 260 varieties of cherry trees in Edo alone (Hayashi 1982: 54–55). Edo represented Japan, which became "the land of cherry blossoms." For the propagation of this representation, woodblock prints played a crucial role. In a famous print series, *One Hundred Celebrated Places of Edo* (*Meisho Edo Hyakkei*), the artist Andō Hiroshige (Smith and Poster 1986 [1988]: 9–10) chose the places he portrayed based on the beauty of their cherry blossoms.[37] The government even sought to confirm the uniqueness of the cherry tree, which in fact is common in many parts of the world, by having Kaibara Ekken (1630–1714), a Confucian scholar-botanist, testify to it in 1698, after interviewing a Chinese from Sichuan province, where the tree did not grow, although it grew elsewhere in China (Saitō 1982: 28–29). The uniqueness of the tree to Japan was thus established.

When urbanization, modernization, and Westernization overtook Japan, cherry blossoms, together with a few other symbols of Japan, such as the fan, sumō wrestlers, rice paddies, Mount Fuji, and geisha, became powerful symbols of Japanese space—the land—and Japanese time qua history.

These were the symbols with which the Japanese represented themselves to Westerners, often in response to Western reactions to Japan. For example, when Commodore Perry arrived in 1853 and 1854, he and his men were fascinated by geisha and sumō wrestlers. The well-known 1887 painting of *Le Père Tanguy* by Vincent van Gogh (1853–1890) at the Musée Rodin in Paris is a self-portrait against the background of Japan, symbolized by cherry blossoms blooming above rice paddies, as in the woodblock print by Hiroshige of Mount Fuji and two geisha figures.

Within a few years, when the government and the people were thrust into the project of "modernization," cherry blossoms as a symbol of Japan took center stage in public discourse. Some proponents of "modern Japan" claimed that the hitherto popular expression "Cherry blossoms among flowers and warriors among people" epitomized the undesirable feudal Japan that must be shed (Yamada 1977: 115). Some began chopping down cherry trees and replacing them with more useful species like camphor trees, which were commercially profitable since camphor protects silk, rice paper, and other items from worms and moths. On the other side were enthusiastic supporters of another, equally "modern" Japan, including prominent politicians, who went out of their way to protect cherry trees, claiming that now that Japan had reopened and foreigners would be visiting, the country should be kept beautiful (Yamada 1977: 115). It was a turbulent period when the idea of "civilization and enlightenment" was enthusiastically embraced not only by the elite but also by the folk. Coined by Fukuzawa Yukichi in his *Bunmeiron no Gairyaku* (An Outline of a Theory of Civilization) published in 1875, the term referred to the wholesale adoption of Western culture, including the Western lifestyle, in the drive to modernize. An opposite force at work was heightened by political nationalism. Shintoism, the only indigenous religion of Japan, was elevated to the national religion in an 1870 decree that purported to eliminate "foreign religions," including Buddhism, which originated in India. Even the most famous temples and treasures were recklessly destroyed (Saeki 1988),[38] together with many famous cherry trees in temple compounds (Kyōto-shi, ed., 1975: 274; see also Kyōto-shi, ed., 1981: 604–5). During the early Meiji, then, the state had already begun the politicization of cherry blossoms, and the battle over the flower involved both the people and politicians, all trying to define new or modern Japan.

While cherry blossoms were involved, as it were, in Japan's raging struggle between cosmopolitanism, modernization, and nationalism, they became a state gift to other countries. The practice began with Mrs. Eliza Ruhamah

Scidmore, who was to become the first female board member of the National Geographic Society. The blossoms captured her attention during a trip to Japan in 1885. After twenty-four years of unsuccessfully trying to convince the U.S. Army Superintendent of the Office of Public Buildings and Grounds to plant Japanese cherry trees along the Potomac River, in 1909 she wrote to then First Lady Helen Herron Taft to inform her of her intention to buy cherry trees from Japan and donate them to the District of Columbia. Mrs. Taft responded that she had "taken the matter up" personally. This led to her acceptance of 2,000 trees as a gift from Mayor Ozaki Yukio of the City of Tokyo on January 6, 1910. However, an inspection team from the Department of Agriculture judged the trees diseased, and with the approval of President Taft they were burned on January 28. Mayor Ozaki then made another shipment—this time 3,020 trees, which arrived on March 26, 1912, and were planted along the Tidal Basin. In 1935 the District of Columbia commissioners sponsored a three-day celebration—the beginning of the world-famous Cherry Blossom Festival held annually, except during World War II (National Park Service 2009).

There have been other instances of the use of cherry trees to establish friendly relations with other nations. At the request of Ōtani Kōzui, the head monk of Honganji monastery, 100,000 seedlings were planted along the Siberian railroad, a multinational endeavor undertaken from 1891 to 1916 in which not only the Russians but also the Japanese, Chinese, and Koreans were involved. The monk's intention was to link the Far East to Europe with cherry blossoms in order to establish peace throughout the world (Sano 1998: 54–57). The practice of offering cherry trees intensified after World War II.[39]

The dominant meaning of the flower as the life force was vividly expressed after the tsunami and nuclear disaster in Fukushima on March 11, 2011. In the town of Kasugachō the government had set up temporary housing for those who had lost their homes in Tomioka City. A man interviewed on television told the reporter that not knowing their future—how long they would stay in the temporary housing nor when they would return to their own home—had been very hard for him and his wife, but the blossoms of one of the three most famous of Japan's cherry trees consoled (*nagusameru*) them. The tree, Takizakura, in Kasugachō, which has lived for a thousand years and keeps blooming, symbolized the disaster victims' zest for life. In addition, local people began inviting evacuees to their homes, establishing a social bond with them.[40]

The Aesthetic in Communicative Opacity

A host of phenomena, activities, emotions, and concepts represented by the flower's polysemy are assigned various aesthetic values because of their association with cherry blossoms, and their aesthetic quality becomes *naturalized* so that it is not articulated in people's minds. The "beautiful" of the blossoms against the blue sky could represent young women, but their threatening, eerie beauty at night stands for the alternative universe of the geisha. These different aesthetic values may be an expression of an ontological plurality, upholding the norm and yet offering provocative alternatives. If cherry blossoms are polysemic, they are equally polyvalent in reference to aesthetic values—the sublimity of healthy vigor, seductive gorgeousness, mysterious eeriness, the pathos of a short life, and so on.

By the time Japan embarked on its course toward modernization, cherry blossoms had become an important symbol at three different levels: the individual, social groups within Japanese society, and Japan and the Japanese as a whole. The penetration of the symbolism of cherry blossoms into life processes and human relationships at all levels of society was crucial in facilitating the military manipulation of this cherished image. The military did not need a novel symbolism to appear profound, sublime, and central, and could not have mapped all the changes it set in motion by embracing and using the symbol of the cherry blossom.

When Nitobe Inazō equated cherry blossoms and the warrior's way, he transferred the beauty of the flower to the Japanese soul, believed to be endowed with the unique capacity to meet death without hesitation. The flower came to represent the sublimity of the act of the warrior's sacrifice. But beauty also has the power to subvert, or deceive people into believing in its sublimity, which may be made into a weapon of oppression and war. It was hard for the people to realize that the warrior's way indeed meant killing themselves, since the act had been elevated to an aesthetic level.

Cherry blossoms were called to duty to aestheticize deaths of soldiers on the battlefield, followed by their resurrection at Yasukuni Shrine. Like cherry blossoms, which fall after a brief life, young men sacrificed their lives for the emperor, but they were promised rebirth as cherry blossoms at the national shrine where the emperor would pay homage. The military construction of blooming cherry blossoms as apotheosized soldiers at the national shrine is most astonishing in that it represents a reversal of the pre-Meiji symbolic structure: the same *blooming* cherry blossoms, which once stood for living warriors, went through a life cycle to become the souls of fallen soldiers.

For Sasaki Hachirō, a *tokkōtai* pilot, explicitly skeptical of the war ideology and critical and sympathetic to Marxism, cherry blossoms first appeared as a sunny symbol of youth and beauty. Later the flower became a counterpoint to the prevailing frenzied atmosphere in wartime Japan. Still later, cherry blossoms became a symbol of an ideal society and an ideal human being of modesty and purity, reminding Sasaki of the negative side of himself that sought and enjoyed honor and recognition from others. Ultimately, as the time of his sortie approached, cherry blossoms became the symbol of pilots, including himself, falling like petals. At this point Sasaki directly linked cherry blossoms and soldiers' deaths, but not as part of the *pro rege et patria mori* ideology (Ohnuki-Tierney 2006a: 49–50).[41] As their deaths became immanent, these student soldiers desperately tried to rationalize why they had to die in their youth. During this process, to aestheticize their deaths as sublime was comforting.

The rich and complex symbolism facilitated the flower's "natural" progression from cultural to political meanings and then to military nationalism and imperial colonialism, representing all these diverse ideas along the way, while its aesthetic contributed to the lack of articulation of the semantic changes in the mind of the people.

Conclusion

Cherry blossoms have stood for a large array of complex and overtly contradictory concepts: human reproduction; agrarian production; nonreproductive geisha and *chigo*; young women; warriors; life; death; madness, and a host of other important meanings in Japanese culture. The universe represented by cherry blossoms is full of paradoxes that become a generative power operating at both the individual and the collective level—simultaneously subverting and upholding the cultural and societal structure.

The many meanings assigned over time demonstrate that this symbol does not stand for an object in a neatly demarcated category, but for meanings embedded in overlapping layers of *processes* and *relationships*: life and death, women and men, the collective identity, which is always defined in opposition to the other. Within this complex nesting of concepts, emotions, and aesthetic, a slight tip of the scale can transform this symbol of life into a symbol of death, as happened during the military regime.

The symbol of cherry blossoms is pregnant with meanings that belong to an alternative imagination, a counterpoint to normative society and the received wisdom of its conceptual structure. The institution of the medieval temple boys, who underwent a period during which they took on the role of court ladies, poses the most fundamental questions about gender dichotomy and the permanence of gender identity. Likewise, the institution of the geisha, who are by definition nonreproductive, defies societal norms by celebrating the ephemeral world and the absence of regeneration. This intensely heterosexual world is represented in kabuki by all-male actors, defying the biological boundary between genders.[42]

The annual cherry blossom viewing by the elite upholds every normative value of Japanese high culture, including poetry and music, whereas the folk version is carnivalesque, with the use of masks, disguises, and slapstick, running counter to societal rules and cultural values. Not just a temporary change of social persona but a permanent loss of the self—madness—is also symbolized by the full bloom of this flower.

Cherry blossom viewing is also an arena for developing collective identity—as a member of a school, class, etc., all the way up to a nation as a whole. This group ritual links individual sentiments and thoughts to the collectivity; it laid the basis for cherry blossoms to become a symbol of cultural nationalism, which was then transformed into virulent political nationalism. This progression, or, rather, digression in the symbolic representations of the flower is an example of how symbolism undergoes profound changes in shifting geopolitical and historical contexts. The tidal wave of modernization and urbanization forced the Japanese to articulate their self-identity by projecting their land as the land of cherry blossoms. Western colonialism forced Japan to strive to be a militarily strong modern nation—leading to phantasmagorical tragedy for the Japanese and others through its own imperialism and wars.

These changes in the flower's meaning did not strike the Japanese, even the soldiers, as odd, let alone frightening, since they all shared a vast and rich field of meanings and images associated with "beautiful" cherry blossoms from which they could choose in a given context. The switch in emphasis was not consciously perceived, especially since the military simultaneously used blooming cherry blossoms as military insignia, celebrating the youthful vigor of the soldiers, and falling petals as the metamorphosed souls of fallen soldiers at Yasukuni Shrine. In other words, the same physical object—*blooming* cherry blossoms—came to represent both soldiers at the height of their power and their rebirth, predicated upon death.

Through many historical changes, the polysemy of cherry blossoms has served to articulate important concepts. Yet it has also contributed to communicative opacity, leading to unawareness on the part of the Japanese, who were not cognizant of their own exclusion from the representation by the flower and unable to realize that the drastic change of its meaning signaled that they were heading for their own destruction.

European Roses

From "Bread and Roses"
to the Aestheticization of Murderers

Just as cherry blossoms are a dominant flower for the Japanese, roses are for many other peoples. The rose, genus *Rosa*, is native to Asia, including China, Europe, the Middle East, North America, and northwest Africa. In these regions, the cultivation of roses started early in history. Unlike the Japanese cherry, which has limited utilitarian value, the rose has proven useful in many ways. Perfumes made from attar of rose or rose oil are highly valued. So too is rose water, used for cooking, cosmetics, medicine, and in religious practices. Like cherry blossoms, different species of roses, especially in reference to single or double layers of petals, are important. Also like cherry blossoms, the stages of the growth of roses—from a bud to full bloom—are significant in providing the flower with meaning. But, above all, it is the colors of roses—red, white, pink, dark pink, light pink, yellow, orange, burgundy, blue, or perhaps some other colors—that provide the basis for a rich and complex array of polysemy. Red and white are the most important among many European peoples, as discussed below. Most important, the rose, like cherry blossoms, is a quotidian symbol, used by ordinary people no less than by the elites in political spaces in most of these European societies.

Studying cherry blossoms in Japan is relatively easy since one is dealing with but a single culture/society. In Europe, however, roses are important symbols in many societies and cultures. What links the role of roses in different societies in Europe is what I refer to as their horizontal spread and vertical transmission. First, for the ruling class, in much of the history of empires, all of Europe, from the United Kingdom in the west to Russia in the east, was rendered borderless through intermarriage, and political boundaries were frequently redrawn through political conquest. Thus, for example, the pink rose symbolism associated with Marie Antoinette at Versailles may be more closely related to Austrian culture than to French culture, although the rose as a feminine regal symbolism seems to be more French than Austrian (see below).

Even more significant were the transnational movements of people across vast areas, transmitting religious, philosophical, and literary movements as well as material goods, including roses and their products, spices, and others. I point to three such movements, each of which will be detailed later. The symbolism of the rose is of central importance in most forms of Christianity, which in its enormously varied forms and practices is shared by so many peoples and classes such that German Catholicism and its symbols, for example, are shared by Catholics in other countries. Therefore, the symbolism of the white rose, discussed below, of the anti-Nazi movement seems closely related to the symbolism of the Virgin Mary, represented by the white rose, in Catholicism, as well as the symbolic space it occupies in German culture.

The spread and sharing also included important intellectual/literary movements. Enlightenment philosophy, with its formal expression in Paris, had a most profound and lasting impact in the intellectual history not only of the so-called West, but also of many other parts of the world, while encountering partial acceptance and resistance both in Russia and Japan. The same is true of romanticism. *Die Romantik* was officially founded at Jena in 1796 by A. W. von Schlegel and others. The longing or even romantic passion for nature and resistance to capitalism and materialism are some of the themes common to *die Romantik* in Germany, *le romantisme* in France, and the Russian romanticism of *narodnost* (national originality), each fusing with nationalism in each country. The symbolism of romanticism in reference to nature, in particular, flowers, therefore relates more to this movement and its sentiment against materialism and capitalism than to an individual cultural tradition. This literary movement reached Japan a century later. Beginning in 1890, *roman-shugi*, its Japanese designation, produced some of the best and internationally known literature. Its fusion with ultranationalism did not take place until 1935 and after.

Perhaps the most spectacular instance of horizontal global spread is the Socialist International, which was a worldwide movement and one that, more than any other movement, made systematic use of the red rose as a symbol. In this case, the red rose is related to workers in general, rather than in a particular society.

Second, not only has the sharing of the rose as a symbol been a result of horizontal spread, it has also been the result of historical transmissions. Thus some of the basic themes of rose symbolism sprang from the Egyptian and Greco-Roman cultures, which were transmitted to some of the latter-day Latin cultures. Needless to say, the transmission was never straightforward. One of the best-known examples of rose symbolism is *sub rosa* (under the rose). This Latin phrase refers to the use of the rose at a meeting room, where a flower is often hung from the ceiling, as a symbol of the sworn confidentiality of the participants, similar to the Chatham House Rule, originated in 1927 at the Royal Institute of International Affairs. The modern derivations of *sub rosa* have little to do with Egyptian or Greek myths from which it derived, although the precise genealogy is not known.

On the other hand, there seem to be some parallels among Latin cultures of France, Italy, and Spain, where roses enter communal activities, such as flower festivals, as well as expressions of love and other feelings between individuals. My cursory study hints that in Germany and Russia, the rose remains an extremely powerful symbol between individuals—the red rose as an expression of love being the singular most important meaning.

Below I offer only a sketch of this vast field, with particular emphasis on the nature of polysemy and its roles in political spaces.

The Rose in Religion, Literature, and Art

Both wild and cultivated roses appear in the Greek and Roman classics, the Bible, and the Zohar. The Romans were known to have been obsessed with roses. They were used at both private and official banquets and rose festivals were common, though not on fixed days. The most regularized use of roses was in commemoration of the dead (*dies rosationis*) (Hornblower and Spawforth, eds., 1996: 1335). In terms of rose symbolism, Venus, the goddess of love in Roman mythology, later combined with the Greek goddess Aphrodite, looms prominently, not least in the well-known painting *Venus* by Sandro Botticelli (c. 1444–1510). The complexity of rose symbolism starts early, as the following account by Goody (1993: 56) succinctly explains:

> Roses in turn became symbols of luxury. Zeus had slept on a bed of saffron, lotus and hyacinth, but it was a bed of rose petals that became the epitome

of the good life in Rome. However, the rose had its more melancholy side, not only because it had a place in funerals, nor even because of its thorns, but because, like other cut flowers in later centuries, it represented the evanescent nature of pleasure. So the flower not only stood as a symbol of luxury, but carried a message of warning about life itself; a canker lay within the rose.

After the fall of Rome and the intensification of asceticism, flowers in general and the rose in particular suffered a partial eclipse, since the rose was associated with Venus and earthly love as well as voluptuousness and debauchery (Goody 1993: 88–89). Those who wished to uphold the morality of society prohibited the symbolism of the rose.

In Judaism, the Thirteen-Petalled Rose in the opening of Zohar symbolizes the "collective souls" of the Jewish people (Steinsaltz 2006). Islam is well known for its strong opposition to images (see Chapter Six). The title of the chapter on Islam by Goody (1993: 101–20) is "Flowers without Representation in Islam." Yet, as Goody points out, Islam made a clear distinction—images were allowed or even encouraged in secular life but sacred space was virtually without icons (Goody 1993: 108). Abundant flowers in gardens were signs of royalty and luxury.

Due to the prohibition of iconographic representation in Christianity, the rose disappeared from religious iconographies of Western Europe until medieval times (Goody 1993: 120–65). During the Middle Ages, the red rose with five petals came to be seen as akin to the five wounds of Christ on the cross, becoming a symbol of Christ and Christian martyrdom. The white rose stood for the Virgin Mary and her purity and innocence, although she "did not herself become a rose" until her twelfth-century devotee, Saint Bernard of Clairvaux, together with Catholic writers, established her as "the most elaborate of ecclesiastical roses to date" (Seward 1960: 22). The Crusaders, as they fought for two centuries (1095–1291) to regain Jerusalem from the Muslims, brought back roses along with other items. Although the history of the association of the rose with the round stained glass window is not well established, the rise of the cult of the Virgin coincided with the birth of the High Gothic cathedrals, with their rose windows and their association with the Virgin. Although the first documented use of the term "rose window" is dated to the seventeenth century, the Virgin, who is referred to as a "rose without thorns," was often depicted in rose gardens or surrounded by garlands of roses in the late medieval period. Every rose window has a center in which either Christ or the Virgin is depicted (Cowen 2005: 19, 200, 222).

The round stained glass window symbolized Christ, the sun/son. The role of the rose in Christianity is well articulated in paintings such as *The Madonna of the Rose Garden*, variously attributed to Stefano da Verona (c. 1379–c. 1438) and *The Madonna in a Rose Garden* (1473) by Martin Schogauer of Germany. Martin Luther (1483–1546) created a design with a black cross in the middle of a heart surrounded by white roses, which he explained in 1530 to Lazarus Spengler: "The rose is to be white, not red, for the color white is the color of the spirits and all angels. Such a rose stands in a field the color of heaven, for such joy in spirit and in faith is a beginning of the heavenly joy which is to be" (Löwith [1964] 1991: 19).

On the other hand, the rose is celebrated as a metaphor of female sexuality in the widely popular medieval French poem *Le Roman de la Rose*, whose original 4,058 lines were composed by Guillaume de Lorris circa 1230; an additional 17,724 lines were written by Jean de Meun around 1275 (de Lorris and de Meun 1982–1984).

Like cherry blossoms, the rose blooms for only a short time before it withers and falls to the ground. Its thorns are a physical expression of the negative opposites of love and life. With this complex set of meanings, the rose became a prominent trope in literature and music, appealing to people of all walks of life. In *The Divine Comedy*, especially *Paradiso*, by Dante Alighieri (1265–1321), there are many references to the rose, such as the eternal rose (XXX.124), equated with eternal spring.

The symbolism of flowers, including the rose, reached its height with German romanticism. Perhaps the best-known reference to the wild rose appears in "Heidenröslein" by Johann Wolfgang Goethe (1749–1832), a poem written around 1770. It is said that Goethe composed it after leaving a young woman with whom he was in love. The poem has a prominent reminder of the thorns with which the rose will prick. More than 150 melodies were created for this poem. Among them the one by Franz Schubert, composed in 1815, and the one by Heinrich Werner were the best known and gained popularity outside of Germany.[1] Goethe regarded a cross garlanded with roses as the symbol of his idea of the "purely human" (Löwith [1964] 1991: 16–17). *Blaue Blume* (the blue flower) that appears in the unfinished *Bildungsroman* of Friedrich von Hardenberg (Novalis) (1772–1801) represents the meaning and imagery of flowers that occupied a central space in the literature of German romanticism.

René Karl Wilhelm Josef Maria Rilke, the poet of roses, chose as his epitaph:

> Rose, oh reiner Widerspruch, Lust,
> Niemandes Schlaf zu sein unter soviel
> Lidern.

> Rose, oh pure contradiction, delight
> of being no one's sleep under so many
> lids.

Even Georg Wilhelm Friedrich Hegel used the metaphor of the rose: reason is a "rose within the cross of the present."[2] There are countless other examples in poems, novels, and music in which rose symbolism is prominent, including in English literature (e.g., William Shakespeare's sonnets) and in French writing (e.g., the works of Paul Valéry).

With the advent of modernity, as discussed in the Introduction, the beautiful was coupled with the ugly. In nineteenth-century France, Charles Baudelaire (1821–1867) and French symbolists ushered in a radical transformation of the symbolism of flowers as symbols of *le mal* and *le spleen*—representing illness, afflictions, and the aftermath of the revolution. The movement also foregrounded the sublimity of the quotidian, for example, the red lipstick of prostitutes, as a striking antithesis to traditional aesthetics.

In sum, whether in high culture or in folk culture, a striking feature of rose symbolism is its representation of opposites. If the flower symbolizes love, its thorns embody the opposite—potential lethality; its gorgeous bloom is the celebration of life at its fullest, yet also a reminder of ephemerality and decay, and "pale death," which indiscriminately knocks at the door of the mighty as well as poor, as warned by Horace ([23 BCE] 1999: 16–17).

The Rose in Political Spaces

Although the imagery and meanings of the rose in art, literature, and religions are often so powerful as to overshadow its political uses, the rose has occupied important political spaces in many societies and in different historical periods. Its symbolic association with aristocratic splendor and political power began early. The cherished flower of Cleopatra VII (69–30 BCE) was the rose, and Claudius Caesar Nero (r. CE 54–68) adorned himself with garlands and crowns made of roses. This tradition continued well into later periods, as exemplified by the emperor Elagabalus, who ruled the Roman world between 218 and 222 CE, and who gave a dinner party accompanied, according to one Roman writer, by such a large number of rose petals, released from the ceiling, as to smother some guests to death (Arrizabalaga y Prado 2010). Although there is no proof of the authenticity of the records of his life, or, even his name, what is certain is that the legend attests to the symbolism of roses as regal power, in his case in excess.

The symbolic representation of regal power continues well into the medieval period. For example, Jeanne-Antoinette Poisson, the Marquise de Pompadour (1721–1764), the favorite mistress of Louis XV; Marie Antoinette (1755–1793), queen of France and consort of Louis XVI; and Joséphine de Beauharnais (1763–1814), the first wife of Napoleon Bonaparte and empress of France (1804–1809)—all indulged in the use of roses as a motif of interior decoration and clothing design, as well as cultivating them in their gardens, the best-known example of which is Joséphine de Beauharnais, who created the most luxurious rose garden at her Château de Malmaison. Abundant use of roses by the elite meant that instead of raising food crops peasants were forced to produce flowers, a luxury predicated upon the vast social stratification in Europe.

The first association with wars that comes to mind is the Wars of the Roses between the houses of Lancaster and York for the throne of England between 1455 and 1487; a red rose and a white rose, respectively, were their heraldic motifs (Hicks 2012). The last member of the House of York who actively sought the crown of England was nicknamed "White Rose" (Seward 2010). Although roses were the emblems of the houses, they became the symbol of the wars themselves. Even today in European cultures flowers are closely associated with wars, battles, and death, such as the red poppy as a symbol of soldiers who fell on the battlefields of Flanders during World War I. A German postcard from World War II called *My Regiment* features a machine gun lying in a bed of roses (Mosse 1990: 67).

THE ROSE AS AN ANTIESTABLISHMENT SYMBOL

Despite its association with political power, the rose has a long history as a prominent antiestablishment symbol beginning in medieval times. May Day was celebrated as a traditional early summer holiday, with flowers, including the rose, expressing abundance of life and energy even during pre-Christian days. Some believe that the Roman equivalent, Floralia, "was instituted about 242 B.C.," or derived from the Druids (Warren 1876: 179–80). The major theme was the celebration of fertility (Davis [1965] 1975: 138; Wheeler 1932: 34–39; see also Warren 1876: 179–92); this festival included the spectacle of prostitutes (Goody 1993: 88).

Of particular interest for this book is the relationship between the folk festival of *la fête de la rosière* (crowning of the "rose queen") and the festival of the French Revolution, in both of which rose symbolism was prominent. Using an example of *la fête de la rosière* at Suresnes in 1789–1780 near Paris as described by N. M. Karamzine, Mona Ozouf ([1976] 1994: see esp. 1–12) points out how utopian primordiality as the theme of this folk festival formed the basis for the people believing in the utopian vision of the Festival of the Supreme Being, unaware of the Terror lurking underneath Robespierre's Floréal text. François Furet ([1988] 1996: 147) writes that on the morning of June 8, Robespierre presided over a ceremony that started as "processions from the forty-eight *sections* [italics in the original] [and] converged on the Tuileries, men and boys on the right with their branches of oak, women and girls on the left with their bouquets of roses and their baskets." Indeed, this is a supreme example of the rose, celebrating life and its vigor, turning into "flowers that kill."

According to Hobsbawm (1984: 78), the adoption of May Day by the international socialist movement was "doubtless due to historical accident." However, Natalie Zemon Davis, historian of sixteenth-century France, convincingly argues that village festivals, including May Day and charivaris, in Lyon, Dijon, and elsewhere in France, were not "safety valves," as some functionalists have proposed. She argues that "festive life can on the one hand perpetuate certain values of the community (even guarantee its survival), and on the other hand criticize political order" (Davis [1965] 1975: 97). She shows that the Abbots (Abbeys) of Misrule (Abbés de Maugouvert), which originated as a youth group, were quite robust around 1500. The urban Abbeys of Misrule lost much of their vitality by the eighteenth century, but the tradition continued in the practice of "making noise," as in charivaris, to express political complaints; this lasted well into the nineteenth century in both cities and the countryside (Davis [1965] 1975: 97–123).

During the Second Socialist International in 1889 in Paris, the workers in attendance chose May 1 as International Labor Day as a form of protest. They demanded the worldwide adoption of the eight-hour work day (Flett 2002; Hobsbawm 1984: 76–81; Krivoguz 1989: 56–57). May 1 was selected as the closest date to May 4 in commemoration of the Haymarket affair in Chicago in 1886, during which a peaceful rally in support of workers striking for an eight-hour day turned into a clash between the workers and policemen, with casualties on both sides. The Haymarket affair is generally considered the origin of workers' observance of international May Day. We can be certain that, contra Hobsbawm, the adoption of May Day was no accident but a continuation of the antiestablishment ideologies and practices that became organized as a movement of the working class, not confined to a country but internationally.

Beginning in 1891, the May Day celebration became increasingly popular among workers in Russia, Ireland, Greece, and beyond (Krivoguz 1989: 97). As the color of "blood of the workers," representing the suffering of the proletariat, red had been associated with revolutionaries even before the European revolutions of 1848. Workers celebrated May Day with flowers— especially red carnations in Austria and Italy, red (paper) roses in Germany, and sweet briar and red poppies in France (Hobsbawm 1984: 78). The adoption of May Day as Labor Day inspired many artists and others, who produced various forms of representation of roses. Well known is *Cartoons for the Cause, 1886–1896*, by Walter Crane. *The Worker's May Pole*, dated 1894, has a maiden suspended at the top of the maypole at the center, with a garland of roses adorning her torso. Flowing down from the pole are several ribbons inscribed with words such as "Eight Hours," "Leisure for All," and "A Life Worth Living." A one-page poem accompanies this cartoon, which was published in *Justice* in 1894. In the poem, Crane characterizes the maypole as a symbol of spring, life, freedom, hope, and workers united.

Another cartoon by Crane, *A Garland for May Day, 1895* appeared in *Clarion* in 1895 (Figure 11). A maiden is at the center, holding a garland with roses over her head, with many ribbons flowing down to the ground on which demands not only for employment, but also for art and leisure and other shibboleths of the labor movement are written. In these shibboleths, one sees clearly the antecedent of "Bread and Roses"—workers wanted art and leisure.

The Russian revolutionary Grigory Gershuni (1870–1908) famously escaped in a sauerkraut barrel from a Siberian prison and went through Japan, where he met Sun Yat-sen, then exiled in Japan (Shillony 1981: 149–50), eventually reaching San Francisco on December 3, 1906.[3] He gave a speech on December 14, 1906 (*New York Times*, December 15, 1906, p. 2) at Carnegie Hall, where thousands of workers flocked to hear him. He spoke in Yiddish, and most in the audience were Jewish workers. Writing on Gershuni's

·A·GARLAND·FOR·MAY·DAY·1895·

·DEDICATED·TO·THE·WORKERS·BY·WALTER·CRANE·

FIGURE 11. *A Garland for May Day, 1895*, by Walter Crane. The drawing shows the long history of the relationship between rose symbolism and workers, dating back to medieval times. Source: *Clarion*, 1895.

visit to New York in her article "Bread and Roses," Rose Pastor Stokes (1919) quotes him: "I want you to wear this symbol of the joy and the beauty of life because we demand not only bread, but roses." She continues:

> Yes, Bread and Roses! When the Revolution was successful, did our fellow workers think only of bread? No. Great and terrible as the need was, they lost no time securing to themselves: in the fullest measure possible—Roses! Roses! The flowers of Song, the Dance, the Opera, Drama, and flowers of Science— of Knowledge.

Most importantly, she points out: "The Orchid of Culture, a hot-house plant nurtured exclusively for the Few, has been transplanted in Russia to the fields and the meadows, where it blooms freely as the common daisy for all the common folk to pluck at will."

In other words, by the turn of the twentieth century this most regal/ imperial flower of Nero and Cleopatra that once symbolized the political power of kings and queens had become the flower of workers/proletarians, although, as we will see in the next section, it continued to be used by the politically powerful—for example, Stalin and Hitler.

The rose as a symbol of May Day and workers must have become well established by the early twentieth century, as seen in a colored lithograph dated to 1920, in which roses scattered by a maiden (the May Goddess) are received by workers below (Figure 12 and Plate 7; see also White 1988: 107). This element of the festival was carried on by workers in most countries even after the celebration became International Labor Day. They sang revolutionary songs while drinking and eating (Flett 2002).

A red rose with two leaves and a clenched fist became the symbol of the Socialist International (Figure 13 and Plate 8), likely after 1917 (Hobsbawm 1984: 79), and the association of the red rose with socialism/communism continues today. The rose is in the logo of the socialist parties of most countries. Except for the white stylized rose in the logo of the Social Democratic Parties of Serbia and Montenegro, the rest use the red rose, in two ways: often with leaves, with a hand or without the hand. The former is variously referred to as "a hand holding a rose," "a hand grasping a rose," "the rose with a fist," or "the rose with a clenched hand." This is used as the logo of the International Union of Socialist Youth, the Social Democratic Party of Russia, the Spanish Socialist Workers' Party, the Democratic Labor Party of Brazil, the Socialist Youth of Turkey, and the Social Democratic Radical Party of Chile. The logo without the hand is used by the Party of European

FIGURE 12. *The First of May. Long Live the Festival of the Workers of All Countries*, by S. I. Ivanov. The May Day Goddess sprinkles roses, with workers below receiving them. Colored lithograph, 1920. 106×65 cm, BS 427. Russian State Archive.

Socialists, the Social Democratic Party of Bosnia and Herzegovina, the Social Democratic Party of Croatia (though it was abandoned in 1994 when the party merged with the SDP), the New Space of Uruguay, the Social Democratic Party of Ukraine, and the Grand Unity Party of Turkey. When a party has changed its logo, the rose usually has been added or retained. In 1983 the original "liberty" logo of the Labour Party of the United Kingdom, adopted in 1924 and featuring the torch, shovel, and quill, was replaced by the New Labour Party's logo of a red rose on a stem with leaves in a circle. The Spanish Socialist Workers' Party changed its logo from the fist and rose to a red stylized rose on white. In France, however, the red rose became the symbol of socialism only recently, when it was made the emblem of the French centrist political party of François Mitterrand, and the British Labor Party adopted it as its emblem (Goody 1993: 295–96).

In Russia, the color red (*krasnyi*) also means "beautiful" and had been a favorite color since prerevolutionary days (Lane 1981: 200–201). A number of objects became "red": for example, the red calendar, together with the hammer and sickle, introduced in 1918 (Lane 1981: 154); the red banner, red star (the emblem of the Red Army), and red kerchief, in all of which red represented the blood of the fathers and grandfathers who fought for the revolution. The Soviet Union held many celebrations and parades in Red Square, filled with red flags—May Day, the anniversary of the Great October Socialist Revolution (Lane 1981), Victory Day, etc.

FIGURE 13. The Socialist International logo: a red rose with a clenched fist. Source: www.socialistinternational.org.

In Russia, as elsewhere, the emphasis on the rose did not exclude other flowers (Goody 1993: 296–99). The carnation had been the flower workers offered to party functionaries on November 7 (October 25 in the Julian calendar, the date of the October Revolution) and on May 1. The carnation was associated with Saint Peter, although it originally was the flower of Zeus and therefore was important to the ancient Greeks.

THE ROSE/FLOWERS AS NONVIOLENT REVOLUTION

When the nonviolent nature of a revolution is to be foregrounded, flowers are often adopted as an emblem. For example, the coup d'état in Lisbon which started on April 25, 1974, and eventually led to a democratic Portugal, used the red carnation as its symbol, and in fact the coup was dubbed the Carnation Revolution. During the nonviolent Velvet Revolution in Czechoslovakia (November 16–December 29, 1989), which overthrew the communist government, demonstrators offered flowers to police to express their willingness to extend their good wishes.

The Rose Revolution was a peaceful movement in Georgia on November 23, 2003, during which Mikheil Saakashvili and his supporters, carrying roses as a symbol of nonviolence, seized the parliament building, interrupting a speech by President Eduard Shevardnadze, whom they succeeded in ousting. With a photo of Mikheil Saakashvili with red roses, the *New York Times* (January 5, 2004) reported: "A bouquet of red roses lay beside the clear plastic ballot box in polling station 66 here [Kutaisi] on Sunday, and nobody seems to mind that the emblem of Georgia's energetic new president was already in place before the first vote had been cast." In May 2004, when Saakashvili successfully drove Aslan Abashidze, the virtual dictator of the Autonomous Republic of Adjara, back to Moscow, he called the event the Second Rose Revolution.

The nonviolent revolution in Ukraine from late November 2004 to January 2005 was named the Orange Revolution, following the names of these earlier nonviolent uprisings, although the reasons for choosing that color were multiple (Wilson 2005: 72–73). Orange was the color of Viktor A. Yushchenko's campaign coalition. Amid banners, flags, and other decorations all in orange, red roses, red carnations, and other flowers were featured prominently. Yushchenko and his supporters handed out flowers at a rally in Kiev on December 27, 2004 (*New York Times*, December 28, 2004; January 9, 2005; *Newsweek*, December 6, 2004; Wilson 2005). Tulips have also been used as symbols, as in the Tulip Revolution of Kyrgyzstan in 2005, although this involved some violence.

Although the rose became the symbol of the labor movement and comradeship among workers, its appropriation and deployment by some leaders whom John Borneman (2005a) characterizes as representing "totalizing" and "patricentric" authority followed as a natural course. The cult of personality of Joseph Stalin was to build Stalin as the caring and benevolent father of the people, for which an emotional tie between the father and his people was crucial, as Borneman (2005a) stresses.

What could be a better ploy than using roses—the symbol of interpersonal love, deeply embedded in the quotidian lives of the people for centuries and even extending to the bonds among comrades? Yet, roses as an expression of love was so ordinary that its adoption to *control* the people escaped the notice of the people themselves—it was "so natural." In this regard, I look at three examples: Lenin, Stalin, and Hitler.

Vladimir Ilyich Lenin (1870–1924)   At the time of the death of Lenin, making use of his enormously popular appeal, the Soviets laid not only the conceptual foundation of the *Vozhd* (Great Leader) but also the technical apparatus for its delivery (Smith 1989: 122). In a chapter entitled "Lenin's Death and the Birth of Political Photomontage," Margarita Tupitsyn (1996) reproduced a series of photomontages in which Lenin's image is arranged among children in various ways. These photomontages were made by Gustav Klutsis and Sergei Sen'kin for the book *Deti i Lenin* (Children and Lenin) (1924) (Tupitsyn 1996: 19–23) and include Lenin lying in state and mourned by three children (figure 15 in Tupitsyn's book). Tupitsyn writes: "One image depicts a fragment of the country estate in Gorki where Lenin spent most of his time after he was shot and became sick [figure 14]. But the artists have placed the smiling leader on top of the roof, overturning the reality of Lenin's incapacity in the years just before his death" (Tupitsyn 1996: 20). In the caption for this photomontage, a little girl whose father worked in the rest home where Lenin stayed explains how she gave him a bouquet of flowers.[4] The photo shows they are roses.

Joseph Vissarionovich Stalin (1879–1953)   Despite some changes in the presentation of Stalin in poster art over the years, Stalin as the beloved father of the people—*otets narodov*—is the stock image that "indiscriminately manifests throughout the 1929–1953 period, more important and persistent than two other images, an infallible builder of Communism (*stroitel' kommunizma*) and, following the 1943 liberation and eventual postwar victory, a triumphant military commander (*polkovodets*) and 'human' leader" (Rosenthal 2005: 1–2).

Stalin ruled the Soviet Union virtually from 1929 until his death on March 5, 1953, as the "father of the people" and the "great leader of the world proletariat," while engaged in the bloody purging of presumed enemies and rivals. Since the very recent opening of Soviet archival materials, we now have an opportunity to look into how Stalin constructed his image and propagated it through photos, posters, and paintings he commissioned. A most extensive collection, Stalinka, is housed at the University of Pittsburgh Digital Library of Staliniana.

Stalin's "cult of children" was a strategy extensively used throughout the Soviet propaganda machine, which published innumerable photos, posters, and paintings in which Stalin is given roses and bouquets by children, women, members of ethnic minorities, and other groups. The most intensive campaign for "Stalin the Benevolent Father" started around 1935, as seen in the caption for a well-known photo by an unidentified photographer, shot circa 1935. The caption reads: "Smiling girl in sailor suit stands atop a crowd of men, including a smiling Stalin looking on from the right of the photo. In the foreground, a hand offers up a large bouquet of flowers" (Stalinka PH000140; see also Radzinsky 1996: 13th page of plates, between pp. 320 and 321).

A telling image of Stalin's cult of children is a photo taken in 1936 by V. Matvievskii (Stalinka PH000057). Under the title *Young Girl and the Leader*, the caption reads: "Stalin holding a young girl from Asia. The occasion for the photograph was a meeting at the Kremlin, where Party leaders and government officials received a delegation from the Buriat-Mongolian ASSR." The girl is presenting him with a large bouquet of flowers, which he holds in one hand while holding the girl with the other; her arms are thrown around his neck. The photo is a reminder of the brutality with which Stalin exercised his power—the father of this seven-year-old girl, Gelia Markizova, was arrested and shot the following year; the mother was imprisoned and died in 1940.

In a poster by V. Govorkov, dated 1936 and entitled *Thanks to Beloved Stalin for Our Happy Childhood!* (Stalinka GR000005), Stalin stands in Gor'kii Park, surrounded by children whom the caption identifies as coming from different republics. A girl in the foreground holds a bouquet and a boy holds a toy plane. Nina Vatolina created a similar poster in 1950 in which a boy and a girl present Stalin with a bouquet of red roses (Stalinka GR000025). The caption reads: "Thanks to Beloved Stalin for Our Happy Childhood." It carries an explanation that the Stalin cult for children continued in the postwar years when the dictator appeared in military uniform, indicating his role as the architect of victory in the Great Patriotic War (Figure 14 and Plate 9). There are a number of other examples.[5]

FIGURE 14. *Thanks to Beloved Stalin for Our Happy Childhood,* by Nina Vatolina. Chrome-lithograph postcard, 1950. Stalinka GR000025. Courtesy of the Russian State Library.

Since Stalin tried to unite the nations and ethnic groups in the Soviet Union, tributes of flowers by ethnic groups are also depicted in paintings and posters. Reproduced in *Traumfabrik Kommunismus* (Groys and Hollein 2003: 155) is a painting by Pavel Malkov (1900–1953) done in 1938, *Polit-buro of the Central Committee of the Bolshevik Party at the 8th Extraordinary Congress of Soviets*. The painting depicts a person in ethnic peasant clothing presenting flowers to Stalin.[6]

If Stalin adorned himself with flowers in life, his funeral was phenomenal in regard to this emphasis on flowers. In a photo taken by Vasilii Egorov, Stalin lies in an open casket filled with flowers. Outside, in Red Square, rows of flowers were laid out in his honor, as shown in a photo taken on March 10, 1953, by E. Umnof (*Ogonek*, no. 11, March 15, 1953: 30–31). A similar photo appears in Radzinsky's *Stalin* with the caption, "Red Square on the day of Stalin's funeral on March 9, 1953. The crowds were so large that many were crushed to death" (Radzinsky 1996: between pp. 324 and 325; photo: Novosti). Sergei Prokofiev died on the same day as Stalin, but his widow found that all the flowers in Moscow had been sent to Stalin's funeral (Radzinsky 1996: 579).

Adolf Hitler (1889–1945)   Of all the dictators, Hitler, with help from Joseph Goebbels and others, was the most skillful strategist in terms of co-opting the symbolic elements of the Socialist International to buttress his totalitarianism. According to Hobsbawm (1984: 78–29), in addition to "consciously" overlaying the color red of the socialist flag with the swastika, Hitler used "workers' emotional attachment" to May Day and in 1933 turned it into an official national labor holiday (see also Flett 2002).

Following the Soviet protocol for propaganda, Hitler exploited the "father of the people" image to the fullest extent. He was "both pater (source and locus of meaning)" and "'transcendent genitor' of the reproducing Volk" (Borneman 2005b: 80). The *Volksstaat* (state of people), as opposed to the *Rechtsstaat* (state of law), was "composed of men who stood for the Volk and women who stood for its foundation, the family" (Borneman 2005b: 81). The caption for an illustration in a primer for children published during the Nazi period in Germany before World War II depicts a girl offering a bouquet of roses to Hitler and a boy in the background, addressing Hitler as their beloved father (Figure 15).

There are a large number of propaganda photos in which children and women are offering roses, other flowers, and bouquets to Hitler. In addition to innumerable head stamps of Hitler—stamps were a major vehicle of Nazi propaganda—there is a stamp featuring a little girl offering a bouquet to Hitler (Figure 16 and Plate 10). A famous photo of the opening day of the 1936 Berlin Olympics shows him receiving a bouquet of roses from five-year-old Gudrun Diem, the daughter of Carl Diem, the organizer for both the stillborn 1916 Olympics and 1936 Olympics (reproduced also in Griffin 2004: 20, and in Hart-Davis 1986: between pp. 128 and 129).

Mein Führer!

(Das Kind spricht:)

Ich kenne dich wohl und habe dich lieb
wie Vater und Mutter.
Ich will dir immer gehorsam sein
wie Vater und Mutter.
Und wenn ich groß bin, helfe ich dir
wie Vater und Mutter,
Und freuen sollst du dich an mir
wie Vater und Mutter!

FIGURE 15. An illustration in a children's reader published in prewar Nazi Germany: "My Führer: I know you well and love you, like father and mother. I shall always obey you, like father and mother. And when I grow up I shall help you, like father and mother. And you will be proud of me, like father and mother." Source: Otto Zimmermann and Eugen Osswald, *Westermanns Groß-Berliner Fibel* (Berlin: G. Westermann, 1935), p. 65. Courtesy of the Wiener Library, London.

FIGURE 16. A Hitler stamp: Hitler receiving a bouquet of flowers from a little girl, 1940. Source: Colin Welch, "Stamps of the Nazi Era," http://research.calvin.edu/german-propaganda-archive/stamps.htm. Courtesy of Colin Welch.

FIGURE 17. Hitler receiving bouquets of roses from children on his fiftieth birthday, April 20, 1939. Source: Heinrich Hoffmann, *Ein Volk ehrt seinen Führer. Der 20. April 1939 im Bild* (Berlin: Zeitgeschichte-Verlag, 1939). Courtesy of the Wiener Library, London.

The cover photo of Heinrich Hoffmann's three volumes of propaganda photos, published in 1939, *Ein Volk ehrt seinen Führer*, was taken on Hitler's fiftieth birthday (Figure 17). Hitler is receiving a number of bouquets of roses from children and women. In another photo entitled *Blumengruß in Tirol*, Hitler peers out the window of a train to receive a bouquet of roses from a woman (Figure 18) (Hoffmann 1935). Hoffmann's (1938) *Hitler holt die Saar heim* includes three other photos of Hitler receiving flowers and bouquets.

The Propaganda of Adolf Hitler, which Hermann Goering and eleven other ministers of the Third Reich published in 1936 (Goering et al. [1936] 1973), includes a photo entitled *Pictured with Farmer's Family in East Prussia.*

FIGURE 18. Hitler peers out of a train window to receive a bouquet of flowers from a woman. The Alps are in the background. Source: Heinrich Hoffmann, *Hitler holt die Saar heim* (Berlin: Zeitgeschichte-Verlag, 1938), no page number. Courtesy of the Wiener Library, London.

It portrays Hitler with a large family, holding hands with the children; two girls carry a bouquet (Goering et al. [1936] 1973: 19). In another, entitled *His Highways Lead Adolf Hitler to His People*, many young people are extending their hands and flowers to Hitler (Goering et al. [1936] 1973: 82). In still another photo, the caption reads: "She recites a poem for the Führer during campaign tour." Hitler is holding a bouquet, presumably given by a little girl; his hand is on her shoulder as he listens to her recitation of the poem (Goering et al. [1936] 1973: 106). In *Youths Greet the Campaigning Hitler*, a bouquet of roses is offered by a boy (Goering et al. [1936] 1973: 108). In *Little Hands Reach for the Führer*, little girls are reaching out toward Hitler with bouquets of flowers (Goering et al. [1936] 1973: 108).

Without going into detail about Mao's China, let me point out that Mao adopted many propaganda techniques of the Soviet system, including its socialist symbolism. There are a large number of posters in which Mao and other leaders are portrayed with children. For example, in an embroidered banner dated 1978, the portraits of Zhou Enlai, Mao Zedong (in the center), and Zhu De are framed and minority children are dancing on a carpet in front of them (N17; see also N13, and N26, China Posters Online, University of Westminster). The Chinese Communist Party also adopted the propaganda motifs of peasants with stalks of grain and red roses from the Soviet Union. One such poster, dated December 1976, features portraits of Chairman Mao and Chairman Hua in Shanghai, with a woman with a bundle of grain stalks, several people with large bouquets of red roses, and balloons flying in the air (catalogue no. N33, China Posters Online, University of Westminster). This propaganda poster also features the "double-happiness" Chinese character and a peony, the flower of the prerevolutionary upper class, alongside the roses adopted from the Soviet Union as the symbol of the socialists—an interesting juxtaposition.

THE WHITE ROSE: THE RESISTANCE MOVEMENT IN NAZI GERMANY

Between June 1942 and February 1943, a group of students and a professor at the University of Munich distributed leaflets calling for nonviolent opposition to Hitler's regime (Scholl [1970] 1983). They called themselves The White Rose, an epithet with which they signed their leaflets, distributed as secretly as possible to prevent the Gestapo from catching them in action, until February 18, when they found some leaflets they brought to the university still remained undistributed. They threw them in the air from the top floor into the empty-looking atrium. The act was seen by a custodian, who called the Gestapo. The core members were Sophie Scholl and her brother Hans, Christian Probst, Alex Schmorell, and Willi Graf, with Kurt Huber, professor of philosophy. They were all executed by beheading.

Their opposition to Hitler's totalitarianism and militarism was based on their Christian faith and their pride in the German cultural heritage. The leaflets, published by a sister of Sophie and Hans (Scholl [1970] 1983: 73–93), contain frequent references to and citations from the Bible, Laozi, Aristotle, and literary figures of German romanticism such as Novalis (Friedrich von Hardenberg), Johann Wolfgang von Goethe, and Friedrich Schiller. In the first leaflet printed, they quote Schiller's "The Lawgiving of Lycurgus and Solon," in which Schiller cautions that political systems are set up at the price of "all moral feeling," and also Goethe's *The Awakening of Epimenides* in which Goethe warns how "all who stand with him / Must perish in his fall"; "he" refers to "he who has boldly risen from the abyss" (Scholl [1970] 1983: 73–76). The second leaflet begins with their shocked reaction to the extermination of Jews in Poland. It reads: "Since the conquest of Poland *three hundred thousand* Jews have been murdered in this country in the most bestial way" (italics in the original). They accuse the Germans of apathy in the face of "all these abominable crimes, crimes so unworthy of the human race." This leaflet ends with quotations from Laozi, who warns that a ruler who governs by whim will not reach his goal (Scholl [1970] 1983: 77–80). In the third leaflet they declare: "But our present 'state' is the dictatorship of evil." They urge the Germans to oppose National Socialism at all points: "We must soon bring this monster of a state to an end." They specify the method of opposition to be sabotage of all sorts—of gatherings, rallies, war machinery, science and scholarship that further the cause of war. This leaflet ends with a quotation from Aristotle's *Politics*: "the tyrant is inclined constantly to foment wars" (Scholl [1970] 1983: 81–84).

The fourth leaflet (Scholl [1970] 1983: 85–88) warns: "Every word that comes from Hitler's mouth is a lie. When he says peace, he means war, and when he blasphemously uses the name of the Almighty, he means the power of evil, the fallen angel, Satan." The statement, "We *must* attack evil where it is strongest, and it is strongest in the power of Hitler" (italics in the original), is followed by a quote from Ecclesiastes 4. Then they quote from Novalis: "Blood will stream over Europe until the nations become aware of the frightful madness which drives them in circles. . . . Establish the rights of the peoples, and install Christianity in new splendor visibly on earth in its office as guarantor of peace." This leaflet ends with the well-known statement: "We will not be silent. We are your bad conscience. The White Rose will not leave you in peace." The fifth leaflet (Scholl [1970] 1983: 89–90) asks, "Germans! Do you and your children want to suffer the same fate that befell the Jews?" It urges readers to dissociate themselves from "National Socialist gangsterism." The sixth and last leaflet (Scholl [1970] 1983: 91–93), written by Professor Kurt Huber, begins with the horror at Stalingrad: "Three hundred and thirty thousand German men have been senselessly and irresponsibly driven to death and destruction." The concluding remarks return there: "The dead of Stalingrad implore us to take action. Up, up, my people, let smoke and flame be our sign!"

A photo of Sophie with a white rose on her sweater has a caption taken from the fourth leaflet, as quoted above: "We will not be silent. We are your bad conscience. The White Rose will not leave you in peace" (used as the cover photo for Dumbach and Newborn 2006). The same photo appears in Scholl's *The White Rose* with a caption: "Hans Scholl, Sophie Scholl, Christoph Probst, summer 1942" ([1970] 1983: 67). In another photo, Sophie holds a white rose. The caption for this photo with Sophie and her friends in uniform reads: "Farewell at Munich's East Station before leaving for the Eastern Front, July 23, 1942. Sophie sniffs a white rose."

They did not leave any explanation for the choice of the white rose as their emblem (for some speculative discussion, see Dumbach and Newborn 2006: 58). But my guess is that it was because of their Catholicism, with the Virgin Mary symbolized by the white rose, as well as the German color symbolism of white representing purity of the self against oppressive regimes. *Weiße Rose* was an intellectual group which chose the white rose as their emblem. Similarly, *Edelweißpiraten* was a proletarian group, tending toward violence, etc., but was opposed to Hitler's regime. The *Edelweiß* is a white flower. The white rose came to oppose Hitler's red rose.

Conclusion: Polysemy of the Rose

Barbara Seward, author of a book on the symbolism of the rose, with a focus on modern British roses (1960: 6–7), writes that the rose is "capable of bearing a vast range of meanings," and lists some of the concepts it represents in Western European cultures: Christ and the Virgin, birth and rebirth, eternity, love, beauty, life, joy, creation, and human ideals on the one hand, and, on the other hand, sorrow, death, the evanescence of earthly beauties, the blood of martyrs, and early death.

Likewise, J. C. Cooper (1978: 141) emphasizes the opposite meanings assigned to roses, leading to complexity: heavenly perfection/earthly passion; time/eternity; life/death; fertility/virginity. "The evanescence of the rose represents death, mortality and sorrow; its thorns signify pain, blood and martyrdom. As funerary it portrays eternal life, eternal Spring, resurrection."

This cursory survey of the symbolism of the rose tells us that this flower has been deeply embedded in people's day-to-day lives and has been an important trope in religion, literature, and philosophy, as well as in music and the visual arts. The rose, however, has never been a symbol of the collective self, unlike cherry blossoms, which became emblematic of both cultural and political nationalism, unlike the British rose which became a symbol of cultural nationalism but not of political nationalism. It is a polysemic symbol par excellence, with its meanings embedded in relationships and processes. The rose as a symbol of love—between God (heaven) and his people (the earth), a woman and a man, a leader and his people, and all other meaningful sociality—is foremost in importance. "Love" means, above all, a positive human relationship, involving more than one individual. The sacrifice of Christ for humanity, symbolized by the red rose, or sacrifice in general is an act of love and dedication. The rose stands for life in its relation to death as part of a process, rather than an isolated phenomenon. These major characteristics of the rose's meanings are the very fabric of the polysemy that facilitates communicative opacity.

Along with its role at the individual and interpersonal level, the rose has been a regal and political symbol since Roman times—this has continued throughout history, most recently with modern European dictators of the late nineteenth and early twentieth centuries, who used the rose and its symbolism of love to their political advantage.

Most fascinating is its parallel development as an important symbol of the common people against the establishment. This significance as the flower of opposition was already present in the May Day festivals in medieval Europe, which led to its importance in the Festival of the French Revolution. Still later, at the end of the nineteenth century, the rose became *the* symbol of the Socialist International, as expressed in the famous motto "Bread and Roses." Some say the red rose became politically prominent because it symbolized blood—the suffering of workers. This tradition of the rose representing the workers, or the people as a whole, has continued to the present, as evident in the emblems of almost all socialist parties all over the world.

If the red rose stood for the common people, struggling against the establishment, the white rose in Germany stood for the Virgin Mary in Catholicism and purity of the self of those who opposed the Nazi regime but also actively fought against it. Japanese cherry blossoms and European roses carried different meanings and played different roles. On the other hand, in both cases polysemy facilitated the fluid transference of meanings from one end of the spectrum to the other, and this made it possible for both flowers to become *flowers that kill*. On the other hand, polysemy prevented people from recognizing how meanings had been so transmogrified that, in the end, the result was their own destruction. This came to pass because, in both cases, the meaning of life and love had such a strong grip in the mind of the people.

THREE

The Subversive Monkey in Japanese Culture

From Scapegoat to Clown

Throughout history the monkey has been an important and complex symbol in Japanese culture. It is the animal considered most similar and therefore closest to humans, and like humans it is a social animal. The *social* self in Japanese culture is defined in relation to the other, either collectively in relation to other peoples or dialogically in relation to other persons in a given social context. This notion is succinctly expressed in the two characters that stand for humans, *ningen*: the character for *nin* means "humans," and that for *gen* means "among." Thus humans are by definition among humans; an individual human cannot be conceived of without reference to others (Watsuji 1959: 1–67). For the Japanese, the monkey, the social animal par excellence, mirrors human sociality.[1] In addition, the animal is very clever, sharing many capabilities with humans.

Because the monkey's depiction in art, literature, and other sources has sensitively reflected Japanese deliberations about self and other throughout history, we can tap a significant part of Japanese culture and society by examining how the meaning of the monkey has undergone changes in important historical contexts. The monkey is another example of how the meanings of a symbol sensitively register geopolitical events and changes in society.

If cherry blossoms symbolize both the normative world and its reversal, portrayed in an alternative imagination, the subversive forces underlying the normative world are more overtly shown in the symbolism of the monkey, which challenges the stratification not only in Japanese society but in the universe, in which humans occupy the apex.

In ancient Japan the very proximity of the monkey as perceived by the Japanese made it a revered mediator between humans and deities. As a mediator, it fetched the positive power of deities to rejuvenate and purify the *self* of humans. However, seeing an uncomfortable likeness between themselves and the monkey, people in later history considered the monkey a threat to the human-animal boundary. This prompted people to distance themselves from the monkey by turning it into a scapegoat, a laughable animal that in vain imitates humans. The term "monkey imitation" (*sarumane*) refers to someone trying to imitate a person of higher status, or the Japanese trying to imitate foreigners regarded as having a superior culture.

The monkey continues to be an important symbol today, when most urbanites see living animals only in the "monkey parks" established as nature preserves. As if to reaffirm the centrality of the monkey in the Japanese structure of reflexivity, a new meaning is emerging—the monkey as a clown who turns itself into an object of laughter while challenging the basic assumptions of culture and society. A clown is a truly reflexive figure who can distance himself from the self rather than simply be an actor in the existing social structure, as the mediator and the scapegoat are.

The meaning of the monkey—historical changed from mediator, to scapegoat, to clown—creates ambiguity, opacity, and even an absence of communication as the Japanese read different meanings.

Polysemy

THE MONKEY AS SEMI-DIVINE MEDIATOR

Saruta Biko—the Monkey Deity (*saru* means monkey)—appears in Japan's oldest myth-histories, the *Kojiki* and the *Nihongi*, dated to the early eighth century. In an episode where the Sun Goddess (Amaterasu Ōmikami), presumed ancestress of the Japanese, orders her grandson to earth to govern there, the grandson, accompanied by several other deities, is ready to descend when a scout sent earlier to clear the way returns to report on his encounter with Saruta Biko at "the eight [many] crossroads of Heaven," indicating that Saruta Biko is a mediator between deities in heaven and humans on earth. The scout describes this deity as having a nose seven hands long and a back more than seven fathoms long; his eyeballs glow like an eight-sided mirror, and light shines from his mouth and from his anus (Sakamoto et al., eds.,

1967: 147–48; see also Kurano and Takeda 1958: 127; Philippi 1969: 138, 140, 142; Shimonaka, ed., 1941: 118).

In Japanese culture, light and mirrors symbolize deities (Ishibashi 1914; Ohnuki-Tierney 1987: 133–36). The mirror-like eyes and light emitted from bodily orifices identify Saruta Biko as a deity (Matsumae 1960: 44; Minakata 1972: 401, 410–11). His physical characteristics include red buttocks, a prominent trait of Japanese macaques (Shimonaka 1941: 118). In the *Kojiki*, Saruta Biko's hand gets caught in a shell while fishing (Kurano and Takeda, eds., 1958: 131; Philippi 1969: 142). Macaques gather shellfish at low tide, as frequently described in folktales (Inada and Ōshima 1977: 392).

Another expression in early Japanese history of the monkey as a sacred mediator is the development of a folk religion, *kōshin*. Since the sixteenth century, the *kōshin* belief and associated practices have become closely tied to the monkey and fused with the worship of the Mountain Deity called Sannō Shinkō. In this religion, the primary role of the monkey, who was referred to as the Monkey Deity (Sarugami), was as the messenger from the powerful Mountain Deity (Sannō) (Blacker 1975: 329; Orikuchi [1918] 1982: 324–25; Orikuchi [1924] 1982: 299; Yanagita, ed., 1951: 196–97, 240, 642–44; Yanagita [1947] 1982b). The monkey thus became closely associated with the belief in the sacredness of Mount Fuji (*Fuji-shinkō*), as shown on amulets that depict Saruta Biko and more than sixty monkeys worshipping Mount Fuji at its foothills (Miyata 1975: 148). The meaning and the role of *kōshin* centered on mediation—between temporal cycles, between humans and deities, and between heaven and earth.

The monkey was also a mediator as the guardian of horses. In Japan, the monkey performance originated as a ritual at stables during which a trained monkey performed to music, either sung by the trainer or played on the three-stringed shamisen or a drum (Ishii 1963: 39). The monkey harnesses the sacred power of the Mountain Deity to enhance the well-being and healing of horses. Later in history the ritual was performed on the street and at the doorways of individual homes on New Year's, symbolizing a visit by the Mountain Deity, who blessed the people with health and prosperity (Oda 1980: 2). The *Ryōjin Hishō* (1169–1179) is possibly the earliest description of the monkey performance. Several sources dated to the mid-thirteenth century attest that the monkey performance was popular. The monkey danced with an *eboshi* hat, the type worn by aristocrats and warriors, which became the trademark of performing monkeys (Yanagita [1947] 1982b: 336–37). Even though the monkey is endowed with the ability to harness sacred power, its trainers were from a marginalized social group whose occupations dealt with culturally defined impurity, such as death, and animals, including butchering and tanning (see Ohnuki-Tierney 1987: 75–100).

Toward the end of the Muromachi period (1392–1603) and the beginning of the Tokugawa period (1615–1867), the performance took on an additional role: blessing the rice harvest. At this time a genre of paintings depicting rice harvesting emerged in which a dancing monkey is depicted, showing how the monkey as mediator/messenger facilitated the blessing of the rice crop by the Mountain Deity, who becomes the Deity of Rice Paddies in the spring.[2]

The belief in the religious power of the monkey was shared by political leaders, including Toyotomi Hideyoshi, the feudal lord who in 1590 gained control over the entire nation of Japan, uniting it for the first time in history, and became regent. He was nicknamed Kosaru (little monkey) or Saru (monkey), not only because his face looked like a monkey's but also because he eagerly sought identification with the monkey (Ooms 1985: 285–87). Tokugawa Ieyasu, the first shogun of the Tokugawa Bakufu, officially designated the Monkey Deity as the guardian of peace in the nation. The festival for this deity was elaborately carried out in Edo during his reign (1603–1616) (Iida 1983: 65) and included a procession led by a monkey cart (*saru dashi*).

The Meiji Restoration in 1868 eliminated the legal codification of the four caste/class system that was instituted by Toyotomi Hideyoshi in 1582, and hence dissolved the warrior class, which had been the patron of monkey trainers. The last monkey performance at the emperor's stables was conducted in 1871 (Oda 1968: 35) in Kyoto, although the emperor had already moved to Tokyo. Yet, the religious meaning of the monkey and the monkey performance survived. As Yanagita Kunio ([1955] 1982: 163) notes, monkey trainers were protected at Nikkō, where Tokugawa Ieyasu's mausoleum is located, because of the religious significance of the Mountain Deity. The stable ritual became less common as the warrior class was abolished and the nation became industrialized, but it continued to be held in rural areas, such as Shinshū (Matsuyama 1941), and was performed for the welfare of the ox, an important animal for farmers (Oda 1980: 18).

THE MONKEY AS BEAST AND SCAPEGOAT

The demarcation line between beasts and humans is delineated in every culture in its own complex manner. In the normative picture of the Japanese universe, humans live in a harmonious relationship with "beings of the universe," including nonhuman animals, many of which are Shinto deities. Conventional Buddhist doctrine offers a fluid boundary between beings: since humans and nonhuman animals alike undergo transmigration, there is no essential distinction between them. The line can be crossed by metamorphosis of an animal into a human and vice versa (for details, see Ohnuki-Tierney 1987: 32–34). The Japanese notion of the relationship between humans and animals is in stark contrast to the Christian biblical tradition: "And God said, Let us make man in our image, after our likeness: and let them have dominion over" all the creatures of the sea, air, and earth (Genesis, 1, 26:17–18).[3] In the Bible, the categories were created by God and thus the transgression of their boundaries is blasphemy.

There is another aspect to the Japanese notion of animals, especially in later history: animals are lowly beasts without superhuman power. Indeed, perhaps the most potent curse word in Japanese is "Beast!" (*chikushō*). As the closest animal to humans, the monkey has been seen as threatening the distinction in Japanese cosmology between humans and nonhumans, challenging the throne on which the Japanese have sat, unique as humans and as a people, prompting them to reaffirm a distance from animals. It is no accident, then, that the monkey is seldom involved in the tales of metamorphosis between humans and animals.[4] Distance is created by emphasizing the dissimilarities between monkeys' bodily and behavioral features and the corresponding features of humans. In a monkey performance, a trainer, representing his monkey, sings a song in which the monkey laments its inferiority to humans: "Because of the karma of my parents, my face is red, my eyes are round, and, in addition, my nose is flat and ugly" (Yamaguchiken Kyōiku Iinkai Bunkaka 1980: 41). When the Japanese wish to accentuate the monkey's animality, they laugh at its "ugly" eyes, nose, buttocks, and so on, whose equivalents in humans are "superior." As in most cultures, eyes are not simply physiological organs of vision but the critical organ for thoughts and feelings.[5] "Monkey eyes" (*sarume*) are not just ugly but beastly, revealing the incapability to think and feel.

The eyes in Japanese culture represent another crucial difference between humans and animals—the capacity for emotion, especially sadness, expressed by the shedding of tears. Emotions, rather than rationality, have always been considered unique to humans, as recorded in the literature of the late Nara (646–794) and early Heian (794–1185) periods (LaFleur 1983: 34–35). Stylized ways of crying are an important element in kabuki theater, and replications of these are included in the traditional repertoire of the monkey performance.

Similarly, a "monkey hip" (*sarugoshi*) is a human hip that looks like the hip of a quadruped trying to be bipedal. The vital step in training monkeys for performance is teaching them a bipedal posture, which symbolizes the uniqueness and superiority of humans over quadrupedal animals (*yotsuashi*). In colloquial Japanese, the term *yotsuashi* is a synonym for *chikushō*, the commonly used curse word. Red buttocks represent the monkey's inability to control its sexual and other bodily functions. Also significant is the Japanese description of the monkey as "a human minus three pieces of hair." Head hair is a powerful metonymic symbol, representing a person's essence in Japan (Yanagita, ed., 1951: 121–22), as elsewhere. Through this definition, the monkey is characterized as an animal close to humans but without the quintessential characteristics of humans.

A major transformation in the dominant meaning of the monkey from a sacred mediator to a scapegoat took place during the three or four centuries between the medieval (1185–1603) and Edo periods (1603–1868). The monkey came to represent people who engaged in silly imitations of others and, during the Edo period, those who tried to achieve beyond their capacity, or more specifically, to go beyond their ascribed status in the increasingly rigid social stratification.

The three-monkey theme was a form of self-mockery of the common people, who were deprived of freedom as society came under increasingly strict governmental supervision and therefore resigned themselves not to see, hear, or speak evil.[6] The monkey is depicted as a scapegoat in folktales, literature, and art. One of the best-known examples is a proverb, *Tōrō ga ono, enkō ga tsuki* (The axe of a praying mantis is like the moon for a monkey), which originated in a Chinese story called *Sōshiritsu*. A praying mantis trying to crush the wheel of a cart with its forelegs (wielding them like axes) is as ridiculous as a monkey mistaking the reflection of the moon in the water for the moon itself and trying to capture it. The theme is depicted also in a well-known painting, *Enkō Sakugetsu* (Monkey Capturing the Moon), by Hasegawa Tōhaku (1539–1610), and is found on the cover of a lacquerware stationery container made by an anonymous artist during the nineteenth century,[7] in which three macaques, all wearing glasses, are opening a scroll while night falcons hover over them. The picture carries a moral message: do not attempt things beyond your capacity. The monkeys lack the ability to read, which to the Japanese distinguishes humans from animals. While the monkeys are attempting the impossible, they are risking their lives by letting their chief predators, night falcons, approach. A night falcon (*yodaka*) is also a euphemism for a prostitute or a night stalker. During this period, the meaning of the monkey seems to have been extended from an undesirable imitator of people above his station to all types of undesirables, including beggars and prostitutes.[8] In the seventeenth century, the monkey became a scapegoat for human victims of smallpox. It was believed that the monkeys kept at the Sakamoto Sannō Shrine suffered from smallpox while the emperors recovered from the disease.[9]

Monkey symbolism came to be associated with a social group, the *hisabetsu burakumin* (discriminated hamlet people), which became increasingly marginalized starting in the latter half of the eleventh century. They engaged in non-agrarian occupations, several of which dealt with animals, including the monkey. Contra a prevalent view, they have not constituted a well-delineated, unilinear social group throughout history. In the ancient period, despite the negative value assigned to such occupations as handling corpses and arranging funeral rites, these people were considered to have religious power (Akima 1972, 1982). During the medieval period, flexibility in the sociocultural system provided them, both as a group and as individuals, with considerable freedom. However, the concept of impurity was naturalized as moral evil. In 1582, Toyotomi Hideyoshi, the regent, codified a rigid, so-called four-caste system: warriors, farmers, artisans, and merchants; the emperor was placed outside of this system but on top and two outcastes were at the bottom (for details, see Ohnuki-Tierney 1987: 93–94). During the Edo period, the dominant Japanese view of outcastes as naturally impure and hence morally inferior was firmly established. Intense aversion to impurity justified the devaluation of their occupations dealing with culturally defined impurity or dirt. Increasing occupational specialization elevated some religious and artisanal occupations, relieving those who engaged in them of outcaste status. Others, such as street entertainers, including trainers for the monkey performance, remained *Fremdkörper* until legal emancipation in 1889.

The two opposing meanings assigned to the monkey coexisted during much of Japanese history, sometimes with subversive play between them. For example, a pamphlet posted in the streets of Kyoto in 1591 reads: "The end of the world is nothing but this: Watching the monkey regent under the tree" (Masse to wa bechi ni wa araji ki no shita no saru kanpaku o miru ni tsuketemo). As George Elison (1981: 244) explains, the poster was a satirical commentary on Toyotomi Hideyoshi, the commoner who became regent (*kanpaku dajōdaijin*, a position above the "shogun"). Hideyoshi eagerly sought to identify himself with the monkey, which remained a semideified figure. "Under the tree" is the literal meaning of Hideyoshi's alleged original family name, Kinoshita. The poster laments the approach of the end of the world, a degenerate era when a commoner can be a regent and, worse yet, a monkey governs humans. During this period, although the monkey continued to be a semideified mediator, promoting peace in the nation and ensuring a bountiful rice harvest, its associations turned increasingly negative.

Polysemy and the Play of Subversion

The afore-mentioned monkey performance has been an important cultural institution throughout most of Japanese history.

First, I introduce a monkey performance during the medieval period as depicted in *Utsubozaru* (Quiver Monkey), a piece of *kyōgen*, a genre of comic interludes staged between classical noh plays. My second example is the monkey performance in contemporary Japan. They show how polysemy creates communicative opacity, which masks the important message of the performance—subversion of received wisdom and the hierarchy in Japanese society as well as in the universe in which humans occupy the throne.

THE MEDIEVAL MONKEY PERFORMANCE

Both kyōgen and noh are performing arts developed independently of each other during the Muromachi period (Hayashiya 1981; Matsumoto 1981). Noh was created by the warrior class, who gained power over the imperial court and aristocrats after a long and bitter struggle in the Nanbokuchō period (1336–1392). Noh represents the perspective on life of the new elite in Japanese society (Matsumoto 1981: 192), whereas kyōgen was produced by lowly warriors and farmers, who were finally freed from the old regime but were still under the newly created ruling class (Hayashiya 1981: 204–6; Koyama 1960: 13; Satake [1967] 1970: 110).[10] Kyōgen was characterized by the motto *gekokujō*, "the below conquering the above." This emerging ethos at the time gave rise to a genre of literature called "the literature of *gekokujō*," which became popular among the common people (Satake [1967] 1970; Sugiura 1965) and was translated into a pragmatic philosophy of life that enabled capable individuals of low social status to surpass those above them, especially in religion and art. This period saw an efflorescence of all forms of art.

The Quiver Monkey (*Utsubozaru*)[11] vividly portrays the monkey performance as a highly developed street entertainment that nevertheless accords a
very low status to the trainers. In this play a daimyō (feudal lord) announces
to his servant Tarōkaja that he plans to go hunting. As they set out, they
encounter a monkey trainer with his monkey. Impressed by the animal's
beautiful fur, the lord asks the trainer for the monkey in order to cover his
quiver with its hide, since monkey hide was believed to protect horses from
the enemy's arrows. The trainer begs the lord to spare the monkey since it
is his only means of livelihood. As the trainer stalls, the lord, becoming en-
raged, tells the trainer that he will shoot both him and the monkey with one
arrow. But the trainer points out that if the monkey is shot, the scar from
the shot will ruin the hide. He then volunteers to strike the monkey with
a stick, explaining that he knows how to kill it with one stroke. In tears,
he begs forgiveness from the monkey for what he is about to do and keeps
stalling. The lord and his servant become impatient and order the trainer to
take immediate action. As the trainer is about to hit, the monkey snatches
the stick and starts to perform rowing a boat, which he has been trained to
do since he was a baby. The trainer, breaking into tears, laments, "It is a sad
fate for a creature when it cannot tell that its life is in immediate danger."
Observing this scene, the lord too breaks into tears and tells the trainer not
to hit the monkey after all. Overjoyed, the trainer has the monkey perform
a dance in gratitude for the lord's mercy. As the monkey starts to dance, the
lord, enthralled, begins to offer the monkey his fan, and then his sword and
even his kimono top (it was customary at the time to offer one's possessions
to performers) (Tierney n.d.). *Utsubozaru* ends with the lord's servant begging the monkey to stop dancing so that his master will stop dancing. The
lord has been transformed—from a barbarian who only knows how to use
force and weapons to someone who appreciates culture, i.e., dancing. This is
also a satirical commentary at the very time when warriors, who only knew
how to use their military power, were taking over power from the emperors
and the aristocrats, who were cultured.

The play depicts both the normative hierarchy at the time and its reversal.
The lord's threat to kill the monkey and the trainer with one arrow reveals his
equation of the two. At the beginning of the play, the trainer also views the
monkey as an animal too stupid to know when its own death is approaching; in contrast to humans like himself and the lord, it cannot understand
language, the epitome of culture. Despite the identification of the monkey
as a lowly beast, the lord wishes to acquire its hide because he acknowledges

its supernatural power, not available to humans. As the story progresses, the monkey upstages both the trainer and the lord, becoming a performing artist who transforms his natural body into rhythmically controlled movements and transforms the savage lord into a peaceful man who enjoys dancing.

The message of the play subverts not just the social structure but the entire universe. Although the lord and his servant and the trainer and his monkey each constitute a master-subordinate relationship, the four are hierarchically ranked within the Japanese universe: lord, servant, trainer, monkey. The monkey, which starts out at the bottom and was to be a victim of the powerful lord, controls the whole scene at the end; neither the trainer nor the servant can break the magnetic spell cast over the lord by the monkey's dancing. As ritual time progresses during the play, the normative hierarchy becomes inverted. The play ends with the monkey taking command of a new hierarchy: monkey, trainer, servant, lord.

The monkey is a trickster who tricks not only the other characters but also the spectators, who, unaware of how the play will unfold, end up being forced to contemplate the structure of their society, albeit vaguely. The message about the inversion of the social structure is subtle and in the restricted space of a play.

The monkey as a scapegoat-turned-trickster continued to play a role in later history, subtly mocking received wisdom. An important record from the interwar period is offered by Ozawa Shōichi (1978), who recalls that during his childhood, trainers often came to a grassy field in his neighborhood to perform. A particularly memorable act was entitled "Three Brave Soldiers as Human Cannons" (*Nikudan San Yūshi*). A monkey in military uniform carrying a toy land torpedo would pose at attention, salute the spectators, and then make a mock dash toward the presumed enemy territory. The monkey always dropped the torpedo before reaching it, and the spectators burst into laughter every time.

In that period, this act was utterly sacrilegious. The "three brave soldiers" refers to three Japanese soldiers who gave their lives by carrying a land torpedo into a barbed-wire barricade, blasting through it thereby facilitating the advance of their unit against formidable Chinese resistance.[12] Until the end of World War II, the "three brave soldiers" were celebrated as the supreme model of patriotic self-sacrifice to be emulated by every Japanese. Yet the trainer turned it into a comic act. The monkey in Ozawa's description is a clown who fools spectators into laughing while covertly making jibes at a society that treats militarism and imperialism as sacred.[13]

THE MONKEY PERFORMANCE IN CONTEMPORARY JAPAN

The monkey performance on the streets and in parks virtually disappeared after the 1920s due to continued discrimination against *hisabetsu burakumin*, who were identified only through their occupations; they were physically indistinguishable from the rest of the population. With the more liberal attitude in general in postwar Japan, especially with a worldwide resurgence of ethnic and minority movements in the 1970s, some fundamental changes took place, and they were expressed in the emergence of new types of monkey symbolism. For example, "cultural monkeys" (*bunkazaru*) (Miyaji 1973) appeared. Sold as souvenirs at monkey conservation parks and elsewhere, these figurines are carved with exaggerated gestures of the monkeys "to speak, to see, and to hear"—the opposite of the traditional three-monkey theme. Sometimes called the "three monkeys of the Showa period" (*Shōwa sanzaru*) or the "inverted monkeys" (*sakasazaru*), they encourage speaking out, examining closely, and listening carefully, indicating an attitude considered to represent the "modern, progressive" stance of new Japan.

In this atmosphere, two brothers, Murasaki Tarō and Murasaki Shūji, resurrected the monkey performance in 1977.[14] Murasaki Shūji revived the traditional repertoire of dancing, and Murasaki Tarō adapted it to keep pace with contemporary youth culture, frequently performing at Yoyogi Park in Tokyo, a favorite park among youth. He succeeded in bringing his performance to New York City's Lincoln Center in 1992, when the monkey reenacted U.S. President Bush's vomiting incident at a state dinner in Japan. Tarō, a name given to a first-born male, named his monkey Jirō, a name given to a second-born male. The Japanese immediately recognized the brotherhood, with Tarō above Jirō within the family hierarchy.

One of the standard acts consists of Tarō giving Jirō a tissue to wipe away tears. Often Jirō would put the tissue on his head or some other place instead of dabbing his eyes. Tarō would chide, "You fool, where do you think your eyes are? Tears don't come out of your head." Traditionally, trainers endeavored to teach their monkeys sixteen ways of crying. Tarō, however, emphasizes the monkey's clumsiness and turns the act into a comic scene. Similarly, when Jirō does not perform on command, Tarō chides him: "If you don't know how to perform, you'll be sent off for an animal experiment." Or, every now and then, Tarō tells Jirō, "Don't make a monkey face." In other words, Tarō enacts an extremely clever job of simultaneously establishing an equal status with the monkey, challenging the received wisdom of human superiority over nonhuman animals, on the one hand, and establishing a clear hierarchy between the two, on the other.

Jirō's cleverly staged disobedience is even more successful in a routine involving jumping from one wooden block to another. After he successfully jumps from the ground to the first block and then to the next, Tarō moves the next block farther away. At about the third or fourth jump, when Tarō issues the same order, "Go!," Jirō leaps only onto the first block, clinging to it while making a miserable face. The staging of "disobedience" always draws laughter from the spectators.

Tarō's dialogue with Jirō is sprinkled with such remarks as "Listen and follow what I say" (*Yūkoto o kike*) and "Concentration!" (*Shūchū*). When Tarō tells Jirō, "Be well-mannered" (*Gyōgiyoku shiro*), Jirō, sitting on a stool, pulls his two hind legs closer together. At Tarō's command, "Attention!" (*Kiotsuke!*), Jirō stands at attention. These are rules of manners Japanese children are taught at home and at school. When Jirō does not follow Tarō's order, usually spontaneously but at times as a part of the act, or carries out the order clumsily, Tarō immediately transforms Jirō's act into a comic scene. Jirō's disobedience is immediately followed by an act of "self-examination and repentance" (*hansei*), as Jirō puts his hand on Tarō's lap and lowers his head. *Hansei* is an important form of moral behavior taught to the young and continues to be reinforced throughout one's life. At the staged acts of "disobedience," the spectators invariably roar with laughter.

After each performance, while the crowd lingers, Tarō and Jirō sit together and sip a cup of barley tea. Spectators smile, and some offer bananas and other goodies to the monkey, which is assuming an equal status with its trainer.

Spectators' interpretations of the performance vary widely. The majority did not give it much thought afterward. The most common view was that the monkey was "cute" (*kawaii*) or "admirable" (*erai*) because it was clever and performed so many tasks with humanlike skill "though it is only a monkey." This was most clearly expressed in compositions written by second-graders who watched the performance of two monkeys and trainers from this group at an elementary school in Tokyo in 1983. All but one of twenty-two short compositions commented on the human-monkey relationship. Most praised the monkeys for performing tasks usually assigned to humans so well. These comments emphasized good manners, skills, and the ability to work hard, which are central to early childhood education in Japan.

Today, most Japanese know monkeys only in zoos or in nature conservation parks specifically designed to protect macaques. In fact, Tarō told me that a kindergartner once asked if the monkey was a stuffed monkey with remote control. In this highly industrialized and urban nation, people live in the company of other humans and are increasingly in contact with foreigners, but no longer live alongside animals. No longer familiar with monkeys in natural settings, the spectators at a monkey performance cannot think of the animal without reference to themselves as humans.

Further Deliberations

The transformations of the polysemy of cherry blossoms and roses show the direct impact of militarization in Japan and Germany respectively. The Japanese monkey registered gradual but basic historical change in Japanese society, providing us with a clear and invaluable example of how polysemy works in real history and geopolitics. The monkey performance shows in a most succinct way how a simultaneous presence of multiple meanings creates communicative opacity.

MONKEY SYMBOLISM AND GLOBAL HISTORICAL CHANGE

In broad historical context, the transformation of the monkey from a sacred mediator to a scapegoat entailed a process of secularization. However, this process in Japanese history does not conform to Western theoretical models of the "disenchantment of the world" and "rationalization" (Weber [1930] 1992), the "decline of magic" (Thomas 1971), or the "mechanization of the world picture" (Dijksterhuis [1950] 1986). The Japanese never ceased to embrace a pantheon of deities. A profusion of what I have called "urban magic" continues to be present today even in the most urban and modernized of Japanese cities, Tokyo (Ohnuki-Tierney 1984: 144).

Although Japan has often been thought of as an isolated country, its history is in fact a series of conjunctures in Ferdinand Braudel's sense. Japan has always been affected by developments in northeast Asia. The transition from the ancient period (250–1185) to the medieval period (1185–1603) was part of a broader transformation of the northeast region in general. Japanese society underwent a series of fundamental changes with the introduction of key developments from China, including a cash economy (Amino 1986). During this period, the Japanese were open to outsiders and curious about foreign lands and cultures. They established extensive trade and cultural contacts with China from about 1342 under the leadership of Zen monks (Putzar 1963: 287). They visited foreign countries in their ships and even founded Japanese colonies. Extensive trade with other peoples brought in foreign goods, which were endowed with positive symbolic meanings.

At the same time, opposing forces—an emphasis on ascribed status, hierarchy, and the system of meaning that included purity and impurity as moral values—continued to be important or even intensified (Kuroda 1972; Ohnuki-Tierney 1984: 35–38), especially at the beginning of the Edo period. The shogunate government enforced the boundaries of the nation by restricting trade and closing ports to most foreigners. It tried to eliminate influences from outside, as manifested in the proscription of Christianity. Internally, during this period Japan developed into a feudal society in which social stratification became rigid under the Regent Toyotomi Hideyoshi, who codified the system of four classes and two groups of outcastes below.

This historical transition in Japanese society coincided with the transformation of the monkey from mediator to scapegoat. The mediator brings in fresh energy from the other: deities in the ancient period and other peoples in later history. The closure of society to outsiders meant the elimination of foreigners who, like the stranger-deities, supplied vital resources for the rejuvenation of the collective self. In their absence, another method of rejuvenating life was needed; hence the emphasis on scapegoats, who provided a means whereby the people could remove their own impurity by placing it on the scapegoats—*hisabetsu burakumin* and the monkey, as further discussed in Chapter Four.

The fall of the Tokugawa shogunate in 1868 was brought about by lower-class warriors, who used the restoration of the imperial system as an excuse to overthrow the shogunate leadership blind to the threatening geopolitical situation, in which Japan was the only Asian nation that had not succumbed to Western colonial powers. Japan reopened to the outside, propelled by the visits of Commodore Matthew C. Perry in 1853 and 1854. This change was therefore the result of a combination of internal forces and external pressures.

With the opening of the country, the Japanese conception of self in relation to other peoples underwent a fundamental transformation. Just as they had been awed by Chinese civilization during the fifth and sixth centuries, the Japanese were overwhelmed by Western civilization. The other, represented first by Chinese and then by Westerners, continued to be seen as a source of positive energy—in effect, the transcendental self of the Japanese.

The post–World War II period has been similar to the late medieval period, a phase of adopting and incorporating technological and other advances from outside. The country's defeat in what most Japanese realize was a "wrong war"—a war undertaken for the wrong reasons—provided an opportunity to fundamentally reassess the received wisdom of their culture and society and make changes accordingly. The fluidity of contemporary Japan is manifested both internally and externally. The American occupational forces eradicated the prewar class structure almost completely, introducing coeducation, equal rights for women, and other universal rights. The Japanese public today is open to outside influences. Japanese tourists now travel all over the world, especially to other Asian countries, rather than exclusively to the United States and Europe. Popular culture incorporates and transforms foreign forms. Conversely, manga, anime, and various other forms of Japanese popular culture constitute soft power reaching many other societies.

The symbolism associated with the monkey shows that it has served the Japanese as a sounding board in their deliberation about their own identity. The monkey prodded the Japanese to question human uniqueness as they had conceptualized it, often challenging the hierarchy in which humans have placed themselves above other animals. The behaviors enacted by the monkey to impress spectators exemplify characteristic Japanese manners, moral principles, and ethos. For example, teaching the monkey to imitate crying, or more specifically, the shedding of tears—part of the traditional repertoire—captures an important emphasis in Japanese culture on emotions, especially sadness.

Given that the collective self of a social group, including a nation-state as a whole, is always defined in relation to the other in a particular historical context, the monkey has played an intriguing role, mirroring how the Japanese conception of the self has changed both after encountering different others and when their country was closed to the outside world. The shifting monkey symbolism reflects the search for a distinctly Japanese identity at important historical junctures, as well as deeper questions about what it means to be human.

SUBVERSION THROUGH COMMUNICATIVE OPACITY

The meanings of the monkey are closely tied to boundaries: mediator, between categories of beings, such as deities and humans; scapegoat, at the margins of society; and trickster/clown, sitting, as it were, at the edge of society, offering meta-social commentaries on received wisdom (for a theoretical discussion, see Ohnuki-Tierney 1987: 226–28). The liminality of these figures is the very basis of their subversive power. Although these three meanings are conceptually related, changes from one to another have been related to changes in the larger historical context.

The role of trickster/clown is an abiding dimension of monkey symbolism and the dominant meaning today. According to some scholars, Saruta Biko represented shaman-actors in ancient Japan (Matsumura 1948: 6–7, 32–36; Matsumura 1954; Takasaki 1956). They argue that his unusual physical appearance, with a long nose and mirror-like eyes, is like that of a shaman wearing a mask and a disguise. They interpret the term *saru* as "to play" or "to perform a comic act causing laughter." Still, comic acting when performed by a shaman had magical power, and laughter holds a prominent place in Japanese culture, including in Zen (Hyers 1973) and in the rich folk tradition of clowning. Contemporary monkey performances have followed this tradition of causing laughter while chiding the people for their follies. Although the class structure has been eliminated, status differentiation continues to be important, for example, in business and in academia. The monkey satirizes boss-subordinate relationships by staging deliberate disobedience.

Laughter has been the monkey figure's weapon of subversion, especially when Japanese society traversed critical times. Some scholars have stressed the impotence of clowns and tricksters in facilitating social action. T. O. Beidelman (1980) argues that the intellectual and symbolic centrality of the trickster seldom translates into social centrality. James Fernandez (1980: 22) states that symbolic productions in general "act more to excite the moral imagination than to alert it to its duty." Clowns have neither led revolutions nor mobilized crowds in mass demonstrations. Pierrot or Tonio Kröger muses at the periphery. But there is more power in the acts of clowns and tricksters than we give them credit for, not only at the ontological level but in real history, especially if we try to understand the long-term significance of their performances without anticipating an immediate or direct effect upon culture and society. I suggest that their voices do not simply fade out on the edge but reverberate at the core of the structure, transforming it, albeit gradually and quietly, like raindrops silently and slowly transforming the shape of a rock on which they fall. Both the monkey charming the lord into compassion during the medieval period and the monkey "accidentally" dropping a torpedo during its mock dash into enemy territory at the height of militarism attest to the strength and resilience of subversive forces.

The subversions brought about by the monkey as a clown, however, do not constitute structural reproduction. In the medieval play, the monkey's targets were the social stratification and the hierarchical positioning of humanity and animality. During the military period, the monkey mocked the sanctity of Japan's militarism and imperialism. Contemporary monkey performances also prod the audience to deliberate upon humanity and animality but also the nature of the collective identity of the Japanese—in an increasingly globalized context, the question posed during the performances is exactly how to be a Japanese—obeying the teacher-trainer, how to bow properly, etc. Yet, these presumed characteristics of being uniquely Japanese are also presented with a sense of reflexive mockery.

On a higher level of abstraction, the monkey performance in its variations over the centuries does not simply present the inversion of the existing social hierarchy. Rather, it portrays both the essential ambiguity and the ephemeral nature of hierarchy: the trainer and the monkey constantly exchange positions so that neither holds permanent hegemony over the other. This forces both spectators and performers to question human uniqueness and superiority. The hierarchy of the trainer over the monkey, and its inversion, were simultaneously present in the medieval play as well as in the staged performance of an "order for disobedience" during the contemporary monkey performance. The "order to disobey" given by the human trainer to the monkey created a situation in which the monkey occupied a higher position, forcing spectators to question the uniqueness and superiority of humans. Tarō took on the role of a clown, offering himself as the target of Jirō's disobedience and spectators' laughter. Indeed, he became a metaphysical trickster, getting unsuspecting spectators to laugh at themselves by making them believe they were laughing only at the monkey.

The monkey's subversion has been staged not as overt political protest but in playful settings—in medieval kyōgen, outdoor performances in wartime Japan, and contemporary monkey performances. The author or the trainers may not have intended the action to be subversive, and audiences likely have read the performances in many different ways. Or, more likely, they have not really tried to interpret. All these enactments of subversion have been facilitated by the polysemy of the monkey as symbol—sacred mediator, beast/scapegoat, trickster/clown. Spectators may have only consciously reacted to the animal as "cute." Diverse meanings and the structure of subversions and inversions have remained opaque not only to the audience but even to the trainer. Communicative opacity in fact has prevented open confrontation among those whose interests are at odds with each other.

FOUR

Rice and the Japanese Collective Self

Purity by Exclusion

After introducing, in the last three chapters, how polysemy and aesthetic have contributed to communicative opacity, this chapter shows quite a different path to communicative opacity—how Japanese rice, with virtually one meaning as a dominant symbol of the collective self, has created communicative opacity by misrepresenting the collective self, without awareness on the part of almost all Japanese, including those who are excluded from the misrepresentation. Put another way, this chapter shows a symbolic pathway, as it were, to the problem pointed out by poststructuralists of "totalization" by the use of the words, such as the Japanese and the Germans.

In Japan, rice has been perhaps the most important symbol of the collective self throughout history, not only because the Japanese as a whole have upheld it as a dominant symbol of their identity but also because this symbol has served as a mechanism of communicative opacity to exclude non-agrarian social groups, with few noticing the misrepresentation. In addition, since the twin metaphors of rice and rice paddies have been the dominant symbols of Japanese identity, changes in their meanings have mirrored the historical changes in the conception of the collective self as geopolitical tidal waves inundated Japanese society and the Japanese encountered various external others—the Chinese followed by Westerners. These contacts in turn created two types of non-agrarian social groups, turning them into internal others: *Fremdkörper* (*hisabetsu burakumin*) with non-agrarian occupations, and the Ainu, a foraging population.

In addition, rice as a symbol of collective identity gives us an excellent opportunity to examine the dialectic between symbolic structure, political economy, and geopolitics. Unlike in the case of cherry blossoms and the monkey, the state has been involved in the production, distribution, and consumption of rice, and also in maintaining it as symbolic capital, ever since the seventh century. Two important findings emerge. First, the symbolism and political economy of rice were mutually constituent during most of Japanese history. Today, however, the strength of the symbolic meaning of rice continues without a firm foundation in political economy—a phenomenon begging to be explored. Second, the aesthetic values of purity and impurity are not abstract products, arising out of classificatory schema, but are products of the necessity to define and redefine the notion of the collective self as various others emerged during historical vertigoes.

The origin of rice cultivation remains controversial but the most recent archaeological investigation points to the middle Yangzi River Valley (Normile 1997). Wet-rice agriculture was introduced to Japan via the Korean Peninsula to Kyūshū, the southernmost major island of the Japanese archipelago, around 400–350 BCE. From there, it spread northeastward in three successive waves, reaching the northeastern region (Tōhoku) by the beginning of the Common Era (Kokuritsu Rekishi Minzoku Hakubutsu-kan, ed., 1987: 14). From a sociopolitical perspective, there has arguably been no other historical event as significant for the development of what we now know as the Japanese nation. Subsequent developments were similar to those in other parts of the world where foraging economies were replaced by agriculture, which enabled permanent settlements with large populations and property accumulation, eventually leading to the formation of nation-states. Until 1978, when evidence of wet-rice cultivation was found in Fukui Prefecture in Kyūshū at a site belonging to the late Jōmon period (Sasaki 1991: 299–305), it had been commonly thought there was a clear break from the Jōmon culture (14,500 BCE–300 BCE) (Kobayashi 2008: 28, 35), exclusively based on a hunting and gathering economy, to its successor, the Yayoi culture (350 BCE–250 CE), which, it was assumed, initiated a wet-rice economy. This assumption has been challenged and some scholars find continuity between the Jōmon and the Yayoi, and, also, Ainu peoples and cultures. At any rate, wet-rice agriculture enabled the development of a large society with social classes, and parts of the country began to politically unite under landowners. During the subsequent Kofun (tomb) period (250 CE–646 CE), political leaders living in the central and western regions, where wet-rice agriculture had penetrated, controlled large territories. One of these regional lords was ancestral to those who established the Yamato state, whose leaders founded the imperial family.[1]

This chapter begins with a sketch of the agrarian cosmological scheme that has been hegemonic in the past and remains powerful even today. I show how the agrarian cosmology has played an important role in the interpretation of historical forces, as the Japanese have reformulated their concepts of self and others.

Agrarian Cosmology

RICE AS JAPANESE DEITY

The Japanese deities in the agrarian cosmology are succinctly described as the *marebito* (strangers), who come from outside the village and are endowed with both a peaceful and benevolent soul (*nigimitama*) and a violent and destructive soul (*aramitama*). When the deity visits, the villagers perform a ritual to ward off its negative energy, which would otherwise inflict harm on them, and to harness its positive energy in order to replenish life, which otherwise would become stagnant and impure. The ritual is related to the different stages of the growth of rice plants. In addition, the villagers consume rice, thereby internalizing sacred power, which then becomes part of the human body and rejuvenates it and promotes its growth. As elsewhere in the world where the concept of "stranger deity" exists,[2] it offers a model to interpret outside forces—including foreigners, envisioned to have both positive and negative powers (Ohnuki-Tierney 1993a: 44–62).

Among the beings of the universe that constitute the deities in the Japanese pantheon, rice occupies the central space. The Mountain Deity, the most important in the pantheon, comes down to the villages in the spring and becomes the Deity of Rice Paddies. Fundamental to the meanings assigned to rice in Japanese culture is the belief that each grain has a soul (*inadama* or *inadamashii*)—a view shared by other peoples for whom rice is a staple food.[3]

Since the Japanese universe is populated by soul-bearers, what is important about the soul of rice is that it is sacred. The eighth-century myth-histories of the *Kojiki* and *Nihongi* are replete with references to rice as deities, whose names include words for the grain and stalk. In one version in the *Kojiki*, Amaterasu Ōmikami (the Sun Goddess) is the mother of a grain soul whose name bears reference to rice stalks. The legendary Jinmu emperor, the so-called first emperor, is the son of the grain soul and the grandson of Amaterasu Ōmikami, who sends him to earth—the episode is known as the "descent of the heavenly grandson" (*tenson kōrin*)—in order for him to transform a wilderness, that is, the Japanese archipelago, into a land of rice stalks with succulent ears of rice (*mizuho*) and abundant grains of five types (*gokoku*), as introduced in Chapter One. He brings the original seeds given to him by Amaterasu Ōmikami, whose rays nurture rice and other plants (Kurano and Takeda 1958; see also Murakami 1977: 13). This episode explains why the most important role of the emperors, even after their power was taken away by the warlords, has been as officiant of the rituals involving the growth of rice (Saigō [1967] 1984: 15–29; Kawasoe 1980: 86).

The rice harvest ritual is a cosmic gift exchange in which a new crop—a few grains of divinity—is offered to the deity in return for the original seeds he gave to humans. The mode of exchange takes the form of commensality—eating together—between the deity and humans at a feast. On another level, the ritual cycle constitutes a cosmological exchange of the soul and the body. Since the grain embodies the soul of the deity, by offering rice grains to humans in the spring, the deity offers his own body-soul as a sacrifice—the ultimate "gift of self"—in the same way as "a man gives himself" (Mauss [1925] 1966: 45). Humans in turn nurture the sacred soul, that is, rice grains, with the rays of the Sun Goddess and at harvesttime make a return gift—the first crop of rice, plus a greater amount of grains as "interest" (Amino 1987). This is a generalized exchange between the deity and humans as a group—a gift that does not entail an immediate return.[4]

RICE AS FOOD FOR COMMENSALITY

The major cooperative effort required for rice cultivation is a powerful means whereby people came to identify themselves with a social group whose members help each other at labor-intensive times, such as the planting of seedlings and the harvest. Rice paddies are a spatial symbol of group identity. However, even more significant is that rice, rice cakes, and rice wine (*sake*) have been the most important food in Japan for commensality between humans and deities and among humans (Yanagita [1940] 1982). For farmers, agricultural rituals have always been a time for relatives residing elsewhere to gather, dine, and drink together. Today, this is often the only occasion when young family members working in cities come back home to rural areas. The New Year's celebration in contemporary Japan is a nationwide ritual during which mirror rice cakes (*kagamimochi*) are placed in the alcove (*tokomona*) as an offering to the deities and then shared among humans, who internalize their sacred power (Yanagita, ed., 1951: 94–95). These cakes are made of layers of round flat rice cakes in the shape of a mirror, symbolizing Japanese deities (Ohnuki-Tierney 1987: 135–36; 1993a: 54–55; Ishibashi 1914; Nakayama 1976).

Rice and rice products are also central to commensal activities in day-to-day life. As a symbol of a commensal act between deceased members of the family, the "ancestors," and the living, the daily offering in the family ancestral alcove continues to include cooked white rice. Rice is the only food shared at daily meals and served by the female head of the household, while other dishes are served individually. In the past in some regions, the wooden spatula used to scoop rice was handed down from a mother to her daughter or daughter-in-law as a symbolic expression of the transfer of the role and power of the woman head of the household (Nōda 1943: 52–56; Yanagita, ed., 1951: 264–65).

Rice stands for "we," for whatever social group a person belongs to. For example, "To eat from the same rice-cooking pot" (*onaji kama no meshi o kuu*) is a common expression for close human relationships, emphasizing the strong sense of bonding arising from sharing meals. Those who eat together become "we" as opposed to "they." Commonly used expressions today refer to the opposite situation. "To eat cold rice" (*hiyameshi o kuu*) is to endure hardship, since rice must be served hot, unless used in sushi or in a lunch box. "To eat someone else's rice" (*tanin no meshi o kuu*) refers to the ill fortune of going through hardship among strangers.

Rice wine (*sake*) is the most important item of commensality in social settings, especially among men, although today it is increasingly common among women. A basic rule of social drinking is that one never pours sake for oneself; one pours it for someone else who, in turn, pours sake into one's own cup in a never-ending series of taking turns. The phrase "drinking alone" (*hitorizake*) is an expression of the loneliness of a socially disconnected person—there is nothing lonelier than having to pour one's own sake. Unlike in some Western cultures, where the independent and autonomous self is regarded as the ideal model of personhood, in Japanese culture the socially localized self does not exist without the social other; the self is always dialogically defined in relation to the other in a given social context. A lone individual who must pour his or her own sake is on the verge of becoming nonself, without a socially localized identity.

The power of food as a symbol of self-identity derives from two interlocking dimensions. First, each member of the social group consumes the food, which becomes embodied in each individual and operates as a metonym by being part of the self. Second, the members of the group eat together. Commensality is the basis for food becoming a metaphor for "we"—the social group. This practice renders food a powerful symbol not only conceptually but also, so to speak, at the gut level. "Our food" versus "their food" becomes a potent way to express "us" versus "them." The purity of "we" is in the food that is consumed collectively and thus becomes embodied in "us." Conversely, "their" undesirable qualities are embodied through the consumption of others' inferior/impure food.[5]

RICE AS JAPANESE SPACE, TIME, AND THE PRIMORDIAL SELF

Another important dimension of the evocative power of rice is that rice and rice paddies represent Japanese time and space, that is, "nature," and thus ultimately signify the primordial Japanese self. Although the valorization of the countryside, epitomized in rice paddies, began earlier, its systematic development occurred during the Edo period, when Edo (Tokyo) became an urban center, as vividly depicted in woodblock prints (*ukiyo-e*). For example, in the famous illustrations by Katsushika Hokusai (1760–1849) for *One Hundred Poems by One Hundred Poets*, the most common motif is rice and rice agriculture, such as rice farmers at work, sheaves of harvested rice, and flooded rice paddies, which appear in 26 out of the 89 prints. Harvested rice fields, flooded rice paddies, bundles of rice (*komedawara*), and rice sheaves appear in the woodblock prints of Andō Hiroshige in his *Fifty-three Stations along the Tōkaidō* (*Tōkaidō Gojū-San Tsugi*) (Gotō 1975).

These recurrent motifs represent more than rice and rice agriculture per se. At the most obvious level, they signal the seasons of the year. Flooded rice fields, like rice-planting songs, are the most familiar signs of spring or early summer, a time of birth and growth. Rice-harvesting scenes, including sheaves of rice stalks—the most frequently used image—represent fall and its joyful harvest, the culmination of the growing season. Strikingly, the cycle of rice growth came to mark the seasons for all Japanese, including urbanites, fishermen, and all other non-agrarian people.

At a more abstract level, the travelers depicted in these woodblock prints, headed toward Edo (Tokyo), symbolize the transient and changing Japan epitomized by the city. In contrast, rice and rice agriculture stand for Japan in its pristine, unchanging form. Far from the reality of mud, sweat, and fertilizer, rice agriculture was valorized aesthetically, in much the same way that rural France and its hardworking peasants were idealized by Claude Monet, Jean-François Millet, and other French impressionists (Brettell and Brettell 1983).

Inherent in these depictions of landscape and subsistence activities are temporal representations. Agriculture symbolizes the vanished past in many industrial and postindustrial societies. This is ironic, since agriculture was the first human endeavor to completely erase "nature," replacing it with farmland (Ohnuki-Tierney 1993a: 125–26). In Japan, in addition to the centrality of the seasonal cycle, the idea of a pristine past suggests a distinct national identity unchanged by foreign influences and modernity, symbolized by the city, as in many other cultures. The valorization of the primordial self of the Japanese, epitomized by agrarian life, reached a high point among intellectuals from the late Edo period (Harootunian 1988: 23) through the Meiji period (Gluck 1985: 175, 181). It continues today, with the Japanese searching for nature in the countryside, now nostalgically referred to as *furusato* (literally, old homestead, one's home region), just as English urbanites construct their own "English countryside" (Newby 1979; Williams 1973).

From a temporal perspective, the ancestral land for rice cultivation, family farmland, and fundamentally untouched nature, stand for a pristine past, the time before the land's purity was contaminated by modernity and Western influences. The twin metaphor of rice and rice paddies became the ultimate symbol of Japan and Japanese culture in its purest form.

THE AESTHETIC OF RICE IN AGRARIAN COSMOLOGY

Rice stalks have been described in literature as bearing lustrous, golden ripe ears waving in the autumn wind in the domain of a feudal lord, the symbol of his wealth and political power, literally expressed by the yield of rice in his territory. Rice paddies with green seedlings in crystal-clear water are another frequent motif in poems, essays, and the aforementioned woodblock prints and other visual arts. Not only the plant and grains but also cooked rice is beautiful. The most important characteristics of cooked rice are the related qualities of luster, purity, and whiteness. In his *In-ei Raisan* (In Praise of Shadows), Tanizaki Junichirō, an important novelist of the twentieth century, extols its beauty:

> Cooked rice in a shining black lacquer rice container, placed in the dark, is
> highly aesthetic to look at it and is most appetizing. When you lift the lid [of

the lacquer container], you see pure white rice with steam rising from it. *Each grain is a pearl*. If you are a Japanese, you certainly appreciate rice when you look at it this way. (Tanizaki [1933] 1959: 17–18, italics added)

Even in contemporary Japan, the aesthetic of rice is extolled. Ripe heads of rice stalks continued to be described as having a "beautiful" golden luster. A pair of ¥60 stamps, one with a picture of succulent ears of rice and the other with a poem by the renowned poet Matsuo Bashō, written in brush strokes, praising the fragrance of new rice grains, was issued on November 11, 1988. The visual message of the stamps is powerful: not only is rice beautiful, but its beauty is as quintessentially Japanese as the brush strokes, often chosen for special occasions, especially among older people. Brush strokes impart a quintessentially Japanese aesthetic to written characters, not attained by writing with a pen, let alone a computer.

Rice is called "pure rice" (*junmai*) or "white rice" (*hakumai*), highlighting its aesthetic quality. The two kinds of rice preferred by most Japanese today are labeled *koshihikari* and *sasanishiki*. The term *hikari* means light or luster and *nishiki* means gold. Both names emphasize luster, which, together with whiteness and purity, constitutes the aesthetic of rice.[6] This is so even though many consumers never have seen rice plants in the field; they see "beautiful rice" in advertisements and on TV. The purity of rice is in turn translated into the purity of the Japanese self.

The above history of rice shows that purity has long been an integral part of the conception of the Japanese self, the emergence and presence of which antedates the birth of the state as a political unit.

The Japanese creation myth centered on the transformation of wilderness into the land of succulent rice. That is, rice paddies gave birth to the land of the Japanese. They stand for the ancestral land at the family level, and for a lord's power, expressed through the image of golden ears of rice in paddies stretching across his territory. Above all, rice paddies stand for "our land," "our history," and thus the pure, original Japanese self.

The Political Economy of Symbolic Production

The process whereby the symbolic meaning of rice was developed and embraced by the Japanese, even those in non-agrarian sectors, has *not* been a "natural" development. Rather, state control of production and distribution has been intensive and extensive from the very beginning. According to the *Nihongi*, on April 10, 675 CE, Emperor Tenmu issued an ordinance to enforce the performance of two rituals, perhaps the first national rituals, to ensure the promotion of rice agriculture—one for the Wind Deity and the other for the Water Deity in charge of water in rice paddies. On April 17, seven days later, the emperor issued another important ordinance, against meat eating (Sakamoto et al., eds., 1967: 418). It prohibited the eating of five beasts: cows, horses, dogs, chickens, and monkeys. Cows and horses are useful for agriculture, and the others are domesticated, and hence close to humans. It is noteworthy that the list excludes deer and wild boars, which were game animals. The official reason for the prohibition was the Buddhistic doctrine of mercy for all living beings, underscored by the defilement incurred by contact with the dead body, either of a human or of an animal, which had been an important belief in Japan's native religion of Shintoism.

Harada Nobuo (1993: 69–76) introduces a number of scholars who argue that Buddhist teaching was used to justify the prohibition of meat eating, which was in fact to protect the agricultural/rice crop, because meat eating was a threat to agriculture. These ordinances testify that state control of agriculture, especially rice production, started quite early. The ammunition for state intervention was supplied by the nativist scholars of the seventeenth century through the nineteenth century. Placing Hirata Atsutane (1776–1843) in a broader context of the nativist movement, Harootunian (1988) details how agricultural work was reconstituted and valorized as a practice of the "ancient way" and became an ideological/symbolic weapon for the exclusive emphasis on agriculture, when the wheel of modernization was turning rapidly toward industrialization and other modern economic activities.

After the ordinance of Emperor Tenmu the official diet of the Japanese consisted of fish and vegetables.[7] The prohibition against meat eating was removed in 1871 when Emperor Meiji announced the adoption of a meat diet at the Imperial Palace (Harada 1993: 17).[8]

The 1942 Food Control Act (*Shokuryō Kanrihō*), which regulated food production and distribution, and the rationing system (*haikyū*) during World War II brought rice to islands and remote regions where only "miscellaneous grains" had been grown (Tsuboi [1982] 1984: 68). State control has continued even to the present, with rice as almost the exclusive focus. Today, rice farmers are often paid to leave fields fallow to prevent overproduction (Ohnuki-Tierney 1995), which leads to a lower price.

That the symbolism of rice held its grip on most Japanese is clearly seen by the fact that only after World War II did scholars, even those of the most liberal persuasion, begin questioning the assumption that Japanese culture should be equated with rice culture. Such scholars as Amino Yoshihiko (1980; 2000: 237–330), Miyamoto Tsuneichi (1981), Sasaki Kōmei (1983, 2009), and Tsuboi Hirofumi ([1982] 1984: 85–86) have challenged the thesis that the cosmology based on rice agriculture is *the* Japanese culture. An influential interpretation is that for many Japanese other grains and various kinds of tubers were more important as staple foods than rice.[9] These grains included wheat (*mugi*), buckwheat (*soba*), Italian millet (*awa*), true millet (*kibi*), Deccan grass (barnyard millet, *hie*), and sesame (*goma*). They grow in poor soil and require far less attention than rice. It is important, however, that these were called "miscellaneous grains" (*zakkoku*), that is, they were a residual category. Scholarly debates about Japanese culture as a "rice-cultivation culture" (*inasaku bunka*) versus a "non-rice cultivation culture" (*hi-inasaku bunka*) continue. The latter is sometimes referred to as the "miscellaneous-grain culture" (*zakkoku bunka*) because of its emphasis on various non-rice grains as staple foods (see Amino 2000; Sasaki 1985; Tsuboi 1984).

An important question is to what extent farmers were rice producers, as opposed to producers of other grains. Even more significant is the question of who consumed the rice. Were the producers, i.e., the farmers/peasants, also consumers? Or were they producers without the opportunity to be consumers, since rice was taken away as tax by the lord? It is difficult to generalize in different historical periods across different regions in Japan (for details, see Ohnuki-Tierney 1993a: 34–43). We have more information on the subject during the Edo period. For example, on the basis of a detailed examination of Fukushima district, Vlastos (1986: 30–41) concludes that peasants during the Edo period "retained at least part of the increase in output" that resulted from an expansion of arable land, improved technology, and a more intensive input of labor (Vlastos 1986: 30).

Undoubtedly the tax system, with rice as the major commodity subject to taxation, affected peasants adversely in many regions. However, peasant uprisings paradoxically serve as evidence that rice must have been a significant part of the daily diet during the Edo period, at least in some areas; there is no reason to assume that peasants demanded rice for ritual occasions alone. Of 2,755 uprisings in Japan between 1590 and 1867, 158 (5.7 percent) were rice riots in rural areas. "Rice riots" (*komesōdō*) were outbreaks over the high price of rice, resulting in attacks on rice dealers, wealthy people, and the police. Another 214 (7.7 percent) incidents constituted demands for rice without outbreaks of violence. Thus, a total of 371 (13.5 percent) were related to rice issues. While these figures are for rural areas, in cities during the same period, 214 outbreaks were rice riots, and in 34 the people demanded rice, which accounts for 73.3 percent of the total city riots (Aoki 1967: 39–45).

The circumstances of farmers' lives changed little during the Meiji and Taishō periods (Koyanagi 1972: 162–89; cf. Yanagita [1931] 1982: 168), and peasant disturbances continued.

If rice was not part of the diet for Japanese throughout history, the question is when it became the staple food in terms of either quantitative value or being the defining and thus indispensable feature of Japanese meals. Scholars' opinions vary widely on this issue. According to Sasaki (1983: 292), urbanites began eating rice three times a day only in the middle of the Edo period; other scholars date it much later.[10] What is certain is that not all Japanese farmers either grew rice exclusively or relied on it as a staple food. Yet the rice symbolism in the agrarian cosmology has represented the Japanese and their culture without competition.

The Self and Others in Historical Conjunctures

EXTERNAL OTHERS: CHINESE AND WESTERNERS

Few groups have lived in isolation from historical flows of peoples and goods. Intensive interaction through trade, warfare, and religion occurred in ancient as well as modern times all over the world. Any encounter with another group, either directly or indirectly, through an exchange of cultural artifacts and institutions, prompts people to think about who they are in relation to others.

In any process of dialectical differentiation between the self and other(s), staple foods often play a powerful symbolic role. Consider, for example, the wheat-eating northern Indians versus the rice-eating southern Indians; the dark bread of the peasants versus the white bread of the upper classes in the European past; French versus German versus Italian breads; the sorghum of the Pende contrasted with the maize of the Mbuun in nineteenth-century central Africa (Vansina 1978: 177). Rice—or, more appropriately, rices—have played a major role in Japanese deliberations on their own identity in relation to other peoples.

Japan's history is a series of conjunctures during which internal developments occurred to a large degree in response to the flow of world history. These conjunctures have been interpreted through the Japanese concepts of self and other, and in turn have forced the Japanese to repeatedly reconceptualize their notion of self.

The two conjunctures that sent the most profound and lasting shock waves throughout the country were Japan's encounter with the high civilization of Tang China between the fifth and seventh centuries, and its encounter with Western civilization toward the end of the nineteenth century. In both instances, the Japanese were overwhelmed by the civilizations of the respective others and hurriedly and earnestly attempted to learn about and imitate them. The previously illiterate Japanese adopted the Chinese writing system even though the two spoken languages were totally unrelated, which meant that the writing was not readily transferable. Similarly, the Japanese eagerly adopted metallurgy, city planning, and a whole range of other features of Chinese civilization. In addition, they took the Chinese designation for Japan, *Nihon* (the base where the sun rises); from China's perspective, Japan is situated on the horizon, where the sun appears in the morning (Amino Yoshihiko, personal communication). In short, the Japanese conception of self was born in the encounter with the Chinese, who represented the stranger deity at a cosmological level and therefore became the transcendental other.

At the same time, the Japanese strove to protect their own culture and their self (Pollack 1986). In this climate, the aforementioned Emperor Tenmu (r. 672–686) commissioned scholars to compile the *Kojiki* and the *Nihongi* myth-histories in order to establish a Japanese identity in opposition to Tang China (Kawasoe 1980: 253–54; Sakamoto et al., eds., 1967: 6–12). For this purpose, the imperial court selected from competing oral traditions the myth that its own deity—the Food Deity—grew the first crop of rice and compiled the first texts in the Chinese writing system it had appropriated. To define Japanese identity as distinct from that of the Chinese, the Japanese added various prefixes such as *kan* (Han), *kara* (Tang), and *tō* (Tang) to items imported from China, as with *kanji* (Chinese characters). In contrast, prefixes such as *wa*, *hō*, and *nihon* were used to designate items of Japanese origin. The phrase *wakan secchū* meant a combination of Japanese and Chinese ways. The most revealing expression is *wakon kansai*, the Japanese (*wa*) soul (*kon*) and Chinese (*kan*) brilliance (*sai*), referring to the best of the two worlds; the phrase represents the Japanese people's effort to preserve their identity as "the Japanese soul." As we will encounter repeatedly in later chapters, the Japanese chose the soul, rather than the mind or the body, as the essence of their own existence and identity.

The second major conjuncture was in the nineteenth century. When the country reopened after three centuries of isolation, it again went through the painful experience of encountering a "superior" other, this time the West, with a host of scientific and technological advances. China had suffered internal conflicts and succumbed to Western colonialism, and as a consequence lost international standing. The West now replaced China as the transcendental other in whom Japan sought its own image (Pollack 1986: 53). Not only did the Japanese eagerly adopt Western science and technology, but they also took up Western clothing, hairstyles, food, and ballroom dancing, as well as Western styles of music, painting, and writing—in short, just about every transferable aspect of culture.

To complicate the matter, the Japanese had to face the fact that the West indiscriminately labeled them "Orientals," just as the Japanese lumped all Westerners together. The more complex international scene required the Japanese both to separate themselves from other Asians, especially Chinese and Koreans, and to distinguish themselves from the West (Tanaka 1993).

Japanese Rice, Chinese Rice   In order to distance themselves from other Asians, who also consume rice, the Japanese engaged in a "war of rices"—domestic rice vs. Chinese rice. The distinction was not simply a matter of Japanese short-grain versus Chinese long-grain varieties. The difference was of moral significance, assigning Japanese rice and Japanese people moral superiority.

Toward the end of the Edo period, the twin metaphor of domestic rice (*naichimai*) for the Japanese and foreign rice (*gaimai*) for other Asians surfaced in public discourse, even though foreign rice had been introduced much earlier, at least by the thirteenth century (Sansom 1961: 183). Championed by nativist scholars, who sought the pure Japanese spirit, Japanese rice was chosen to represent the pristine Japanese way, while Chinese rice was denigrated as "inferior" and "those who eat [it]" declared "weak and enervated" (Harootunian 1988: 211–14). Motoori Norinaga (1730–1801), a nativist scholar of the Edo period, claimed that the aesthetic of rice derived from the fact of its being grown in Japan, which was superior to other nations (Motoori Norinaga, *Kojikiden*; cited in Watanabe Tadayo 1989: 89). It was "our" rice grown on "our" land, made beautiful by the rice plant.

The distinction underscored by the prejudice against the Chinese apparently came to be shared by common folk, as described in *Kōfu* (The Miners), a novel by Natsume Sōseki ([1907] 1984), one of the best-known writers of the period. The novel summarizes life in a coal mine, the lowest type of existence, as "eating Chinese rice (*nankinmai*) and being eaten by Chinese bugs" (*nankinmushi*, bed bugs). The term *Nankin* refers to Nanjing and thus to China. Chinese rice is depicted as tasting like mud and being too slippery to manage, while Japanese rice is called "silver rice" (*ginmai*). The symbolic opposition of /domestic rice: Chinese rice:: silver: mud/ represents the basic opposition of the Japanese self and the marginalized external other.

Japanese Rice, Western Meat   At the time of the encounter with the West, the metaphor of rice versus meat replaced the metaphor of domestic versus foreign rice. As shown above, meat had been a highly problematic item of food and therefore a striking feature of the Western diet. Some people who favored the unabashed imitation of the West advocated the abandonment of rice agriculture and the adoption of animal husbandry. They argued that as long as the Japanese continued to eat only rice, fish, and vegetables, their bodies would never become strong enough to compete with the bodies of meat-eating Westerners (Tsukuba [1969] 1986: 109–12). They also associated a diet dominated by rice with country hicks and uncivilized habits (Tsukuba [1969] 1986: 113). Those who opposed the imitation of the West emphasized the importance of rice agriculture and the superiority of a rice diet, even when the army, which adhered to the rice diet, suffered enormous casualties from beriberi, far more than on the battlefield, while there were no casualties among sailors, whose diet included barley and bread. Vitamin B1 deficiency as the cause of beriberi was discovered only in 1910 (Matsuda 2007: esp. 322–39, 372–76; Takaki 1888, 1905).

Throughout the period of militarization, the construction of the Japanese national identity by the state involved the use of symbolically significant foodstuffs, especially rice. For example, the rising sun flag motif was frequently used in the well-known rising sun lunch (*hinomaru bentō*), which consisted of a bed of white rice with a red pickled plum in the center. The purity of white rice (*hakumai*) or "pure rice" (*junmai*) became a powerful metaphor for the purity of the Japanese self. During World War II, white rice, symbolically strong despite its nutritional deficiency, had to be saved for the most precious sector of the population, the soldiers. The state used the shortage of Japanese rice to motivate the rest of the population to work hard for victory, which promised a return to good times with plenty of white Japanese rice instead of foreign rice.

Just as Chinese objects are distinguished by prefixes, objects of Western origin are marked by *yō*, as in *yōshoku* (Western cuisine), as opposed to *washoku* (Japanese cuisine). At times foreign words are retained to distinguish them from their Japanese counterparts, as in the case of *wain* (wine), which refers to Western wines, in contrast to Japanese sake. Today, there is a profusion of foreign foods throughout Japan. Fast food such as Big Macs and Kentucky Fried Chicken, pizza and bagels, and haute cuisine from every culture of the world—all are available and eagerly sought.

Precisely because of the abundance of Western foods, Japanese cuisine has made a phenomenal comeback. Streetcars and newspapers are full of advertisements for restaurants and inns featuring numerous Japanese dishes. Rice remains the defining feature of traditional Japanese cuisine. While it continues to be referred to as the main food (*shushoku*), with other dishes called auxiliary food (*fukushoku*), or side dishes, Japanese haute cuisine emphasizes the side dishes, though always with rice, served in small portions. What makes a Japanese dish (*washoku*) is the presence of rice. Japanese-style steak (*washokushiki sutēki*), a popular menu item in contemporary Japan, is steak served with cooked white rice. Many dishes of foreign origin are Japanized by the presence of *raisu* (rice), as in "rice-burger" (*raisu-bāgā*), a hamburger sandwiched between two layers of bun-shaped rice. At restaurants, for dishes of foreign origin, a waiter/waitress usually asks, "Would you like *raisu* or *pan* with it?," using the Portuguese word for bread, which has been adopted by the Japanese. Despite the decreased importance of quantity, rice remains "the king-pin of any meal's architecture" in Japan (Dore [1958] 1973: 86).

California Short-Grain Rice, Japanese Short-Grain Rice President Bill Clinton tried to open up Japan's rice market in the fall of 1993 as the first and symbolic gesture in opening the market for more important products. That year cold weather had drastically reduced the harvest. The world witnessed an enormous drama on both sides of the Pacific. South Koreans protested the importation of rice to their country perhaps even more vigorously than the Japanese did, but international attention was focused on Japanese resistance. America's mass media caricatured the Japanese as xenophobic, clinging to domestically grown rice despite the seemingly obvious fact that rice grown in California using seeds from Japan was identical to Japanese domestic rice and would be much cheaper.

President Clinton and Prime Minister Hosokawa both staged dramatic performances, each keeping his eye on his own domestic front. In Japan, most politicians had realized that rice importation was inevitable, but they could not risk losing the rural vote. The Ministry of Agriculture, Forestry, and Fisheries took a hard line, publicly vowing to fight "until death" against the opening up of the rice market (*Asahi Shinbun*, December 14, 1993), even though it had been quietly trying to open up the market for other food items, such as beef and oranges in 1992. The Ministry of International Trade and Industry as well as Japanese corporations had pushed for rice importation for decades (Calder 1988: 231). They were willing to sacrifice the symbolic value of rice in exchange for reducing the tension that arose from the trade imbalance between the two countries and for facilitating the export of Japanese high-tech products.

While politicians were "performing" for the voters, Japanese consumers, who had been paying several times more for domestic rice than for California rice from the United States, became active participants in the opposition, replicating, for different reasons, the rhetoric of those tied to rice farming and agricultural cooperatives. Japanese short-grain rice as opposed to Chinese long-grain rice, and rice as opposed to meat, constitute materially obvious symbols of "us" versus "them." But for California rice, seemingly identical to domestic Japanese rice, those who opposed opening the rice market needed a different strategy. Their rhetoric was couched in the language of "rice as self" and "rice paddies as our land." They argued that rice paddies are essential for Japan, serving as dams, promoting soil conservation, preserving underground water, *purifying* the air and water, and *beautifying* the land (Inoue 1988). In contrast, California rice, grown in American paddies, served their air, land, and water, not "ours."

Ironically, there has never been any singular, uniquely Japanese rice. Japanese farmers have practiced self-seeding, each family selecting and saving their own seeds for the following year, creating thousands of varieties of rice that the Japanese have grown and consumed throughout much of their history. Only recently have they begun to identify as *the* Japanese rice two types (*koshihikari* and *sasanishiki*) grown in northeastern Japan, where rice agriculture penetrated the latest. These varieties have been regarded as *the* Japanese rice only for a couple of decades. Furthermore, as noted earlier, Japanese rice has always been predicated on the presence of foreign rice, without which there is no concept of domestic or Japanese rice (Ōbayashi 1973; Miyata 1993).

The equation of self-sufficiency (*jikyū jisoku*) with an exclusive reliance on domestic rice (Ōshima 1984: 40) has been frequently stressed. Self-sufficiency in rice production has been the almost exclusive emphasis of the state's food control policy (*shokuryō kanrihō*) throughout Japan's history (Tōkei Kenkyūkai 1969: 4). Other metaphors used in 1993 include rice as the life-blood crop (Yamaguchi 1987: 40); rice as the lifeline (*seimeisen*); rice as the last sacred realm (*saigo no seiiki*) (*Kōbe Shinbun*, July 6, 1990); rice as the last citadel, a phrase used by the minister of agriculture and fishing (*Asahi Shinbun*, June 27, 1990); and rice as the national life and the prototype of Japanese culture (*Zenchū Farm News* no. 5, January 1987: 2). The opponents of rice importation equated foreign rice with *impurity* caused by chemicals from insecticides and processing, although Japan's own rice was not chemical free.

Consumer groups such as the All-Osaka Consumer Group (Zen-Ōsaka Shōhisha Dantai Renrakukai) became intensely involved in checking foreign rice for chemicals (Shimogaito 1988: 76–78). Individual consumers, especially women, voiced their fears in newspapers (*Asahi Shinbun*, June 13, 1990) and introduced the English phrase "postharvest chemicals" into daily parlance. One consumers' organization even conducted an experiment, putting worms in a sack of foreign rice to see how soon they would die from pesticide residues (*Asahi Shinbun*, October 30 and November 17, 1993). Some demanded that the government investigate the processing methods used for all imported rice (*Asahi Shinbun*, October 30 and November 12, 1993). Consumers also opposed the government's plan to mix imported rice with domestic rice.

On December 15, 1993, Prime Minister Hosokawa announced that "for the future national interest" he would allow a minimum of 4 to 8 percent of the country's annual rice consumption (40 to 80 tons) to be imported tariff-free for the next six years. No riot took place. Japan's mass media quickly shifted its attention to the issues of electoral reform and the sales and consumption tax.

In early 1994, despite opposition from consumers (*Asahi Shinbun*, November 11, 12, 17, and 19, 1993) and female members of the Lower House (*Asahi Shinbun*, March 10 and 11, 1994), the government began promoting *burendo-mai* (domestic and foreign rice mixed). The mass media reported how consumers lined up to stock up on domestic rice (*Asahi Shinbun*, March 11, 1994). But this too quickly passed away, as the following year's rice crop was abundant.

The image created during the California rice incident was that the Japanese have consumed their own domestic rice from time immemorial, and the Uruguay Round of the General Agreement on Tariffs and Trade (GATT, which then became the World Trade Organization, or WTO) was forcing them to open their rice market for the first time. In this scenario, President Clinton became the contemporary counterpart of Commodore Perry, the U.S. naval officer who forced Japan to "open its door" to foreign trade in 1853 and 1854. Centuries after the original construction of the Japanese self in a discourse of opposition to China, the 1993 rice importation issue rearticulated the Japanese sense of self in relation to the United States (for details of the 1993 rice importation issue, see Ohnuki-Tierney 1995).

INTERNAL OTHERS

The development of the collective identity of the Japanese, as expressed in "rice as self" and "rice paddies as Japanese land," represents a historical process that wrote off two social groups, the Ainu (Ohnuki-Tierney 1974; 1981a) and the *hisabetsu burakumin* (Ohnuki-Tierney 1987).

The Ainu are a group of people in Sakhalin and Hokkaido, and in the past, also on the Kuriles and northern parts of Honshū (the main island of Japan). Before colonization by the Japanese and Russians in the eighteenth century, they engaged in a foraging economy—hunting land and sea animals, fishing, and plant gathering. Although they did not develop a writing system, they enjoyed a highly developed oral tradition, which included lengthy epic poems.

The other marginalized group, now officially called *hisabetsu burakumin* (discriminated hamlet people), has never constituted a separate population from the rest of the Japanese. They are heterogeneous people with diverse but non-agrarian occupations, such as trading, religious, artistic, and entertainment activities, as well as occupations that deal with animals, such as butchers, tanners, and manufacturers of leather goods, and the death of animals and humans, such as undertakers and tomb caretakers. In ancient times individuals in some of these occupations were thought to have a special power as mediators between humans and deities. There is no clear descent line linking the people or their occupations from one historical period to the next (Harada 1978a, 1978b; Noguchi 1978; Ueda 1978a, 1978b). The meaning and cultural valuation assigned to them have gone through significant changes over time.

During the medieval period, two significant developments—one in society and the other in aesthetic values—changed their fate. First, social stratification was intensified, with minute details regulating the people in each category. The most basic division was between "residents" (*teijūmin*) and "nonresidents" (*hiteijūmin*). Called *heimin* (common people), residents were full-fledged members of society who were free, that is, not owned by others, and were allowed to carry arms and to move freely. They were obliged to pay taxes. "Nonresidents," on the other hand, "did not have the right to be taxed," as described by Amino (1980: 22–23). In this category were placed many of the people now called *hisabetsu burakumin*; they either were without a permanent residence or resided in marginal spaces (for details, see Ohnuki-Tierney 1998: 36–39).

Another decisively adverse development for them was an extreme negativity assigned to the symbolic/aesthetic value of impurity. Perhaps the strongest taboo in Japan's agrarian cosmology, which is based on the native Shintoism and has been integral to Japanese culture from the very beginning, is impurity. However, during the latter half of the late medieval period, impurity took on an intense negativity and was permanently attached to individuals who engaged in occupations dealing with culturally defined defilement, most of which were their so-called traditional occupations (for details, see Ohnuki-Tierney 1998: 39–42). This negative association and the concomitant prejudice and marginalization continued until and even after the legal prohibition of discrimination against these minority groups was issued in the promulgation of the Meiji constitution in 1889.

These two social groups were marginalized at different periods, due to different historical forces. The Ainu were "discovered" primarily during the eighteenth century, at the time of imperial expansion into the northeast corners of the world, rich in natural resources, by the Russians and the Japanese, while Japan itself was under the threat of Western colonial expansion. The Japanese, having adopted wet-rice agriculture, the writing system, and a host of other items from the Chinese, by then wished to raise their own status in the social evolutionary scale, also adopted from the West. By pushing down the Ainu as hunter-gatherers without writing, the Japanese could elevate themselves. The felt need for this came from the geopolitical situation—at the time when Japan reopened itself to the world, it faced the urgent task of catching up with the science and technology of the West. In order to fully join the "civilized" nations of the world, the Japanese had to denigrate one of their own social groups—the Ainu.

These two internal others were not "landed/residents," at a time when Japanese society increasingly emphasized residency; they were non-agrarian; and they dealt with animals for their livelihood. The Ainu were foraging people who had no concept of territory, and they were meat eaters. The *hisabetsu burakumins'* occupations brought them close to animals. Thus, neither group belonged to the tropic representation of the Japanese—"rice as self" and "rice paddies, our land."

Conclusion

An advantage of following the life course, as it were, of the symbolism of rice is that it enables us to examine the complex relationship between symbolic structure and political economy. In most historical periods, the state strongly intervened so that symbolic meaning and the aesthetic of rice would uphold the political economy. The strength of this symbolism derives in large measure from its aesthetic, which may have been created and maintained by the state and yet it became naturalized and was transferred to the people. The 1993 rice importation affair clearly showed that rice as a symbol of the Japanese self had remained powerfully evocative for the people. The symbolic importance of rice has outlived both the imperial system and rice agriculture in contemporary Japan, where virtually no full-time farmers remain.

Many parallels across societies concerning state intervention in agriculture (see Chapter Five), especially staple food production, on the one hand, and the symbolic importance of staple food, especially as the symbol of the collective self, on the other hand, call for a careful consideration of the relationship between symbolic systems and political economy, neither of which is a natural historical process.

Purity has been the most important aesthetic value assigned to rice in Japan's agrarian cosmology, and this value was translated as the sublimity of the Japanese. Purity, however, is predicated upon impurity. The dominant Japanese assign the value of purity to themselves by assigning impurity to their internal and external others. The impurity of "foreign rice" has been a weapon against outsiders even until today. Impurity was assigned to those Japanese engaged in work that involves killing animals. Such scapegoating is a familiar technique whereby the dominant group purges itself. In the Hitlerite cult of anti-Semitism, the Germans "ritually cleansed themselves by loading the burden of their own iniquities upon" the Jews (Burke [1945] 1969: 406–7), and the major slogan of the *Futurisme* in Italy was "hygiène" (Marinetti 1909). Ethnic cleansing continues, as in the case of the former Yugoslavia.

For the purposes of this book, rice—as a symbol primarily with one meaning—shows an entirely different path by which a symbol creates communicative opacity. The symbol of rice, imbued with the aesthetic of purity, was transferred to the Japanese as a whole, when in fact the symbol conceals that it represented only the dominant Japanese—those in the upper sectors of agrarian Japan—and excluded the non-agrarian Japanese. Yet, most Japanese, including those who have been excluded in this representation, have not been aware of it. In post-industrial Japan when full-time rice farmers have virtually disappeared and the quantitative value of rice has been drastically reduced, the partial representation of the Japanese through the metaphor of "rice as self" remains not only viable but emerges strongly when the other presses the self of the Japanese, as happened during the 1993 rice importation incident. Rice symbolism is an example of the creation of communicative opacity, which hides its strikingly partial representation.

PART II

Collective Identities and Their Symbolic Expression

FIVE

The Collective Self and Cultural/Political Nationalisms

Cross-Cultural Perspectives

In each of the previous chapters I have examined a particular symbol over a long period to show how each created opacity in its delivery of meaning. This chapter continues to explore how symbols conceal and/or misrepresent the referent. The examples chosen in this chapter are the symbols of the *collective* self of Nazi Germany and imperial Japan primarily as expressed in each regime's propaganda. I use the singular, "identity," most of the time in this chapter, since the collective self is usually expressed as a singular attribute, although another attribute may be chosen as the self encounters another "other." While an individual always carries a bundle of identities based on ethnicity, nationality, race, gender, age, etc., anyone of which emerges as one encounters a specific other, my focus is on collective identity.

Granted that the term "identity" covers too many concepts and can thus lose its analytical utility (Brubaker and Cooper 2000) and that some believe the vertigoes of globalization diminish the utility of the concept, I nonetheless argue to the contrary that there is an urgent need for further studies of collective identity and for the development of fine-tuned interpretive tools, without treating collective identity as a hermetically sealed entity in the singular, unchanged throughout history. The heightened sense of Japanese and German collective identities took place at particular historical periods when they were threatened by the other. Global forces have not created a singular global village or global culture. Instead they have reinforced local identities. Precisely because of globalization, ethnicity and nationalism have become virulent forces (Tambiah 1996a). To abandon the study of collective identity altogether ignores the vigorous assertions of ethnic, religious, and national identities that we witness today all over the world. This happened well before the dissolution of the USSR, disproving Marx's belief presented in his *Manifesto* that nationalism is a reactionary bourgeois ideology and that "national differences and antagonisms between peoples are daily more and more vanishing" (Marx and Engels [1852] 1989: 26). Geopolitical forces have never been singular. When the wind of globalization blows hard, counterforce blows even harder, tightening national borders, be they the U.S. walls against the Mexicans, the security at every airport, or immigration policies in Europe, Japan, and the United States. As many have already pointed out, the golden arches of McDonald's have not produced a homogenized world culture. Instead, they have reinforced local/ethnic/national cultures, which have strengthened their own identity without reproducing it. Today, the European Community and its constituent nations wrestle, on the one hand, with "their" own identity vis-à-vis recent immigrants, and on the other hand, with the force of American cultural, economic, and political hegemony. Peter Geschiere (2009: 155–57) emphasizes the complex but strong sense of identity of Africans, especially Cameroonians, with autochthony (born from the soil) as the symbolic and emotive dimensions of their belonging, which he views as "the flip side of globalization."

This chapter explores the complexities of identity and its historical vicissitudes, inherent inconsistencies, internal contradictions, and, in particular, its misrepresentation, hidden underneath the seemingly apparent singularity of "we." Although the collectivity could be that of a religious or ethnic group, my examples are primarily of the collective self of the people belonging to a state, a political unit defined in terms of the presence of a government, territory, sovereignty, and a few other attributes (Young 2012: 35), or a nation, a nonpolitical unit consisting of people who are enclosed within state boundaries and believe they share a common culture and society, inhabiting an "imagined community," in which all the members "imagine" their connections to each other without face-to-face contact (Anderson [1983] 1991: 6; Young 2012: 41).[1] I follow popular parlance in which the technical distinction between a state and a nation is mostly ignored and the term "nation" is most frequently used, as in the case of the "United Nations." My use of the terms "nation," "state," and "nation-state" by no means ignores a critical point John Kelly and Martha Kaplan (2001: 3–4, 8–9, etc.) most forcefully argue, namely that these terms and accompanying concepts have not marched through a "homogeneous, empty time" (Benjamin [1950] 1968: 261) but have been construed in Western scholarship in relation to notions of race, colonization, and decolonization.

The crucial point about collective identity is that its genesis lies at the interface of the self and a specific other, who forces the formulation and/or reformulation of the collective self. Self-other encounters may be through trade or other flows of peoples, objects, and ideas. For example, Japanese collective identity was born in the discourse with the Chinese, whose advanced civilization forced the Japanese to define their previously inchoate identity. They chose rice, a foreign food, as their own (Chapter Four) and identified the aesthetic of cherry blossoms as theirs instead of the aesthetic of plum blossoms, which they had imported from China and had embraced (Chapter One). This took place well before Japan or China became a nation, let alone a state.

Each social group has many identities, one of which is selected depending on the specific "other" who appears in a given social or geopolitical context at a given time (Ohnuki-Tierney 2002a: 245–54). Crawford Young (2012: 291–333) explains Africans' triple helix of identity: Africans as opposed to non-Africans; territorial nationalism for each African nation; ethnicity within a nation. One of the helices becomes the collective self-identity of each social group and the individual in a given social context. Likewise, the Spanish monarchy traditionally rested on a "supranational community" consisting of "a combination of constitutional pluralism with unitary kingship" (Elliott 1985: 155). The legacy of this "fragmented Monarchy" (Elliott 1985: 159) continues even today. Basques, Catalans, and Galicians have dual identities—as a subgroup and as Spaniards. They are now "adding" another identity as members of the European Community after the 2005 European Constitutional Treaty (see Balfour and Quiroga 2007). Thus Basques are Basques as opposed to Catalans, Galicians, or dominant Spaniards, but they are Spaniards as opposed to other peoples in the European Community.

Symbolic Representations of Collective Identity

Identity must be defined in terms of particular qualities or features that express the oneness of a social group based on "assumed 'givens'" (Geertz 1973: 250–69; Tambiah 1996a: 22). Each instance of the collective self represents a presumed stable substance for its identity, unambiguous in its meaning and everlasting. The nature of symbolic representations of the collective identity of the self are discussed below, with special emphasis on how selectively a symbol represents the self and yet this fact is seldom recognized by the people who are supposedly represented. Thus this chapter follows "rice as self," offering a general discussion of this selectivity of symbolic representation.

Common symbols of collective identity are blood and soil: they have become legal attributes of identity in many countries and symbols of political nationalism. These cases allow us to see how real—chiseled in stone, as it were—they seem to the people, although they do not have solid anchors to historical or ethnographic reality. The most common symbols of collective identity with legal consequence in reference to citizenship are *jus soli* (Latin for "right of soil")—place of birth—and/versus *jus sanguinis* (right of blood)—"blood" from one's parents. Soil as a symbol of collective identity represents autochthony (born from the soil), one of the features chosen for self-identity, legal or informal, by many peoples. In the first chapter of his *Perils of Belonging*, Geschiere (2009) presents an analytical overview of various notions of autochthony from classical Athens to Africa and Europe in the contemporary globalizing era in which the feeling of "belonging" has been intensified.

Both symbolic attributes of identity—blood and soil—became the legal basis of French citizenship at different times in the country's history, as it underwent change necessitated by practical pressure, such as demographic needs. Originally, the *droit du sang* (the right of blood) of the ancien régime was replaced by *droit du sol* (the right of the soil) by the Civil Code introduced by Napoleon in 1804. This was therefore an ideological move, breaking away from the power of the aristocracy during the ancien régime. However, when the demand for workers arose, first in the 1850s during the Industrial Revolution and then after World War I, during which 1.5 million men died and some 2 million were handicapped, the law had to be changed to accommodate the economic situation. Between 1927 and 1938, there were an average of 38,000 naturalizations per year in France, rising to a high of 81,000 in 1938 alone. The only attempt to reverse the course was during the Vichy government, which deemed the 1927 law too lenient and abolished it in 1945, denying French citizenship to Jews, following the example of the 1935 Nuremberg Laws in Germany (Pecheur 2002/2003). The legality of belonging was forced to adapt to the hard reality of demographic, economic, and political contexts. While the right of blood frees individuals from spatial constraints in that French blood can reside outside of the national boundaries of France, it excludes individuals within the national boundaries who lack "proper blood." Also the transmission of identity as blood or soil causes problems when the parents do not belong to the same soil or possess the same blood. And, each religious and national community usually has its own rules governing descent groups, which today have come under the global pressure for gender equality, as with the case of Japan, which was forced to change its patrilineally transmitted *droit du sang* so that mothers also can pass their citizenship to their children.

The case of French citizenship illustrates the dynamics of the battle, as it were, between very basic ideological stances and historical and geopolitical realities. If "blood" as the symbol of collective identity presents disjunctions from reality, "from the soil" does as well. It implies that the people have lived on "our soil" from time immemorial. But, more often than not, it is the positive actions of people that create "our soil." "Rice paddies as Japan" was constructed by Emperor Tenmu and his imperial court to buttress a political economy based on wet-rice agriculture. It in fact reveals that the Japanese did not deem the original soil as "our soil" (Chapter Four). Another aggressive creation of "our soil" was when the Japanese military government planted cherry trees in its colonies—an act of transforming *their* soil into *ours* (Chapter One). Even more frequently, "our soil" is acquired through what Young (2012) calls "territorial nationalism," which endlessly changes the map due to various conflicts, including wars. This happened in Africa, Europe, the Americas, and elsewhere.

"Nature" is a dominant metaphor of primordiality—the pure state of the collective self in the pristine past, uncontaminated by urbanization and foreign influences. It is a symbol of *both* the spatial and temporal identity of the self of the people. Nature can be represented by mountains, prairies, lakes, and so on, but cultivated land, that is, farmland, is often thought of as "our nature." The quest for nature leads to the longing for nature-cum-the rural. In a striking cross-cultural parallel, in many societies urbanization created a new need to construct "the rural" (Berque 1990), be it Jean-François Millet's haystacks or rice paddies in urbanizing Japan during the Edo period as depicted in woodblock prints of the time. Modernization propelled people to seek their primordial roots—the pure state of self—in the rural and in agriculture, even when agriculture involves the most thorough removal of nature by felling trees and replacing them with domesticated plants.

The notion of "our soil" leads to its products—plant foods grown from it or animals that graze upon it—becoming "our food." By definition, "our food" is shared by all the members of the "imagined community." Thus, even if they are not eating together as in commensality, members of a society are united by "our food" at the gut level. *Our* food is thus a marker of the self in opposition to *their* food. For this purpose, staple food often plays a powerful role (see Chapter Four).

Consumers today look for pure natural food, uncontaminated by chemicals and pathogens. Consider that only *plant foods* become *natural foods* that presumably are healthy for the body. When it comes to fish, dairy products, and meat, consumers seek the locality of production in pristine nature—clear waters for fish, green pastures where cows graze only on the grass on "our soil," and eggs from cage-free vegetarian hens.

The symbolic importance of the rural, with its agriculture and pastoralism, for post-agricultural and postindustrial countries is in part the source of agricultural protectionism and farm subsidies by the government or by international organizations, such as the former European Economic Community (EEC) and the subsequent European Union. The creation and development of the European Community was hampered by an inability to agree on a common agricultural policy because differentially subsidized food exports affected the common monetary system. The Uruguay Round of GATT (General Agreement on Tariffs and Trade) negotiations had a most difficult time because of disagreements on agricultural policy (Ohnuki-Tierney 1993a: 125–26; 1993b).

CULTURAL/POLITICAL NATIONALISMS AND PATRIOTISM

While the identity of the collective self, as opposed to the other, is important for the reaffirmation of who "we" are, it can easily develop into cultural and then political nationalism. An enduring question in the voluminous scholarship on nationalism has been how to define nationalism and whether there is more than one type (see Gellner 1983: 88–109). One of the most important debates in this regard centers on the question of the relationship between the development of nationalism and modernity/modernization, which is important for the theme of this chapter, since modernization ushered in the age of mass media and propaganda.

There are roughly two camps—those who dislodge the emergence of nationalism from unilinear history,[2] and those who see a linear progression in human history with modernity/modernization occupying the "most advanced" stage and nationalism as part and parcel of modernity. Benedict Anderson ([1983] 1991: 36) considers nationalism a historical product of the West and believes it arises only after three shackles of the past have been broken: 1) script language as the path to the truth; 2) monarchy; and 3) the indistinguishability of cosmology and history. The breaking of these shackles is facilitated by print capitalism, the development of vernacular language, and changing conceptions of time, according to Anderson. Ernest Gellner, an outspoken critic of constructionists like Anderson, nonetheless follows a linear and progressive time scale. He believes that a nation develops through the establishment of equality, shifting away from a hierarchically based society. For Gellner, "nationalism is . . . the consequence of a new form of social organization, based on deep, internalized, education-dependent high cultures, each protected by its own state" (Gellner 1983: 48; for a critique of Gellner, see Hall, ed., 1998).

Others critique this view, as I do, which springs from a unilinear social evolutionary vision based on historical developments in Western Europe, where Enlightenment philosophy and historical "progress" gave birth to modernity after shedding the burden of medieval ontology.[3] The Japanese case detailed below will show a path to modernization that contradicts the unilinear vision on almost every point. Although many scholars treat "modernity" and "modernization" as synonymous, I use "modernity" to refer to basic ontological assumptions, as discussed in the Introduction, in contrast to "modernization," which refers to socioeconomic, sociopolitical, and technological developments.

I differentiate between cultural nationalism and political nationalism. The former is voluntary on the part of individual members of the nation who feel affection, love, and/or attachment to their nation, for example, the Russians' deep feeling of love for the Russian motherland with its birch trees or the Germans' love of their fatherland with its oak trees. Patriotism, on the other hand, involves an act of commitment—service and/or sacrifice of one's life—based on love for one's country.

Political nationalism, orchestrated by the state, strives to disseminate "ideology," that is, "unified schemes or configurations developed to underwrite or manifest power" (Wolf 1999: 4). Although we usually assume that propaganda succeeds in disseminating the state's message to the people, Dominic Boyer (2005: 38), using tropes as examples, points out how "social actors stake their semiotic-epistemic activity in dialogue with others, who may variously construe the intentions and significance of the tropes in question." His meticulous study of the records of the German Democratic Republic shows how functionaries "never successfully rid it of polysemy" and were "sensitized to the limits of their intellectual agency" (Boyer 2005: 147). Nonetheless, an examination of symbols of state ideology tells us a great deal about the presentation and representation of the self of the state.

SYMBOLS OF POLITICAL NATIONALISM: GERMANY AND JAPAN

The period I have chosen in order to highlight the symbolic expressions of political nationalisms in propaganda in Germany and Japan, with some reference to the USSR and fascist Italy, is between the end of World War I and the end of World War II, when there was a heightened need for collective self-representation by the states, deploying an array of dominant symbols. This was a turbulent period during which each state struggled with the world wars and the vertigoes of modernization. Modernization ushered in basic technological, economic, social, and political changes, and advances in military technology brought about basic changes in warfare—World War I with trench warfare to World War II, fought primarily in the air. Technological developments facilitated the unification of national subjects in different regions within the state. People and goods were able to move with hitherto unprecedented speed. Modernization was vital in building up the country, militarily and otherwise. Therefore, European dictators foregrounded the symbols of modernization in order to imprint in the minds of the people that modernization was *their* gift to the people. In Japan the scheme did not work, since modernization was the hallmark of the "other," which Japan was forced to adopt, quickly, in fact. For authoritarian states, mobilization of the masses, or, "nationalization of the masses," to use George Mosse's (1975) phrase, was of vital importance, and propaganda was the major medium. The Soviet Union is known to have provided the protocol for political propaganda. In Germany the process was intensely orchestrated by the state, with Joseph Goebbels as the head of the Ministry of Popular Enlightenment and Propaganda, established on March 13, 1933 (Evans 2005: 121). Goebbels was mainly in charge of inculcating in the people his vision of "cultural revolution." In Japan, where there was no ministry of propaganda, the people were more active participants in creating propaganda (Kushner 2006: 3).

The purpose of state propaganda is to convert political nationalism into patriotism of the subjects. I use the term "patriotism" to refer to the individual's sense of loyalty and dedication to a nation, or a state, a political unit. It is a "political belonging," actively undertaken by the individual.[4]

The analytical distinction between nationalism and patriotism is important not simply for distinguishing between political ideology from above and its embrace on the ground, but also for identifying how political nationalism is often disguised by the state as patriotism, voluntary on the part of the individual, to make it more palatable to the people, as captured in Horace's classic phrase, *Dulce et decorum est pro patria mori* (Sweet and proper it is to die for your country), as discussed in the Introduction. The state's purpose in using propaganda is to fortify the patriotism of its soldiers so that they will not fear death but believe that dying for the nation is the utmost honor.[5]

The mass media had already made inroads into Germany, Japan, and other modern nations. Mass printing began in the mid-nineteenth century. Radio, which involved a number of people before "radio" in its current form emerged, was commercialized in Pittsburgh in 1920. These modern states selectively used a wide range of media for propaganda, including radios, loudspeakers for speeches, newspapers, magazines, photographs, films, posters, stamps, currency, coins, novels, poems, paintings, and sculptures, as well as monuments, buildings, and statues. Different states emphasized different media, and the literacy rate mattered. Unlike in the USSR, Italy, and China, in Germany and Japan citizens were highly literate, enabling their states to use print media extensively and utilize their highly developed school systems for ideological inculcation. In contrast to Japan, where public spaces were limited, in the USSR, Italy, and Germany the presence of public space facilitated pageantry, massive rallies, marches, and parades in the large public squares and plazas where the leaders delivered their speeches. Statues of authoritarian leaders were erected, although Hitler did not have bronze statues made of himself, in contrast to the Soviet leaders, who did.

Auditory propaganda, especially speeches and music, was equally important in many of these states. Radio transmitted state messages. In Germany, by the middle of 1939, over 70 percent of households owned a wireless radio—*Volksempfänger* (people's receivers). Altogether over seven million of them were manufactured (Evans 2005: 133–35). Radio reached Japan in 1925, with three radio stations established in that year. During World War II, national broadcasts always began with the proclamation that they were from the Joint Chiefs of Staff (*Daihon'ei*).[6] Even toward the end of the war, these broadcasts still reported a rosy picture, although the country was in fact rapidly tumbling toward defeat. In contrast to Germany, where it was Hitler himself whose speeches dominated German radio, not a single speech by the emperor was broadcasted until the declaration of the unconditional surrender of Japan on August 15, 1945 (Japan time).

Nazi Germany made extensive use of music by Richard Wagner and Johann Sebastian Bach, but not that by Felix Mendelssohn, who was of Jewish descent.[7] Popular songs, folk songs, children's songs, and school songs were a powerful means of propaganda. The overwhelming importance assigned to music as a propaganda medium by the Nazis derived from the cultural value of music in Germany, past and present, although "Nazi music" as such was never created (Potter 2006). At the beginning of the Meiji period, when Western music was introduced to Japan, the Japanese almost abruptly abandoned their traditional melodic pattern and switched to the Western pattern, and the government adopted the American system of music education. Beginning in 1880, music became a powerful means of propaganda for the war effort, with lyrics full of adulation for the emperor in a generic sense, not specified by name, and the glorification of the war (Ohnuki-Tierney 2002a: 130–42).

Although Japan had had a long history of comics for both adults and children, remarkably, at least from a contemporary vantage point, the attack on Pearl Harbor occasioned the first anime (see below for details). During World War II, the United States also used animation in propaganda; for example, the Walt Disney character Popeye the Sailor was transformed into a white-suited U.S. Navy officer in the film *The Mighty Navy*, produced in 1941. Dr. Seuss too "went to war," with the portrayal of the Japanese with round eyeglasses and slit eyes, as Minear ([1999] 2001) pointed out.

Yet markers of modernization—planes, cars, trains, tractors, etc.—do not represent the unique achievements of a particular people who therefore must present themselves as "unique," calling upon various symbols of "tradition." Nazi Germany and wartime Japan each constructed its own self-portrait, as revealed in propaganda, striving for a delicate balance between reaffirming tradition and emphasizing modernization. Modernization as a part of self-representation posed a particular problem for Japan, since it was introduced from the West almost in toto, when Japan was struggling to cope with or even fight off the Western powers. Thus while the European states could comfortably juxtapose their modernization and their cultural identity, Japan had to Japanize its modernization by, for example, naming battleships after terms for ancient Japan and relying more heavily on Japan's tradition in the presentation of the collective self. Below I discuss the propaganda of Nazi Germany and Japan with a special emphasis on their primordial and modern selves.

NAZI GERMANY: SIMULTANEOUS REPRESENTATION
OF THE PRIMORDIAL AND THE MODERN SELVES

Dubbed "the best propaganda film of all times" (Strötgen 2008: 1, 14), the 1934 film *Triumph of the Will* is a spectacular example of political propaganda, even though Leni Riefenstahl, the filmmaker, denied it. The film, which glorified the 1934 Nazi Party rally in Nuremberg, was commissioned by the Führer and heavily edited by Riefenstahl, with the assistance of Joseph Goebbels, the propaganda minister.

Its central theme is sacrifice for Hitler-cum-Germany, whose collective identity is represented by the juxtaposition of symbols of the modern and the primordial. These themes were replicated, with amazing systematicity, in other propaganda media, such as stamps and posters. The weeklong Nazi Party Congress rally was held at the Zeppelin field, designed by Albert Speer, in Nuremburg. The deployment area, the so-called Luitpoldarena, was situated so that the Ehrenhalle—a memorial for the nearly ten thousand soldiers from Nuremberg who perished in World War I—lay at its far end.

The film is filled with powerful visual and auditory symbolic representations of the central themes. The "Horst Wessel," the anthem of the National Socialist Party, is played as Hitler descends from the sky to earth in a plane—the most spectacular achievement of modern technology. According to Stefan Strötgen, the anthem is the musical equivalent of the swastika, an auditory sign for the Führer. Hitler's voice fills two-thirds of the soundtrack, occupying the "place of a commentator" (Strötgen 2008: 11–13).

In the opening scene, Hitler's plane breaks through clouds, with steeples in the background. After he lands, his motorcade proceeds to the city center through cheering crowds. In Europe, as elsewhere, modernization was characterized by mobility, facilitated by airplanes, automobiles, and trains. Hitler was fascinated by planes and welcomed Charles Lindberg by having Hermann Goering award him the Service Cross of the German Eagle. He was proud of having flown thirty thousand miles himself. He considered trench warfare degenerate and envisioned modern war to be fought with tanks and planes (Eksteins 1989: 321–22).

Automobiles were supposed to signify individual mobility. Hitler promised to deliver the *Volkswagen* (the people's car) in order for the people to understand that the Nazi regime brought personal freedom to the *Volk*. The caption on a 1936 poster links Hitler to the automobile and stresses its economic benefits:

> The Führer promised to motorize Germany. In 1932, 104,000 motor vehicles were manufactured, 33,000 people were employed, and goods with a total value of 295,000,000 marks were produced. In 1935, 353,000 vehicles were manufactured. Over 100,000 people were employed, and the value of goods produced was 1,150,000,000 marks. The Führer gave 250,000 people's comrades [*sic*] jobs in the auto industry and its suppliers. German people: Thank the Führer on 29 March! Give him your vote! (Bytwerk 2007a: no. 42).

Autobahns, advertised on a poster (Bytwerk 2007a: no. 41) and a stamp (Welch 2007: Scott B93), facilitated mobility, although their primary purpose was to move tanks and other military equipment quickly and efficiently.

Spatial compression and national unity were greatly facilitated by the *Volksempfänger* radios (Bytwerk 2004: 60; Bytwerk 2007a; Koshar 1998). A poster with a picture of a radio is captioned: "All Germany hears the Führer on the People's Receiver" (Bytwerk 2007a: no. 38). Despite its name, which tried to create the illusion that people had their own radios and listened to Hitler's speeches voluntarily, the people's receiver was designed to disseminate state propaganda through instant transmission of sound bites.

The city of Nuremburg, the cultural center of the German Renaissance, had become a center of industry, science, and technology. During World War II it was a major site for the production of airplanes, submarines, and tank engines. In 1935, the Reichstag was convened at Nuremburg to pass the anti-Semitic laws that deprived German Jews of civic rights and prohibited marriage between Jews and "Aryans." Indeed, the city epitomized Nazism. The military might of modern Germany was dramatized in posters and stamps depicting fighter planes, tanks, and other war machinery. The Nuremburg rally itself was commemorated on stamps issued in 1935 (Welch 2007: Scott 465, 466).

Side by side with modernized Germany, the primordial German identity was represented through symbols of the Holy Roman Empire and images of Germany as an agricultural state. In the film *Triumph of the Will*, the Holy Roman Empire is established as ancestral to Nazi Germany through the ubiquitous presence of the Roman eagle along with the swastika, itself a symbol suggesting the mythical primordiality of the "Aryan race" (Quinn 1994). The Nuremburg stadium was designed after the Roman model that symbolized imperial power (Smith 1989: 156). Every flagstaff was wreathed with green oak leaves, symbolizing victory. Oak is a sacred tree representing might and longevity (Chevalier and Gheerbrant [1969] 1996: 709) and is the national tree of Germany. The Germans saw the battle between Roma and Germania during the reign of Napoleon as the city versus the forest and the olive versus the oak (Schama 1996: 104–5, 195–96). Although the film does not emphasize a Wagnerian theme, Wagner's *Ring* cycle, tracing the origin of the German people through German and Scandinavian myths, was enshrined on a set of nine stamps, issued in 1933, portraying scenes from the opera (Welch 2007: Scott B49–B57).

The extreme importance the National Socialists placed on their Roman ancestry is told in their quest for Cornelius Tacitus's *Germania*, written in 98 CE, "About the Origin and Mores of the Germanic People"—a 2,000-year-old "proof" of the pristine past of Germanness. The text was taught in schools in Germany and was the cherished source enthusiastically embraced by many National Socialists, high and low. Remarkably, in 1943, as Allied troops began the invasion of southern Italy, Heinrich Himmler, the head of the SS, and his agents launched a desperate search for the original text of *Germania* (Krebs 2011). Facing defeat, they felt it was of paramount importance to locate proof of their primordial identity in *Germania*, a "Roman's imaginative reflection on human values and a political statement" (Krebs 2011: 25).

Triumph of the Will opens with the representation of Germany as a Christian nation and Hitler as a semi-divine ruler. Gothic churches fill the screen, creating the effect of religious verticality, with God and heaven as the ultimate space whence the Führer as God/father descends, just as the Roman eagle is seen soaring toward heaven and columns of smoke and torch flames billow upward. Smoke, rising from earth to heaven, and fire, with its purifying power, are important symbols in many religions. During the night rally, highlighted against the darkness are Hitler and his right-hand men, plus the Roman eagle and the swastika, all in front of the podium qua shrine. The rest of the scene recedes in darkness while the podium where Hitler, the demigod, stands is dramatically lighted and spectacular fireworks illuminate the night sky. Hitler and Hess wear only the Maltese Cross, representing Christian caregiving and military duties simultaneously; they wear none of the badges and insignias that adorn the uniforms of high officers. These two alone are religious figures. Unlike the officers, they carry their cap in hand rather than wearing it.

At this time in Germany, the economic base of agriculture was diminishing in importance, taken over by industry, while, or perhaps because of this, its psychological importance for farmers as well as urbanites was growing stronger than when Germany was in fact agrarian. Especially conspicuous at Nuremburg is the iconographic representation of wheat stalks with ripe grains as part of the design on top of the Roman eagle, and two stalks surrounding the swastika in a half circle. During the rally, farmers paraded with shovels and picks. In 1933, eight months after Hitler seized power, a poster featuring agricultural equipment decorated with a swastika was issued for an agricultural fair. The farmers presented their harvest to Hitler, reenacting the traditional harvest ritual when offerings were made to God. Many propaganda photos show Hitler's visits to agrarian regions, at the Thanksgiving festival at Bückeburg in 1934, for example (Goering et al. [1936] 1973: 18). The emphasis on agriculture lasted through his entire regime: a 1941 Nazi Party poster shows a woman plowing a field while her husband is fighting at the front (Bytwerk 2007b: no. 8).

Other types of workers were represented in propaganda as well. Nazi ideology emphasized equality between blue- and white-collar workers, as shown in a 1933 poster on the German Labor Front (DAF) (Bytwerk 2007a: no. 12) and displayed on a set of nine stamps picturing different occupations (Welch 2007: Scott B59–B67). The images include both people who hold modern industrial jobs and those with traditional artisan and manual skills.

In the framework of "ein Volk, ein Reich, ein Führer," Nazi leaders strove to nationalize diversity within the so-called Aryan sector of the population. The slogan "United we stand" (first used as a political message in 1768 in an American revolutionary song, "The Liberty Song," by John Dickinson) recurs throughout the film. The rally is flooded with flags and banners, which Albert Speer called a "sea" or "storm" of flags. Written on each banner is "Deutschland" followed by the name of the region, e.g., Bavaria, Danube, and Rhine. Men and women in folk costumes with musical instruments are shown prominently, each group wearing the traditional headgear and attire from a specific region, representing its distinctive culture even though it was no longer practiced.

The same was done on stamps. Each stamp in a set of twelve (Welch 2007: Scott B69–B78) portrays regional "traditions." The pristine nature of Germany is emphasized by pastoral and Alpine scenes (Welch 2007: Scott B197), as well as photos of medieval architecture from various parts of the country (Welch 2007: Scott B121, B122, B138, B139, B160–B162, B177–B179,

B180, B194–196). Here, rich cultural diversity is rendered compatible with modern national unity.

According to Nazi ideology, "New Germany" could only be built by able men and women. In order to strengthen soldiers' bodies, sports were encouraged (Welch 2007: Scott B79–B81, B82, B86). In the film's extensive footage of a youth camp outside Nuremberg, young men are shown washing their bodies and shaving their faces, preserving the purity of the self, and engaging in wrestling and other activities to cultivate their physical strength and competitive spirit. At the youth rally in the film, Hitler emphasizes: "You must learn sacrifice." Goebbels, referring to fallen soldiers, preaches: "You are not dead. You live in Germany." A number of stamps commemorated the infamous Berlin Olympics of 1936 (Welch 2007: Scott B79–B81, B82, B86), when the able bodies of the Aryan race were displayed to the world. The Foucauldian "docile body" (Foucault [1975] 1995: 135–69)—the body to be molded into the soldier's body—was in the making, as it was in other twentieth-century authoritarian states, including Japan. Women too were ordered to build their bodies so as to bear as many future soldiers as possible and raise large Aryan families (Welch 2007: Scott B155); many stamps show *Mutter und Kinder*, mother and children (Welch 2007: Scott B246, B253–B256).

Hitler's quest for the purity of the race led him to ban tobacco smoking. In the 1930s German medical scientists established a link between lung cancer and smoking. Hitler, like Mussolini and Franco but unlike Tōjō, Stalin, Churchill, and Roosevelt, did not smoke. The German government launched an aggressive campaign, using posters depicting smoking as the vice of degenerate Africans and Gypsies and showing its economic cost as equivalent to two million Volkswagens every year. A poster of Hitler is captioned: "Our Führer Adolf Hitler drinks no alcohol and does not smoke. . . . His performance at work is incredible" (Proctor 1999: 173–247, images on 174, 200, 220, 224).

The German collective self as constructed in film, stamps, posters, and other propaganda materials is a balanced juxtaposition of the modern and the traditional. As the aesthetic value of the self, purity is of paramount importance, as expressed through Alpine mountains, bodily cleanliness, and above all the Führer, a nonsmoking, teetotaling vegetarian.

Triumph of the Will and other propaganda depict Germans as one happy family, with Hitler as their father. Some of these images clearly contradict historical facts. For example, a stamp commemorating the 1935 "reunion" of the Saar (Welch 2007: Scott 444, A71), an industrial center rich in coal resources, shows a little girl returning to her mother (Welch 2007: Scott 451, A74), suggesting that the Saar is returning to the arms of Mother Germany. This benign familial image belies the military conquest of the region. Ultimately, every "real" German is supposed to be united as *ein Volk*, under *ein Reich*, with *ein Führer*. For this reason the title of the film, *Triumph des Willens*, has "will" in the singular.

There are some significant contrasts between Germany and two other authoritarian regimes of the same period. The Soviet economy was more agrarian and less technologically advanced than the German economy, and the literacy rate was lower than in Germany. From the time of the revolution on, the identity of the Soviet Union was based on the coexistence of the industrial proletariat and agricultural workers. The coat of arms (technically, an emblem) of the USSR, designed in 1923, shows a hammer, symbolizing industrial workers; a sickle and two wreaths of wheat, representing agricultural workers; and the Red Star over a globe, symbolizing the world united by the proletariat. This configuration also appears on a poster of 1923–1924 entitled *Friendship of Peoples*, in which men of visibly different ethnic groups are hoisting a banner with a hammer and a sickle with a bundle of wheat stalks bearing ripe ears (Groys and Hollein, eds., 2003: 213).

It is commonly held that the USSR was the first state to make use of modern propaganda machinery, with colorful posters and dramatic designs. Well known is "agitprop" (short for "agitation," meaning urging, and "propaganda," which then had no negative connotations), which used visuals as well as texts to inculcate the masses with Communist ideology. After the Bolshevik revolution, agitprop teams crisscrossed the country on trains carrying books, pamphlets, newspapers, posters, films, a projector, and a printing press, along with trained "agitators." Artists and actors performed simple plays and broadcast propaganda. Posters were reproduced as needed and thrown out the windows as the train passed through villages (Ebon 1987: 21; Smith 1989: 124; Kenez 1985).

Lenin was relatively unknown when he came to power. His image began to appear on posters in the early 1920s, such as the 1920 poster, *Comrade Lenin Cleanses the Earth of Scum* (Bonnell 1997: 139–58 and figure 4.1). Lenin's reluctance to court public adulation deterred the use of his portrait in propaganda during his lifetime, but his image was extensively deployed after his death. The mass production of Lenin's image created a veritable mania, "Leniniana" (Bonnell 1997: 153). Lenin was projected through the double image of the Soviet, featuring agricultural and industrial production side by side (Bonnell 1997: figures 4.4, 4.6, 4.7, 4.8, 4.9, 4.11).

After Stalin came to power, the juxtaposition of symbols of agriculture with those of modernization, especially planes, tanks, and ships, continued. Technology gradually made inroads into agriculture, as depicted, for example, in images of tractors on collective farms. Stalin developed the cult of the leader most aggressively, first around the figure of Lenin and then around himself. In almost every piece of propaganda, his image appeared alongside symbols of "progress"—planes first, but also tanks, tractors on collective farms, and occasionally a warship[8]—with the message that it was he who modernized the USSR.

While the Nazis traced their ancestry to the Holy Roman Empire, Mussolini's Italy sought its ancestry in the Roman Empire. Its emblem of fasces, a bundle of rods from which an axe protrudes, signified the authority of Roman officials. Mussolini upheld the idea of *romanità*, with the Roman ideal of the citizen-soldier-farmer, even more emphatically than the Nazis did their version of their origins in the Holy Roman Empire. Through the well-known "Battle of Wheat," Mussolini placed wheat at the center of the state's symbolic and economic structure. Despite opposition from farmers who wished to cultivate more lucrative cash crops, Il Duce pushed through his plan and managed to increase wheat production. Simonetta Falasca-Zamponi (1997: 155) states: "Although different reasons and motivations intersected in the campaign, through the Battle of Wheat Mussolini formulated and communicated his ultimate vision of fascist Italy." In July 1934, Mussolini appeared as a thresher in a poster. Wheat came to symbolize the rural, as shown, for example, in a poster for the VIII National Competition for the Victory of Wheat with a man working in a field of ripe wheat while two children play nearby (Falasca-Zamponi 1997: 154, 157).

IMPERIAL JAPAN

Japan's modernization path presents striking departures from the unilinear vision of a historical march toward modernization. Preceded by centuries of wars among feudal lords and virtual closure of the country to the outside world, Japan's modern period began in part under global pressure, epitomized by the visits of the American Commodore Perry in 1853 and 1854 to force Japan to open to the world market. There was no equivalent of the Enlightenment. With the reopening of the country in 1868, Japan entered a period of modernization during which it strove to catch up in science and technology under the motto "civilization and enlightenment" (*bunmei kaika*). Yet these historical developments ran counter to Anderson's vision of modernization. Instead of shedding the monarchy, Japan's "modernity" created an absolute monarchy in its constitution, when the emperor had been a politically impotent shadow under the shogunate ever since the twelfth century.[9] In the 1889 Constitution of Imperial Japan, the emperor was defined as the "imperial soul"—an apolitical identity—and at the same time as commander-in-chief (Ohnuki-Tierney 2002a: 61–101). Instead of entering the period of history, as in Anderson's scheme, Japan entered the period of myth—a period that its imperial system had begun 2,600 years earlier. Thus it replaced history with myth. A host of other beliefs and rituals were created to transform this myth into official History.

When the Japanese were jolted into a nascent political nationalism against the Western colonial powers, they saw an urgent necessity to strengthen their boundaries militarily and cultivate political nationalism in the minds of the people. But like many other Asians, they succumbed to Western *cultural* hegemony. The double-edged sword of threat and adoration of Western civilization played a crucial role in the struggle to establish Japan's modern identity. The Japanese had hardly shed their topknots before they faced their first Western enemy, Russia, at a time when Japan was politically and even geographically unknown to most of the rest of the world. The Japanese felt an urgent need to be "somebody in the world," which is "at the heart of the great cry for recognition on the part of both individuals and groups" (Berlin [1958] 1969: 157). They believed they had achieved this goal by defeating Russia, having been heavily financed by other countries and non-Japanese individuals, such as Jacob Schiff in New York. Almost immediately, the nation was hurled into the geopolitics that culminated in World War I. Amid this turbulence, many Japanese, including liberals, experienced a heightened sense of their own identity as Japanese. For them, liberalism, including cosmopolitanism, and patriotism were not odd bedfellows. Even though many refused to participate in imperial nationalism by defying the state and the military, they were patriotic, that is, they felt a sense of allegiance and even loyalty to their country and were ready to defend it from external attack. Early Meiji liberals who were involved in the Freedom and People's Rights movement (1874–1890), which opposed the Meiji oligarchy, embraced much of Western liberalism, and yet they were ardent patriots who advocated the virtue of the Japanese soul (*Yamato damashii*) and sacrifice for the country.

Below I focus on the self-representations of the Japanese in the propaganda more immediately linked to Japan's twentieth-century wars. Three distinct features of Japanese propaganda are important to identify. First, unlike Nazi Germany, Japan had no single organ for propaganda and no ministry of propaganda; there was no counterpart of Goebbels (Kushner 2006). Second, the Japanese had been inculcated to embrace nationalism and patriotism ever since the opening of the country in 1868. They became active participants in the creation of propaganda, and even originators of propaganda. Barak Kushner (2006: 20–24) points out that Japanese propaganda involved far more participation by the people than did German propaganda. Third, as in Germany and elsewhere, military development was closely tied to business profits, not only in industry but also, for example, in department stores, which sold kimonos and other items with propagandistic designs, such as planes, warships, the rising sun flag, and Mount Fuji, as well as battle scenes, created by different techniques, such as cut-paper stencil dyeing (Atkins 2005: 51–66, 155–203, 259–362; Mitsukoshi 2005: 141–62). Needless to say, kimonos and other objects could not bear any images related to the emperor. Although only a limited number of these items were made, and thus they were not a major medium for war propaganda (Kashiwagi 2005), they illustrate the extent to which businesses were active participants in the war effort.

Japanese leaders were acutely aware of the importance of propaganda and devoted enormous energy to it. In 1921, when the *Yomiuri* newspaper held an exhibition of posters made in Germany after World War I, their intensity and power shocked Japanese designers. The Soviet avant-garde and the magazine *USSR* also made a strong impression (Nanba 1998: 41–42). The realization of the need to build propaganda machinery led to the creation in November 1940 of the Association for Research on Mass Media (Hōdō Gijutsu Kenkyūkai) to educate designers and copywriters on how to produce war propaganda. The association's clients were the Bureau of Information (Jōhōkyoku) of the cabinet and Taisei Yokusankai (Nanba 1998: 7) (see Chapter One).

During its first five years, the Association for Research on Mass Media created about 150 items of propaganda: 60 percent were posters and "wall newspapers" (*kabe shinbun*, a medium adopted from Germany and Italy), 23 percent were traveling exhibits, and 15 percent were pamphlets and graphs. Thematically, 36 percent dealt directly with the war, 35 percent focused on the need for increasing economic productivity, 18 percent treated morality, and 11 percent were devoted to recruitment for the air force. The *kumi-posutā*, a set of three or more posters that together carry a complete message, was chosen as the best format. Far less elaborate in construction than Soviet agitprop, Japan's mobile exhibitions (*idōten*) had some 25 drawings mounted on a bicycle-drawn cart, taken all over Japan, and exhibited on the streets and in factories (Nanba 1998: 139–53; Orbaugh 2007: 214, 149–54).

As Japan's fortunes in the war worsened, mobile exhibits became a major means of disseminating visual propaganda, other methods having become impossible or too costly (Nanba 1998: 139–53). The mobile exhibitions were slightly more elaborate versions of the traditional *kamishibai*, "paper theater"—street theater for children made of wood and carried on the back of a bicycle—that had been familiar to people since the end of the Edo period (Kata 1994). Sharalyn Orbaugh (2007) examines a large number of media for war propaganda and pays special attention to the *kamishibai* (2007: 214, 233–34, 249–54, 264–71). Parking on a street corner, the operator/narrator would sell sweets before the show and then tell stories accompanied by painted cardboard illustrations. Tracing its development, Orbaugh (2005) discusses the government's deployment of *kamishibai* in the 1930s and 1940s and shows how the state transformed it into *kyōiku kamishibai* (education *kamishibai*) in an attempt to inculcate children with the virtue of sacrifice for Japan—teaching them that parents, especially mothers, were willing, or even eager, to see their sons give their lives for the country. Education *kamishibai* were widely distributed to schools, neighborhood associations, and factories and staged by teachers, parents, and neighborhood leaders. As Orbaugh cautions, it is hard to assess the precise impact on children, but the deployment of a familiar, seemingly innocent venue was certainly a clever technique for disseminating propaganda.

In addition to deploying state radio, the Japanese government relied heavily on printed materials, such as newspapers, popular magazines, and school textbooks (Sonobe [1962] 1980: 169–75). The government began to control the media in 1932, in response to growing criticism of Japanese imperialism in the Chinese press. Suzuki Kurazō, whose autocratic right-wing policy earned him the nickname "Little Himmler," later took over the Bureau of Information and imposed extremely tight control of the media (Satō 2004: 293–376). The bureau attempted to eradicate the "languages of the enemies," i.e., English, sometimes referred to as "horizontal writing" (*yokomoji*), since Japanese used to be written vertically. Words that had been romanized or transformed into Japanized English were turned into Japanese terms. During World War II, the government exercised strict censorship and purged intellectuals and artists who did not participate in its ideological campaign (Rubin 1984).

In 1940 sixty manga (comics) artists formed a new association (Shin Nihon Mangaka Kyōkai, or New Japanese Manga Association). In order to use manga for military purposes, the army and navy established research institutes (the Hōdō Manga Kenkyūjo for the army and the Daitōa Manga Kenkyūjo for the navy) (Nanba 1998: 135–39). It was quite clever that comics, which had been a favorite medium for satire and covert criticism of authority in Japan, were being deployed for military purposes. *Private Norakuro* (*Norakuro Jōtōhei*), a comic series, became explosively popular among young adults and children. *Norakuro* means a mongrel stray dog with black spots on white fur. He enters the army as a private and despite making horrendous mistakes, he moves up in the ranks. Children loved the antihero represented by this dog. The series began in a magazine, *Shōnen Kurabu* (Boys' Club), in January 1931. When the military caught on to its antiestablishment undertones, the government denounced it for making fun of the military, and in October 1941 prohibited its publication (Takeuchi 1994).

The 1943 production *The Spider and the Tulip* (*Kumo to Chūrippu*) by Masaoka Kenzō, a pioneer of animation in prewar Japan, was the first anime film in the world. In 1941, in order to publicize the victory at Pearl Harbor, the Imperial Navy commissioned Seo Mitsuyo, a disciple of Masaoka Kenzō, to make an anime of this "spectacular success." Seo superimposed the story on a well-known children's folktale, "The Peach Boy" (*Momotarō*), which centers on an ambitious boy, born of a peach stone, who conquers an island of ogres. The 37-minute anime produced in 1943, *The Peach Boy as a Sea Eagle* (*Momotarō no Umiwashi*), was about Pearl Harbor. It became very popular because the characters were "cute" (*kawaii*), not because viewers were impressed by the Imperial Navy's success (Kōdansha Sōgō Hensankyoku, ed., 1997: 24). Moreover, the story contained a subversive message of hope for peace. At that time, the state proclaimed that there had been only nine pilots lost in action, having plunged into American ships at Pearl Harbor. They did not disclose that a tenth pilot had been captured by the Americans—a national disgrace to be kept top secret. The odd number of nine pilots raised questions even among children, and the truth about the tenth leaked out in some quarters (Yamanaka 1989: 112–15).

As had been done in Germany, the state emphasized its military might in the motifs for postage stamps, such as a castle where warriors of yesteryear had resided, juxtaposed with modern technological achievements, such as planes, boy pilots (*shōnen hikōhei*—young boys trained as pilots), and battleships (Nihon Yūbinkitte Shōkyōdō Kumiai 2003: 161–70). Commemorative stamps had pictures of newly acquired colonies and of scenes of victory, such as the Pearl Harbor attack (Naitō 2004: 87, 88). The "Three Brave Soldiers as Human Cannons" (*Nikudan San Yūshi*) stamp depicted three soldiers who sacrificed their lives by carrying a land torpedo to penetrate a Chinese fortress during Japan's assault on Shanghai. The government proclaimed them heroes and urged others to emulate them (Naitō 2004: 16; see Ohnuki-Tierney 1987: 121–22, 153, 239; 2002a: 113).

In sharp contrast to the Nazis' efforts to ban smoking, Japan used cigarette packages as a vehicle for propaganda. They were provided to soldiers on the battlefield as "cigarettes given by the emperor" (*onshi no tabako*). The exclusive right to produce and sell tobacco had been held by the Japanese government since 1904. In the absence of competition, advertising was not necessary, but the authorities proclaimed: "People's taste is related to aesthetics, and therefore we must pay due attention to packaging" (Tabako to Shio no Hakubutsukan 1985: 148). They carefully chose names and package designs for different types of cigarettes, all of which aimed at presenting the best image of the collective self at a time when Japan was struggling to become a modern nation and expand its empire while preserving its own identity. The names chosen for cigarette brands reflect this effort.[10] Examples are several ancient designations for Japan, the rising sun, and mountain cherry blossoms—all representing the primordiality of the Japanese.

One such design (Figure 19) exemplifies Japan's presentation of itself at the time. It depicts fourteen cherry blossoms, a traditional warrior's helmet, and arrows with a strip of white cloth on which is written "One hundred million Japanese as one soul." This slogan was an equivalent of "United we stand" and tells all the Japanese they had to be part of one Japanese soul to win the war. This was declared by Konoe Fumimaro, then prime minister, on July 23, 1940. With the abolition of the warrior class at the beginning of the Meiji period and the adoption of universal conscription in 1872, many of the modern soldiers of Japan were a far cry from what the helmet represents, i.e., a handful of elite warriors who possessed a castle and a domain with retainers. It was a clever way to aestheticize modern soldiers (see Ohnuki-Tierney 2002a: 13–14). The two words written in characters in the center are "love of one's country" (*aikoku*) and "brocade" (*nishiki*). The character for brocade stands for the flag used by pro-imperial forces since the fourteenth century. Thus, the design foregrounds the power of the patriotism of the Japanese, which enables them to win in modern war.

The train had been the most important symbol of "civilization and en-

FIGURE 19. A Japanese cigarette package from World War II with patriotic symbols: cherry blossoms, a warrior's helmet with arrows, the rising sun flag, and the character for "brocade" (used by pro-imperial forces before the Meiji Restoration) on the right and the two characters for "patriotism" on the left. Source unknown.

lightenment," the motto of modern Japan, ever since Commodore Perry brought along a model train in 1854 when he came to negotiate the opening of Japan. It captured the Japanese imagination. In 1872, the first railroad, between Shinbashi in Tokyo and Yokohama, was inaugurated with great fanfare (Haga 2002: 114). Emperor Meiji rode the train from Shinbashi and as he arrived at Yokohama, he read a decree expressing his satisfaction with this accomplishment and his hope for Japan's continuing prosperity. The common folk, excited about the event, were not admitted to the site of the ceremony. The government called this train "Your Highness' Train" (*omeshiguruma*)—the train for the emperor and the empress. As a symbol of Japan's entry into the modern era, photos of it were frequently displayed, though without the emperor or empress in it. Locomotives of the time often hoisted two rising sun flags at the front.

As a symbol of what we now call globalization, the train became a favorite theme for woodblock prints. For example, one made by Utagawa

Kunitoshi in 1896 depicts the train station at Shinbashi at dusk, as indicated by birds flying against the sunset. The artist emphasized modernized Japan: the station consists of very modern buildings, and the three attendants with rising sun flags are all clad in Western-style uniforms. The title reads *Famous Places in Edo: Shinbashi Station*. It had been customary to designate certain places in Edo (Tokyo) as "famous places" on the basis of more traditional symbols of Japan, such as cherry blossoms. Now the train station, a symbol of modernization, certified Shinbashi as a "famous place" (*meisho*). In the caption, the station's name is written in kana syllabi, usually used for writing foreign words, indicating that the Japanese were ready to construct their new identity incorporating elements of Western technology. Other woodblock prints depict trains with steamships in the background in the bay, a symbol of Japan's trade and communication with other nations. These images show that the Japanese eagerly adopted Western science and technology and were ready to open their country's door to the world.

At a time when militarization of the country to resist Western imperialism was of utmost importance, the railroad came to be used as propaganda for imperial militarization, as reflected in the theme of a popular school song, "The Song of the Locomotive" (*Densha Shōka*) (Horiuchi and Inoue, eds., [1958] 1995: 115–22), published in 1905. The fifty-two stanzas describe the view from a train at different stations, with every station linked to political nationalism. The first two stanzas are about the Imperial Palace, the Tokyo government, and the Ministry of the Interior. Other locations include the statue of Saigō Takamori, a hero at the time of the Meiji Restoration; Sengakuji, where the Forty-seven Loyal Retainers are enshrined; the Ministries of Law, the Navy, and the Army; the military training ground at Aoyama; and the school for officers at Hachimangū. The last five stanzas are about the Yasukuni Shrine, including the Yūshūkan Exhibit Hall, which displayed portraits of soldiers who had died for the nation. The final stanza describes how the souls of those who sacrificed their lives for the emperor (*Ōkimi*) are immortalized at the shrine. In other words, the celebration of the train was used to nationalize and militarize the masses.

Warships constituted another set of propaganda symbols to display Japan's modernization and military strength. Germany gave its fleet of ships and U-boats everyday names or named them after military leaders (Goering et al. [1936] 1973: 100, 98). In contrast, the names for Japanese warships almost exclusively represented the country's primordial identity. Ships were given names used for ancient Japan, or the names of mountains and other places significant in the myth-history of the country's mythological birth. *Yamato*, an ancient name for Japan, was given to the largest battleship ever built. Its existence as well as its name was kept secret throughout the war. Launched in 1940, the *Yamato* was hit first by "friendly fire" during the battle of the Marianas and then was struck by American torpedoes, sinking off Okinawa on April 7, 1945, together with 3,056 sailors. Thus, the pride-of-place battleship failed to attain any military goal and met a dishonorable end. The Japanese people learned of its existence and its embarrassing finale only after the war.[11] The *Yamato* epitomized the utterly anachronistic vision held by the top military brass at the time. Although military strategists and even the civilian population were aware that the war was being fought in the air, the government spent enormous resources building battleships, all named with the ancient designations for Japan.

The names of the 647 *tokkōtai* (kamikaze) planes all also referred to Japan, especially its ancient designations, and to soldiers' loyalty and sacrifice to the emperor, although never a specific emperor (for details, see Ohnuki-Tierney 2002a: 164–66).

School songs and popular songs, along with music for military marching bands, were extensively used as propaganda. The national anthem, hurriedly composed at the beginning of the Meiji era, had only a short passage in praise of "His Majesty" (Ohnuki-Tierney 2002a: 68). It was not an evocative song. Therefore, a dirge-like song, "Umi Yukaba," became the de facto national anthem and filled the air every time the government wanted to remind the people of the virtue of sacrifice, such as when every *tokkōtai* plane took off. Its lyrics read:

If I go away to the sea, I shall be a waterlogged corpse.
If I go away to the mountains, I shall be a corpse lying in the grass.
But I shall not look back if I am dying for your majesty.[12]

Further Deliberations

Multiple attributes of the self-identity of any culture are expressed as concrete symbols, each of which emerges in a particular historical and geopolitical context, as encounters with different "others" necessitate the articulation and rearticulation of identity. In this regard there are some cross-cultural parallels. Many of these symbols represent the primordiality of the self—blood, soil, the origin of the people, the ancient imperial system, the national epic, and the like. This is intensified when the traditional self is threatened by the modern self, a situation faced by all the authoritarian states discussed here. Nazi Germany, the Soviet Union, and fascist Italy all engaged in a two-sided self-representation, balancing the primordial with the modern. Agriculture played a central role in their symbolic identity; bundles of wheat are featured in propaganda photos produced by all three regimes. In all these countries, the modern state was represented by airplanes, with automobiles ranking a close second. These modern means of transportation facilitated unprecedented mobility. Significantly, the propaganda of these regimes emphasized mobility and supposedly delivered freedom of the individual. "Time-space compression" (Harvey 1990: 201–323) served the regimes first by uniting people living in various regions, thereby facilitating state control as well as the rapid transport of military equipment and personnel.

There were sharp contrasts between the European authoritarian states and Japan in the way they projected their image. Germany gave equal weight to the traditional or primordial self and the modern self. Modernization was a sign of proud progress in history. Through what they called *Leistung*, "a discourse of performance," the Nazis aimed to mold and represent new Germany without dichotomizing the two identities (Koshar 1998: 153). It was important to present modernization as a gift to the people from Hitler, as other dictators did as well.

In contrast, Japan had to Japanize its modernization, which had come from the West, the enemy, for example, by naming train stations after important place-names in Japan's modern history and giving ancient names for Japan to battleships and planes. Even consumer goods like cigarettes bore ancient names for Japan. As Kushner (2006: 11) notes, "wartime propaganda often specifically depicted an advanced and modern Japan," but this had to be done through the indigenization of modernization, foregrounding the primordiality of the national identity, including the symbols of the ancient imperial system, when in fact the modern emperor system is altogether different from the ancient system (Ohnuki-Tierney 2002a: 69–80).

In addition to realizing that histories do not march "through a homogeneous, empty time" (Benjamin [1950] 1968: 261), we must keep in mind that similar historical forces find different expressions depending upon the sociopolitical-economic contexts of each nation. An important difference between Germany and Japan was the way mobility, a key dimension of the modern era, was introduced. Both Germany and Japan rushed into the time-space compression brought by new technologies of transportation. However, the sociopolitical and ideational dimensions of these changes were substantially different. Nazi Germany made an effort to convince people that automobiles, autobahns, and radios brought them *individual freedom* and equality— thanks to the Führer. In contrast, Japan's pride was the train as a new mode of rapid transit. People were packed in and passed through stations named for the nationalization of the masses for the war effort, like cogs in a gigantic wheel rolling toward total war. The Japanese people were unknowingly heading toward a collective phantasmagorical self-destruction for the sake of *pro rege et patria mori*. The state did not even pretend to offer any means of individual mobility. This is not to say that the concept of individual freedom had not been embraced by the Japanese; on the contrary, those who believed in and supported it in opposition to state control were severely persecuted, and many died in prison (Ohnuki-Tierney 2002a: 91–92).

Unlike in the European authoritarian states, in Japan the image of the presumed leader, the emperor, was absent from propaganda, which only emphasized the symbols of the emperor and the imperial *system*, whose antiquity was supposed to prove the antiquity of Japan itself. Kushner (2006: 20) reminds us how American studies of the Japanese mobilization for the war failed to produce useful counterstrategies "because Americans had exaggerated ideas of Japanese culture's supposedly slavish devotion to the emperor." He points out that for Japan's wartime professional propagandists "discussion of the emperor seldom figures in their work" and "the emperor rarely made an appearance." No visual images were made and when the word "emperor" appeared in songs it was a generic emperor. This contrasted most drastically with the propaganda produced by other totalitarian regimes, which built a personality cult and equated the dictator with the state itself. During the 1934 Nuremberg rally, while Goebbels shouted, "Hitler is Germany," Rudolf Hess, with "his face glowing with fanatical devotion," shouted, "The Party is Hitler! But Hitler is Germany, just as Germany is Hitler! Hitler! Hail, Victory! (*Sieg, heil!*)" (Evans 2005: 126). What is often referred to as mass hysterical devotion to Hitler was developed through extensive and intensive engineering, including propaganda. Therefore, from the perspective of the collective political self, Hitler represented Germany. But the ancient imperial system, not the emperor, represented Japan.

Collective self-identity consists of a large number of features from which one or another surfaces in relation to a specific other. Each is perceived as the metaphor of a homogeneous "we." Crucial for an understanding of these symbols of the collective self is that they hide other features of the collective and the heterogeneity within the population. The singularity of the self of a nation/state is almost always built upon a contradiction, since a state or other large political organization is usually multiethnic or otherwise heterogeneous. This sometimes leads to a specific effort on the part of the dominant social group to get rid of the "other" within and purge its impurity through scapegoating (Ohnuki-Tierney 1998) as happened with the Japanese, who displaced their own impurity onto a marginalized group (*hisabetsu burakumin*) and their own primitiveness, as they measured themselves against the West, onto the Ainu, formerly a hunting-gathering people in northern Japan (Chapter Four; Ohnuki-Tierney 1998). In Nazi Germany, a "pure" Aryan race was constructed through scapegoating Jews, Gypsies, homosexuals, and the mentally retarded, to whom the Aryan Germans transferred their own impurity (Burke [1945] 1969: 406–7).

A most striking parallel between these examples is that all the symbols of the primordial self—before and after modernization—are not "real," if we use the positivistic term. People have not been on "our" soil from the beginning of time, their blood is never pure, their origin is usually murky, the imperial system had not been in place for 2,600 years, and so on. There is a stark disjuncture between the symbolic construction of the self and historical reality, especially when we examine the symbols of the collective self in these authoritarian states. While the symbols of the modern self are relatively easy to relate to, people "should" have a hard time relating to those of the primordial self, which is almost always purely imaginary if we take a positivistic view.

For this pan-universal phenomenon, we may seek an explanation in the importance of the aesthetic for the image of self. For example, purity is the most important aesthetic value of self-identity for many peoples. The linguistic purity of recent Quebec nationalism (Handler 1988), Mao's slogan "today pure but poor; tomorrow pure and powerful," and the ethnic cleansing in Bosnia are a few examples of the "invention of purity" required for all nation building (Williams 1989). The most unfortunately memorable example is the primordial German *Volk* sought in a putative Aryan or Teutonic past with spiritual strength and purity (Wolf 1999: 236). For symbolic expressions of purity, a successful strategy is to portray the primordial self, uncontaminated by the negative impact of later historical developments. To transfer, in the Kantian sense, this beautiful pristine nature, like flowers, to the collective self at present is uplifting to the people. It is a strategic choice on the part of any state to accomplish the unification of the people as "we" and mobilize them for self-sacrifice, another aesthetic act.

PART III

(Non-)Externalization

Religious and Political Authority/Power

SIX

The Invisible and Inaudible
Japanese Emperor

Instead of quotidian symbols chosen for deliberation as in the previous
chapters, the last two chapters of this book focus on political leaders and
institutions. Regarding the "the center with the symbols," Geertz ([1977]
1983: 143) explains: "no matter how peripheral, ephemeral, or free-floating
the charismatic figure we may be concerned with . . . we must begin with
the center and with the symbols and conceptions that prevail there if we are
to understand him and what he means."

Since the crucial point on the communicative opacity of the symbols of
cherry blossoms and roses is how it took place during war, it is imperative
to probe into the question of *how* or *if* leaders exercised or manifested their
authority and/or power. In Max Weber's well-known distinction, legitimacy
is the principle that distinguishes between authority, which is legitimate,
and power, which is not (Weber 1947: 324–63, 392–407). I use the notion
of power loosely. Rather than focusing on "power" and its functions, that is,
the impact of symbols and rituals upon people's minds or even actions, my
interest is in how religious and political leaders and institutions deploy these
symbols and rituals, or in some cases, deliberately avoid doing so.

The term "externalization" is chosen over "objectification," which has been
used in philosophy, art, art history, and related disciplines. The terms "materialization" and "reification" are deeply embedded in scholarship, especially
by Marxists (Jameson 1992: esp. 16–17). Therefore, I opt for "externalization"
to mean the expression of an idea/concept either as an object, including
signs and symbols, or as sound or speech, since auditory externalization is
not immediately implied by either "objectification" or "materialization."

While the last chapter of this book will discuss political authorities and powers more broadly, in this chapter I introduce the Japanese imperial system and Japanese emperors.

Let me start with a brief account of the emperor system and the emperor to provide an overall picture in order to counter common stereotypes and even gross misunderstandings about the emperor as "God." As Kushner (2006: 20) points out, Americans (and I would say many other non-Japanese) tend to have an "exaggerated idea" of the Japanese people's "supposedly slavish devotion to the emperor." This misrepresentation of the importance of the emperor for the Japanese, in my view, has resulted in an unjustifiable attribution of power to the "Japanese emperor" in the generic sense. I attempt to show the importance of understanding the emperor system and the basic nature of the Japanese emperor, while recognizing that there were enormous differences among individual emperors, a discussion of which is beyond the scope of this book. A fuller explanation of various dimensions introduced below has been published earlier: pre-Meiji emperors and the imperial system (Ohnuki-Tierney 2005); Japanese religiosity and the emperor (Ohnuki-Tierney 1991b); the redefinition of the emperor at the time of the Meiji constitution (Ohnuki-Tierney 2002a: 70–80); and the accession ritual (Ohnuki-Tierney 2002b).

The Japanese Emperor System Before Meiji

As described in Chapter Four, six centuries after the introduction of wet-rice agriculture to Japan, at the end of the fourth century CE, the Japanese emperor system was developed with rice agriculture as the basis of its political economy, which in turn led to an agrarian cosmology with rice as its symbolic center. The early agrarian leaders, including the early emperors, were magico-religious leaders, i.e., shamans whose political power rested on an ability to solicit supernatural power to ensure a good rice crop. The annual harvest ritual thus served to legitimate the local political leader, ensure his symbolic rebirth, and strengthen his political power (see Murakami 1977: 4–6). For this reason, many scholars consider the emperor first and foremost as the officiant in rituals venerating the soul of rice (*inadama no shusaisha*) and looking after every stage of the growth of rice plants. Although other rituals were added in different historical periods, the central ones over which the emperor officiated were established during the ancient period. The annual rice harvest ritual of *niinamesai* becomes the *ōnamesai* when it is performed after the accession of a new emperor. This is so even today.

According to Joseph Kitagawa (1990: 140), "never before or after in the history of Japan did the monarchy reach such a zenith as in the eighth century." Instead of having warrior-kings, the Japanese divided duties between the warlords and the emperors, in stark contrast to the pattern of rule in Europe. Although its opulent life style and florescent high culture continued, the imperial court lost its financial power and began relying on the protection of the warriors. Three emperors (Ōgimachi, Goyōzei, and Gomizuo) and three warlords (Nobunaga, Hideyoshi, and Ieyasu) engaged in intensive negotiations (Fujii 2011) that led ultimately to the victory of the latter. Thus Japan entered a period stretching from 1185 to 1868 under which power was concentrated in the military government and the emperors and the imperial court were pushed into the background (for details, see Ohnuki-Tierney 2002a). However, the military government neither abolished the emperor system altogether nor dared to officiate in rituals related to the growth of rice. That role was strictly reserved for the emperor. When the warlords participated in the rituals, they covered their heads to conceal their blasphemous presence (Ohnuki-Tierney 1991b: 209–10). Thus it was political power that was held by the warriors, while symbolic power continued to reside with the emperors (Fujii 2011).

Dramatic instances of the apotheosis of warlords reveal the limited power of the emperor and the basic fluidity of Japanese religiosity. Both Toyotomi Hideyoshi, the military leader who in 1590 succeeded in uniting Japan for the first time, and Tokugawa Ieyasu, the most powerful of all warlords, left their wish in their respective wills for their apotheosis. Both wishes were fulfilled, under the reign of Emperor Goyōzei in 1599 and Emperor Gomizuo in 1617, respectively (Fujii 2011: 266–70, 333–37; Inoue [1953] 1967; Inoue [1963] 1967: 258–59). That a warlord—an ordinary human—could achieve the status of a deity, for which a semi-divine emperor had to give approval, illustrates a fluid religiosity and religious hierarchy among the Japanese, as well as the limited power of the emperors (for details, see Ohnuki-Tierney 1991b).

The Japanese people have always thought of the emperor as human, as revealed in folktales. For example, when he was a crown prince, Emperor Sakuramachi (r. 1735–1747) enjoyed soba, noodles made of buckwheat. Since the emperor is the official guardian of rice, once he became emperor he could no longer eat other grains, which were deemed inferior to rice.

Nor could he receive moxibustion—the healing technique that uses lighted cones of artemisia placed on certain spots of the body—because no foreign objects could touch his "crystal body" (Miyata 1989). He is said to have expressed great pleasure when he abdicated his throne; he could then eat buckwheat noodles to his heart's content and undergo moxibustion treatment (Tsumura [1917] 1970: 615). This story reveals that a prince is an ordinary human and becomes a quasi-divine emperor, but can revert to an ordinary human.

The Refashioned Emperor System in Meiji

Commodore Perry's arrival in 1853 and return visit in 1854 signaled that Japan could no longer maintain its isolation. Many scholars (e.g., Murakami 1977: 45) believe that the "restoration" in 1868 was not a restoration of the ancient Japanese emperorship but simply an excuse for lower-class samurai to overthrow the shogunate, because the shoguns had been oblivious to geopolitics when Japan was the only East Asian nation not colonized by Western powers. Internally, Japan had been divided into some 260 *han* (a region controlled by a daimyō) and its many territorial lords were independent, often fighting among themselves. It bore little resemblance to a modern, centralized state.

The Meiji oligarchs traveled to several Western nations and consulted a number of foreign experts in order to draft a constitution. Since the urgent goal of the Meiji Restoration was to establish sovereignty to protect the country from Western colonialism, the crucial question was whether ultimate power should rest with the emperor or with state organs. Following the Prussian constitution as a model for constitutional monarchy, the key figures of the oligarchy and their foreign advisors agreed that it should rest with the emperor (Emura, ed., [1989] 1996: 265–71, 482–84; Inada 1960: 589; Mitani 1988: 55–59).[1]

The Constitution of Imperial Japan of 1889 reads:

Article 1: The Emperor belongs to one line from antiquity to eternity (*bansei ikkei*) and he governs Imperial Japan.

Article 3: The Emperor is sacred (*shinsei ni shite*) and inviolable (*okasu bekarazu*).

Article 4. The Emperor is the head of the nation, holding the rights of sovereignty, and exercises them according to the provisions of this Constitution.

Article 5. The Emperor exercises legislative power with the consent of the Imperial Diet.

Article 6. The Emperor gives sanction to laws, and orders them to be promulgated and executed.

Article 11: The Emperor shall command the Army and the Navy. (Emura, ed., [1989] 1996: 430–34)

The Meiji constitution established the emperor as a constitutional monarch and granted him imperial sovereignty with limitless power. Yet at the same time it rejected the idea of direct imperial rule. Political responsibilities were placed in the hands of all organs of the state, which consisted of the cabinet and the two-house Diet, the House of Peers and the House of Representatives. They operated independently of one another.

The constitution as it played out *in practice* reveals that the political and military roles codified in Articles 4, 5, and 11 were in fact devoid of meaning, providing the emperor with virtually no power. This was facilitated by the wording of Article 3. As Mitani Taichirō (1988) explains, the "real meaning" of the expression "sacred and inviolable" is to relieve the emperor of any political responsibility by placing him beyond politics. Institutionally, the announcement by the government in December 1885, that is, prior to the promulgation of the constitution, required that all laws and ordinances issued by the government be signed jointly by the prime minister and the head of the respective ministry. This accomplished the removal of the emperor from active involvement in politics (Beasley [1989] 1996: 648–49).

Stripped of any political role, the emperor was named commander-in-chief of the army and navy. In reality, the ministers of the army and navy, who were directly responsible to the emperor, gained direct access to him without having to clear their proposals with the cabinet or the Diet (Emura, ed., [1989] 1996: 491–92; Mitani 1988: 60–61).

Military leadership—entirely secular—had been held by the warlords since the eleventh century. Now the emperor was thrust into this utterly new and unfamiliar role under the newly created theocracy. To overcome this contradiction, the state attempted to resurrect the myth that the emperor had been a military figure, as demonstrated by the legendary first emperor, Jinmu, who conquered all the barbarians. A hanging scroll was made with a fake photo of Emperor Meiji below and Emperor Jinmu as a warrior with a bow on top, validating the military role as belonging to the emperor from the very beginning of the imperial system. A limited number of these scrolls were circulated among the people.

The Meiji constitution thus provided the legal basis for bureaucrats and military officers to control national policies, excluding the emperor. Ben-Ami Shillony (2005: 119–30) proposes that the modern emperors voluntarily abided by the Confucian model of the "Sage King."[2] The tight control of the decision-making process was facilitated by a fairly easygoing Emperor Meiji. Those in the innermost circle of the government referred to the emperor as "the crystal ball in the palm," which could be easily manipulated (Inoue [1953] 1967: 21, 225–26); the term "crystal" had been used as an honorific prefix for the emperor's body, his voice, and various other objects, such as the seat he sits on. Not only was Emperor Meiji manageable, but the emperor system was an empty vessel that the oligarchs could fill with their strategic plans. The major structural cause for the outbreak of World War II sprang from this codification, which made it possible for Tōjō Hideki and other army officers to seize power.[3]

As for the imperial line stretching from antiquity to eternity as mentioned in Article 1, the statement had no historical or legal meaning, as Karl Friedrich Hermann Roesler (1834–1915), a German legal scholar hired as a consultant at the time of drafting of the Meiji constitution, pointed out (Inada 1960: 248; Ohnuki-Tierney 2002a: 70–72). Its inclusion in the constitution was opposed by every foreign advisor. Yet the Japanese oligarchs insisted, and it became the ideological foundation of the emperor system based on theocracy, a myth that the state made a strenuous effort to inculcate in the people. Although the ritual to commemorate the beginning of the imperial line had been performed annually only since 1872 (Murakami 1977: 80–81), in 1940 the beginning of the emperor system as having taken place 2,600 years earlier was celebrated with enormous fanfare (Ruoff 2010).

Theocracy, based upon myth, was further buttressed in Article 1, which identified the emperor as having the imperial soul, transmitted from one emperor to the next, guaranteeing the continuity of the institutional body, or the "body politic," while leaving the individual emperor's "body natural" dispensable, to use Ernst Kantorowicz's theoretical scheme ([1957] 1981: 7). In short, the focus of the constitution was on the emperor *system* rather than the emperor himself. The same point was stated in the "pledge" (*kokubun*) the emperor made to his ancestors before he promulgated the constitution (Satomi 1972: 160–67; Nagao [1987] 1995: 840). It begins with the emperor reporting to the divine soul (*shinrei*) that resided in previous emperors and now resides in himself (Murakami 1977: 144–45; for details, see Ohnuki-Tierney 2002a).

The *Nihongi*, dated 725 CE, includes a passage in which Emperor Jinmu, the legendary first emperor, performs a ritual for the imperial ancestral soul (Okada [1985] 1997). However, it was only in 1869 that the imperial soul was added to the Hasshinden Shrine, which had housed the eight most important deities, who are guardians of the emperors. The Hasshinden was overseen by the office of the central government in charge of religious matters (Shingi-kan). In 1871, for the first time, the imperial soul was moved to Kashikodokoro in the imperial compound proper, where the Sun Goddess is enshrined. In 1877 the government added the souls of the empress and other imperial family members. In 1900 the designation Kōreiden (Shrine for the Imperial Souls) was officially adopted (Fukuyama [1985] 1997). The performance of *kōreisai*, the spring and fall ceremonies for the imperial soul, was codified in 1908 and revised in 1927 (Okada [1985] 1997). The imperial soul was elevated above all other deities as the Manifest Deity (Arahitogami). Since Japanese religiosity lacks the concept of an all-powerful god, the emperor could never become equivalent to Almighty God in Christianity, though he was often misrepresented as such outside of Japan.

To recapitulate, at a time when feverish efforts toward modernization were taking place in most nations and empires in the world—especially Japan, which had a great deal of catching up to do after the long closure of the country—the Meiji constitution replaced history with the myth of the emperor system, for which the imperial soul was refashioned and elevated in the hierarchy of the Japanese pantheon. The constitution established a theocracy, with the emperor as the high priest of state Shintoism. It even codified, for the first time in history, the ban on females ascending to the chrysanthemum throne.[4]

The Meiji constitution, then, may be an excellent example of Laurence Tribe's point in *The Invisible Constitution* (2008). Tribe argues that in America, what is "written in law" is a figment of our rationalist imagination: "it's the *invisible* Constitution that tells us what text to accept as the *visible* Constitution of the United States" (Tribe 2008: 7, italics in the original), and the written Constitution "floats in a vast and deep—and, crucially, invisible—ocean of ideas, propositions, recovered memories, and imagined experiences that the Constitution as a whole puts us in a position to glimpse" (Tribe 2008: 9).

How the written text of the Meiji constitution yields various versions of the invisible constitution becomes clear when we compare three modern emperors and how they enacted the written codification of their reign.

After Emperor Kōmei's death, Emperor Meiji acceded to the throne at the tender age of fourteen. He had been pampered exclusively by court ladies and was physically frail. In July 1864, when warriors from Chōshū fired cannonballs at the Imperial Palace in order to force a "restoration," he fainted at the sound. The architects of the new government got rid of the court ladies and undertook the masculinization of the rosy-cheeked emperor, who began to enjoy activities such as horseback riding (Ohnuki-Tierney 2002a: 69). Emperor Meiji posed no major obstacle to the oligarchs in carrying out their plans and remained without political, legislative, or military power (for an extremely detailed account of Emperor Meiji, see Keene 2002).

His heir, Emperor Taishō, was enthroned in 1915, but his reign lasted only fifteen years (see Dickinson 2009 for the corrective to the image of Emperor Taishō disseminated by the state). The official statement on "The Condition of the Emperor" announced to the people on November 25, 1921, is worth citing at some length, not only because it was crude and almost cruel, but also because it so clearly shows that the government forgot, as it were, that the emperor was supposedly sacred according to the Meiji constitution:

> Emperor Taishō had suffered meningitis three weeks after his birth. When he was young, he also suffered from the serious illnesses of whooping cough, typhoid, and pleurisy. Consequently, his physical and mental development has been somewhat delayed. However, he labored night and day over domestic and international affairs. In recent years, although his appearance has not changed, his brain power gradually diminished and his speech became impaired. It has been difficult to witness the extreme difficulty he has in expressing his thoughts. (Quoted in Inose [1986] 1988: 30–31).

Needless to say, the statement is full of honorifics, but it ruthlessly dismisses Taishō and explains why the crown prince, Hirohito, had to take over the imperial duties. Hirohito became regent in 1921 at age twenty and emperor in 1926.

Hara Takeshi, among others, suggests that when Emperor Taishō abdicated the throne and Hirohito became regent in 1921, the Japanese emperor system underwent a profound change and the "national body" became more visible through the emperor's personal appearances (Hara 2002: 137). Hirohito, as Emperor Shōwa, created a very different "invisible constitution" from the same written constitution. As Irokawa Daikichi (1995: 75) points out, Shōwa "could not be manipulated easily by the militarists and politicians because of his personal familiarity with the generals and political leaders." His reign coincided with the rise of dictatorship in Europe. At that time the Japanese government felt the need to reinforce the emperor system in the public consciousness, especially after the weak reign of Emperor Taishō. For this purpose, the government resurrected Emperor Meiji by designating the places he had visited as sacred sites, usually by placing a large rock on which details about his visit were inscribed.

As crown prince, Hirohito often appeared before the people. His tours of Europe and, after he became emperor, of Manchukuo (the Japanese-ruled state in Manchuria and Inner Mongolia) were filmed and shown to the people. The emperor began to appear regularly in public, often accompanied by the empress. Although he became visible, he stood at a distance from the people, who gathered and shouted *banzai* (Eternal Life), a customary salute invented in Meiji following the practice in England and the United States (Inose [1986] 1988: 498–500). From November 10 to 14, 1940, the state staged a spectacle on an unprecedented scale to celebrate the 2,600th anniversary of the supposed beginning of the emperor system—the very enactment of Article 1 of the constitution. The presence of the emperor and empress was confined to their appearance in the Outer Compound (Gai'en) of the Imperial Palace (Fujii [1984] 1996; Ruoff 2001). In order to emphasize his role as commander-in-chief, Emperor Shōwa on a white horse became the iconic image of the emperor as semi-divine military commander.[5] This image seems to have been shown more outside of Japan, however.

The invention of radio and its diffusion throughout Japan since 1925 mattered little, since the emperor gave no speeches and he remained virtually silent until Japan surrendered on August 5, 1945, when his "crystal sound" (*gyoku'on*) was broadcasted—the very first time the Japanese heard his voice, or the voice of any emperor.

Japanese Religiosity

For an understanding of the basic nature of the Japanese emperor, three fundamental characteristics of Japanese religiosity must be highlighted. First is its fluidity for secular purposes. As Ozawa Hiroshi (1987) emphasizes, humans (*hito*) and deities (*kami*) constitute a continuum and the notion of

human-deities (*hitogami*)—deified humans—is central to Japanese religiosity, as noted earlier, although it has undergone significant historical change.
Komatsu Kazuhiko (2008: 12–13) points to individual emperors, warlords,
and ordinary people who became deities. Indeed, an ordinary human can
turn even a toothpick into a *kami* (Miyata 1975). Second, the fluid characterization of the *kami* in Japanese religion has led to the ease with which
the Japanese have adopted various foreign religions. When Buddhism was
introduced from India via China and Korea during the sixth century, it was
embraced eagerly by the elites, including the imperial family. Buddhism
is based on the principle that a human being can become a bodhisattva,
a notion that posed no contradiction to Japanese religiosity. According to
Kitagawa (1990: 136), "most people in Japan at that time probably thought
of Buddha as just another kami." Officially, the Japanese tried to reconcile
the two religions by claiming that the *kami* are manifestations of the buddhas and bodhisattvas, a theory known as *honji suijaku*. With equal ease,
the Tokugawa Japanese, especially the elites, adopted Neo-Confucianism
with its emphasis on natural law and the Way of Heaven. Astonishing as
it may be from the perspective of Western religions, the Meiji government
concocted "non-religious State Shinto," which was to be adhered to by every
Japanese subject, "regardless of his or her personal 'religious' affirmation and
affiliation" (Kitagawa 1990: 161). Most Japanese today are at least nominally
both Buddhist and Shintoist (Ohnuki-Tierney 1984; 1991b).

The Japanese attitude toward religion is quite practical—it tends to involve asking the deities and buddhas to ensure recovery from illness, provide
protection from natural calamities, and ensure success in passing entrance
examinations or in business (Ohnuki-Tierney 1984: 145–55). For this reason,
S. N. Eisenstadt (1996) concludes that the Japanese do not have an axial
civilization. Joseph Kitagawa (1990) describes their religions as "eclectic,"
and others use the term "multilayered" or "fused" (Ohnuki-Tierney 1984:
145–49). Importantly, the concept of an all-powerful God, as in Christianity, Judaism, and Islam, has always been alien. When the Japanese refer to
the emperor as a deity (*kami*) or Manifest Deity, it should not be translated
as "God" in these religions.[6]

The third important premise of Japanese religiosity having a direct bearing on the nature of the emperor is the notion that it is the soul (*tamashii*)
that defines and identifies deities as well as other beings of the universe.
At the base of Shinto is the idea that the invisible soul takes up residence
(*yadoru*) in different objects—a rock, a petal of a cherry blossom, a tree—

but only temporarily (Ohnuki-Tierney 1993a: 55). These objects are referred to as *goshintai*, the body of the deities. However, they are *not objectified bodies* but rather a "perch" for the divine soul. When a deity perches on a rock, for example, people place ropes made of rice stalks (*shimenawa*) around the hitherto ordinary rock to give it a new and sacred identity (Ohnuki-Tierney 1993a: 53).

The soul of the deity, however, remains invisible. Proposing the "empty center" as the basic theme of folk Shinto religion, Kawai Hayao points out that in the *Kojiki* there are three sets of three important deities. In each case the most important of the triad is introduced by name at the beginning, but as the narrative of the myth progresses, this most important deity disappears, becoming a void, while the activities of the other two are well described (Kawai 1982: 30–44), and thus they serve as predicates for the invisible deity.[7]

The invisibility of important deities is exemplified in the characterization of the Sun Goddess, Amaterasu Ōmikami. She is arguably the most important deity in the pantheon of the agrarian Japanese, providing light to the universe and warmth for the crops, especially rice.[8] In the Ise Shrine, the Sun Goddess is in the inner shrine, not to be seen. Isozaki Arata (1995) emphasizes the importance of "hiding" (*kakusu*) the goddess. When visitors come to the shrine, they must invite the invisible deity by clapping their hands, talk to her as if she were there in person, and offer her daily necessities such as food.

The concept of the soul as the essence of a deity and the necessity of keeping it hidden make it difficult to apply the notion of externalization in the Shinto context. A rock is not a divinity externalized: it is simply the deity's temporary abode. The soul remains formless, invisible, and inaudible. In fact, the construction of shrines as well as wooden images of deities started only in the ninth century under pressure from Buddhism (Itō 2011: 51, 84; see also Kageyama 1978). At any shrine, worshippers clap their hands to summon the deity enshrined there and pray in silence. This belief and practice continue today.

In ancient Japan, people believed that death occurred when the soul departed from the body. At least until the end of World War II, the notion of the soul remained crucial, so that the Japanese were identified by the possession of a specifically Japanese soul (*Yamato damashii*), which no other people can have. When Chinese civilization engulfed Japan during the fifth and sixth centuries, the people asserted their distinct identity in the phrase

"Japanese soul and Chinese wisdom" (*wakon kansai*). In the late nineteenth century, as Japan embarked on its military course, the state began emphasizing that what was unique about the Japanese as a people was their soul, which enabled them to face death without hesitation.

In his famous book in English, *Bushido: The Soul of Japan*, Nitobe Inazō, a cosmopolitan intellectual who became increasingly patriotic, advocated patriotism and loyalty. In the book's opening sentence, he equated the Japanese soul with cherry blossoms—both indigenous to Japan (see Chapter One). One of the flower's salient meanings had been the brevity of its beautiful life (Ohnuki-Tierney 2002a: 115–21). Since the end of the nineteenth century, this symbolic equation was deployed by the state to mean that Japanese soldiers, supposedly endowed with the Japanese soul, should face death without hesitation and fall like beautiful cherry petals after a short life. This encouragement to die reveals how life was *not embodied* for the Japanese, in sharp contrast to the Germans, who were urged to kill their enemies, not themselves. (On the relationship between the soul and the body in Japanese culture, see Ohnuki-Tierney 1994b; 1997.)

To conclude, the Japanese emperor had been just one deity in a large pantheon, whose divinity had never been as powerful as the supreme deities in the axial religions. The notion of the soul in Japan necessarily precludes the externalization of the imperial soul.

Non-externalization of the Emperor

Yet, as Japan entered the modern era, Meiji officials became aware that in order to use the emperor as a figurehead, they had to make the people aware of his existence, a challenge after he had been hidden behind the warlords since the eleventh century. The following section shows the tortured ways the state struggled to accomplish this task.

PUBLIC APPEARANCES

At the beginning of Meiji, society was still turbulent. Powerful former warriors who opposed the "restoration" were still around, and the policies of the new government created unrest among the people. These policies included universal conscription, which was introduced in 1883; the overhaul of the feudal land tenure system, which created a strong and lingering resentment among members of the former warrior class, who lost their livelihood; and a change in the way tax was paid, from rice to currency, which the peasants resented (Taki [1988] 1990: 75–77).

The government felt the need to appease the public by making the emperor known through his appearance in person (Taki [1988] 1990: 75–80). However, there was no pre-Meiji tradition of such appearances. In ancient Japan, the emperor went up on a hill or a mountain, and his simple act of viewing the land below enabled him to claim it as his territory. This ritual act, known as *kunimi* (Orikuchi [1932] 1976: esp. 165–67, 176–79), together with the control of the agrarian ritual calendar, epitomized the politico-ritual power of the emperors in ancient Japan (Miyata 1992). The practice of imperial gazing continued as the *tenran* (imperial viewing), during which the presiding emperor watched his subjects' activities, for example, sumō. In the *Nihon Kiryaku* (Kuroita and Kokushi Taikei Henshūkai, eds., 1965a), there are frequent references to the emperor watching sumō in 861 and 867, all the way to the present.[9]

Lacking any tradition of the emperor's presence in public, the state adopted a strategy of imperial tours. The model was the British monarchy, although the protocol had been set by processions of the feudal lords from their domains to Edo (Tokyo), as ordered by the shogun. These became occasions to display, or be forced to display, their wealth and power. During Meiji, the government sent the emperor on six extensive tours of Japan, starting in 1872 (Taki [1988] 1990: 75–82; for a complete list of the tours, see Sasaki 1984: 218). On these trips, the emperor rode in the imperial carriage with a phoenix, an imperial emblem, on top; he was not to see or to be seen by his subjects, though his presence was obvious.

Taki Kōji emphasizes that the processions by Emperor Meiji were *not* spectacles. They developed into the opposite of the sixteenth-century European monarchs' tours, which were intended to display and impress people with the power of the monarchy through elaborate rituals (Taki [1988] 1990: 82, 84).[10]

With the acceleration of militarization, the *tenran* was extended to the viewing of troops, but not the public. In 1890, Emperor Meiji supposedly took on the role of commander-in-chief, directing the troops in heavy rain during a large-scale training exercise (*enshū*) organized jointly by the navy and the army. This legend became important as a model for all Japanese, who were not to be deterred by weather and other circumstances from fulfilling their duty (Haga 2002: 123–24).

Clearly, the *tenran* should not be understood as the emperor's personal appearance before the public. It was his staged viewing of a select group of people or activities.

IMPERIAL RITUALS

The Japanese imperial rituals had been agricultural ceremonies synchronized with the growth cycle of rice. None were public rituals. Even today the harvest ritual serves as the accession ritual for the new emperor. It is performed at the Imperial Palace. The crucial part, when the emperor receives the imperial soul from the preceding emperor, has been, and remains, a secret ritual (*higi*), with only the emperor present. It is called the *mitamashizume* (the rejuvenation of the soul), during which the imperial soul of the preceding emperor is captured with the use of a cotton thread (Matsumae 1977: 96–97; for details of this ritual, see Ohnuki-Tierney 2002b, and 2005).[11]

At the beginning of Meiji, following the German advisor Lorenz von Stein's suggestion, the government added eleven rituals to the two existing ones to be performed at the imperial court with the emperor as the officiant (Miyachi [1988] 1996). Local shrines throughout Japan were ordered to perform their version of the same rituals in coordination with those at court. According to Murakami Shigeyoshi (1977: 75), there are two categories: rituals related to the eighth-century *Kojiki* and *Nihongi* myth-histories and those in reference to the imperial soul (see also Shimazono 2010: 98–105). The former celebrate the origin of the Japanese country as described in the myth-histories, beginning with the story of how the heavenly grandson of the Sun Goddess descended to earth, that is, Japan, and the celebration of the accession of the legendary Emperor Jinmu (Murakami 1977: 75–86). Of the rituals added at the time of Meiji, those related to the imperial soul were by far more numerous. By synchronizing their enactment at the imperial court and at local shrines, the state attempted to impress upon the people the importance of the emperor system. Celebrating the emperor's birthday was a custom dating back to 775 CE, but had long been neglected until Meiji, when it was reinstated not as a resurrection of the traditional practice but as an act to follow the custom of celebrating the birthdays of monarchs and political leaders in European states.

None of these events was a spectacle for the display of power and pomp (Ohnuki-Tierney 2002b: 89–91; 2005: 5–9)—a far cry from most political rituals. Nor were they occasions for the emperor to be seen.

PORTRAITS/PHOTOS

The idea of portraits came to Japan from China, where they were made to honor great figures from the past, starting with the first emperor of unified China, Qin Shi Huang Di (259 BCE–210 BCE). The portraits of the two most powerful Manchu emperors—Kangxi (1662–1722) and Qianlong (1736–1796)—are well known. The Japanese learned of the Chinese practice at the beginning of the eighth century but refused to adopt it (Miyachi [1988] 1996: 2). They believed that portraits of the dead would hold their soul in this world, preventing the dead from being at peace in the afterworld. In the mid-eleventh century the Japanese began to adopt the practice of creating portraits of the dead but these were drawn many years after their death and were not supposed to physically resemble the deceased (Miyajima 1996: 2, 5).

Later that century, the practice became more accepted. The first "portrait" of Prince Shōtoku (574–622) was produced in 1065, although the best-known portrait of this prince, with two child attendants, has not been authenticated as his portrait (Hayashi [1986] 1994: 577). During the Kamakura period (1185–1392), portraits of famous monks (Ōtsuka 2013: 168–76) started to appear. The thirteenth-century *Kouke Retsueizu* is a well-known national treasure, on which altogether 57 members of the Fujiwara clan, whose members were court nobility, are portrayed (Kyōto Kokuritsu Hakubutsukan 2012: 34–35, 208–9). Portraits of upper-class warriors began to appear in the fifteenth century, starting with that of Matsu'ura Yoroshi, the daimyō of Hizen (present-day Saga and Nagasaki prefectures) in 1438 (Miyajima 1994: 39, 260). However, portraits of the emperors met the greatest resistance (Miyajima 1994: 37–38). The first was the portrait of Emperor Toba, who died in 1156. The work was commissioned by Emperor Goshirakawa, his fourth son, and displayed in 1174, eighteen years after his death. In the well-known portrait of Emperor Godaigo (1318–1339), the emperor appears as a monk of an esoteric Buddhism (*mikkyō*) (Amino 1989: 184–85). In other words, in Japan the tradition of portraits met strenuous opposition and even after it was adopted the images were never to resemble the faces/figures they portray. The emperors were seldom portrayed and, when they were, it was never for the externalization of their power.

However, by Meiji, Japan had entered the international political arena, and pressure from outside to produce imperial photos intensified. Diplomatic protocol required the exchange of photos of the heads of nations.

Iwakura Tomomi, the Minister of the Right (*udaijin*), who traveled to the United States and other countries on diplomatic missions, needed to be able to do this. In early Meiji, some government officials were still unwilling to circulate images of emperors. In 1872, Thomas William Kinder, the former chief of the currency bureau in Hong Kong and the head of the Bureau of the Mint in Osaka (Ōmori [1984] 1996), suggested placing the emperor's face on Japanese currency, explaining that heads of states had been on coinage and currency ever since Greco-Roman times and that seeing the ruler's image would enhance his stature in the eyes of the people. Inoue Kaoru, the head of the Ministry of Finance, and Shibusawa Eiichi, the most famous industrialist and also an official at the Ministry of Finance, immediately saw Kinder's point. But the Ministry of State rejected the idea as blasphemous because the emperor's portrait would be defiled by being touched by ordinary people (Suzuki 1993: 22). Besides, the Japanese have regarded money as morally contaminating as well as physically dirty (Inose [1986] 1988: 443; Ohnuki-Tierney 1984: 28–29). Even today, people wash their hands after handling bills and coins. However, the idea of putting the emperor's image on currency did not die out. In 1878 the Ministry of Finance planned to hire Baron Raimund von Stillfried from Austria to undertake the task, without carefully checking his background, which included an episode in 1871 of secretly taking two photos of the emperor during his visit to the Yokohama dock in order to make money by selling copies. The negatives were confiscated by the government and the plan to hire him was canceled.

Since then, the government's official policy has been less than systematic. In 1874 a law was passed to prohibit the sale of photos of the emperor in Tokyo, although such sales were permitted in other regions. In 1878 another law prohibited the distribution of photos of the emperor except to foreigners. In 1880 a law was passed to punish behaviors irreverent to the emperor, empress, and crown prince, including disrespectful uses of their photos (for details of this history, see Inose [1986] 1988: esp. 472–76).

Emperor Meiji, who disliked being photographed, allowed three photos to be taken of him early in his reign. The first was taken in 1872, in which he appears in a Shinto priest's attire, without a mustache, and the second was taken in 1873, in which he wears a military uniform, fashioned after the French uniform, and sports a mustache and goatee (Inose [1986] 1988: 424–84). These photos were too old to use as the official photo and otherwise unsuitable, but the emperor kept refusing to have a new photo taken. Hijikata Hisamoto, the Minister of the Imperial Household, resolved the situation by commissioning Edoardo Chiossone to draw a portrait of the emperor. The Italian artist had been invited by the Ministry of Finance to help design the currency. A highly skilled portraitist, using Conté crayon on copper and stone plates, he was overjoyed by this honor. On January 14, 1888, in order to observe the emperor, Chiossone was invited to a dinner after the emperor's visit to the Yayoi Shrine. Although he was seated in the next room, he saw the "dragon face" (in the Chinese-derived iconography, the dragon symbolizes the emperor). He then borrowed the emperor's military uniform and had a photo taken of himself in the uniform in order to reproduce the details as faithfully as possible, but replacing his face with that of the emperor as he remembered it. The resulting portrait of the emperor drawn on a large copper plate belied the fact that Chiossone's own photo was the model. Many observers commented that the face and posture appeared European. However, officials in the imperial household were pleased to see the dignity and yet also compassion for the people shown on the emperor's face (Ōkurashō Insatsukyoku Kinenkan, ed., 1997: 7, 36, 52). Numerous photos of this portrait were taken, and the best was used as the "Emperor's Photo" (Inose [1986] 1988: 428–29; Keene 2002: 417; Sasaki 1984: 59; Suzuki 1993: 23).

The whole process of producing a fake photo was no secret, and is detailed in *Meiji Tennōki* (Chronicle of the Era of Emperor Meiji) (Kunaichō [1933] 1972: 7–8). Kurihara Hitora, the emperor's chamberlain, writes: "even though the drawing was well done, the photo that was 'sent down' was not a photo taken of the emperor; instead it was a photo of the drawing" (Kurihara 1953: 221). The photo of Chiossone himself in the emperor's military uniform and the official "honorable photo" created from it are often reproduced as a pair for comparison in Japanese publications (e.g., Ōkurashō Insatsukyoku Kinenkan, ed., 1997: 36; Sasaki 2001). Unlike the emperor, the empress was willing to have her photo taken and on June 14, 1889, two photographers produced her official photo (Kunaichō [1933] 1972: 287).

By the second decade of Meiji (1887–1896), unrest in the country was severe. Government officials decided that the people had become sufficiently aware of the existence of the emperor and, rather than take a chance, he could be replaced by a "photograph" (*goshin'ei* or *oshashin*) (Taki [1988] 1990: 82–83)—or rather, by a photograph of the portrait drawn by Chiossone (Suzuki 1993: 23). After 1889, the year the Constitution of Imperial Japan was promulgated, this substitute "photograph" of the emperor and a real photograph of the empress were "sent down" to the people in order to generate respect for the emperor as the sacred commander-in-chief. They were given to educational institutions that specifically requested them. This was an important means for the government to develop an emperor-centered society. School principals competed to submit requests for a copy in writing, composing them to express utmost respect for the emperor. Most public and private schools at all levels acquired a copy of the "honorable photo" of the emperor and the empress (Satō [1985] 1997; Taki [1988] 1990: 113–38; Yamamoto 2002), although the practice reached elementary schools only around 1897 (Inose [1986] 1988: 470). Maruyama Masao mentions Emil Lederer, who was teaching at the University of Tokyo and recorded with amazement how many school principals were burned to death trying to save the "emperor's photo" already in flames when their school buildings caught fire. Maruyama ([1961] 1993: 32) thinks that this was likely during the aftermath of the 1923 earthquake. Lederer's observation suggests that the emperor-centered ideology had been so successfully enforced that individuals in an official capacity, such as school principals, feared the consequences of failing to rescue the photo.

However, the "visualization of the emperor" did not take place by "sending down" the honorable photos. School principals' attitude notwithstanding, students and others never really saw these photos, which were housed in a small wooden structure in the form of a Shinto shrine; the doors were opened only during certain ceremonial times to "show" the emperor and the empress to the people. At schools the wooden structure was placed at the far end of the schoolyard or a hall where the students gathered. People who grew up during that time have told me that they never actually saw the images. For the folk, the emperor remained invisible. Thus, that his photo was a fake did not matter. Keene (2002: 586) points out that "not one statue of Meiji was ever erected, although sovereigns, such as Queen Victoria, his near contemporary, had no objection to being immortalized in stone or bronze." Only after his death was a bronze statue of Emperor Meiji made (Kurihara 1953: 225–26), with copies erected at several places, including at the site of his burial at Fushimi Momoyamaryō in Kyoto. These posthumous statues were not meant to display Emperor Meiji's power, but to inculcate the emperor-centered ideology using the legacy of Emperor Meiji, who was far better-liked and celebrated than either Emperors Taishō or Shōwa. Kushner (2006: 20) points out: "The influence that the Shōwa emperor exerted in wartime Japan cannot be completely discounted, but it must be placed in context. . . . Propagandists concentrated on the content of their propaganda, but the emperor rarely made an appearance in it." The practice of not publicly revealing the emperor's image has continued. Even today, "one rarely sees formal photographs of the emperor on display in public spaces" (Ruoff 2001: 131).

WOODBLOCK PRINTS (*UKIYO-E*)

Given that the Meiji "restoration" was extraordinary, events and activities related to Emperor Meiji became themes of commercially successful woodblock prints, reflecting growing interest in the emperor among the people. In a historical event in 1868 known as the "imperial journey to the east" (*tōkō*), the emperor and his entourage left Kyoto, where the Imperial Palace had been located since 794, to enter Edo Castle, which was built in 1457 and had been occupied by the shogunate for three hundred years. One well-known woodblock print commemorating this procession was created two months *before* it took place, demonstrating that these works of art were not meant to be realistic depictions of political events. Most important, the emperor is never visually represented. The phoenix on top of the imperial carriage and the elaborate procession became the predicates for the invisible emperor (Taki [1988] 1990: 19–26). In addition, the woodblock prints of the procession were never labeled as such, even though the convention of the genre is to identify scenes/events by name (Taki [1988] 1990: 95). The scene itself was supposed to enable the viewer to identify the event. Beginning around 1888, the emperor himself began to appear in woodblock prints (Taki [1988] 1990: 94), but he was shown only indirectly. For example, in scenes depicting the time when he was a young boy, an older man is depicted (Taki [1988] 1990: 11), whom the viewers are supposed to identify as the emperor, since the court ladies and others in attendance, identified by their names in the print, indicate who the figure is (Taki [1988] 1990: 95).

When the emperor and empress were depicted, their images were not meant to be portraits. The event in which they participated, rather than their imperial presence, was the motif. For example, in a woodblock print, *Imperial Viewing of the Chiarini Circus*, by Yōshū Chikanobu, created in 1886, the emperor and empress are on the left watching an acrobatic performance by this Italian circus troupe (Taki [1988] 1990: 97). A number of woodblock prints show the emperor watching a sumō match, but again, they were not portraits.

The absence or substitution of the emperor and empress was not entirely due to special treatment of them, however. In various forms of arts and literature, the convention of avoiding direct representation (*mitate*) led to the use of substitution and other techniques (Taki [1988] 1990: esp. 11, 15).[12] The resulting artworks are not meant to be realistic portrayals of events and people.

STAMPS AND CURRENCY

Following the example of the British government, which issued the world's first postage stamps in 1840, the Japanese government began issuing stamps in 1871 (Yamaguchi 1996). Instead of head portrait stamps, like those of the British monarchs and Hitler, no image of an emperor was ever imprinted on stamps or currency bills. Instead, the emperor system and its antiquity, as described in Article 1 of the constitution, were represented and presented, using imaginary scenes featuring legendary or historic figures central to the early development of the imperial system. Perhaps to emphasize its antiquity, the symbols chosen to represent the Japanese imperial system and the emperors were predominantly those introduced from China when its imperial system was adopted by the Japanese. The first stamps bore an image of a dragon, the Chinese symbol for the emperor. The design was changed the next year to cherry blossoms at the four corners, which continued to be used in a variety of ways, and the sixteen-petal chrysanthemum at the center or top center (Nihon Yūbinkitte Shōkyōdō Kumiai 2003: esp. 161–70). The chrysanthemum was originally introduced from China during the Nara period and was favored by aristocrats, including the imperial family, in the belief it promoted longevity. The sixteen-petal chrysanthemum officially became the imperial crest in 1889. After that every stamp, currency bill, and coin had to have it as part of the design.

The avoidance of direct representation of individual emperors was most evident on commemorative stamps. The first was issued in 1894 for the "silver wedding anniversary," a concept adopted from the West, of the Meiji emperor and the empress. It was a pair of stamps, one in red and the other in blue, and each very small (3×2 cm) with an identical design, male and female cranes on either side of a sixteen-petal chrysanthemum. The symbolism of cranes too came from China, where they, believed to be the only bird that could fly over the Himalayas, became a symbol of longevity and prosperity. In Japan, coupled with the tortoise, cranes became a symbol of longevity and marital harmony. Other stamp designs included mythical animals (*reijū*) introduced from China, the ritual headgear worn at the time of the enthronement ceremony, and the Shishinden, where the ceremony was held. Even for the current emperor, a stamp was issued with a phoenix for his accession to the throne and a kylin (Chinese mythical giraffe) to celebrate the twentieth anniversary of his reign. Furthermore, none of these stamps specifies which emperor it is meant to commemorate—all refer to the emperor without his name.[13]

With the rise of militarism, affirming the antiquity of the imperial system became of urgent necessity since the government decided that World War II must be fought in the name of the emperor. In 1940 a set of four stamps was issued to commemorate the mythical origin of the Japanese imperial system 2,600 years earlier (Naitō 2004: 78; Nihon Yūbinkitte Shōkyōdō Kumiai 2003: 6). One bears a picture of the Kashihara Shrine, where the accession to the throne by the legendary first emperor, Jinmu, supposedly took place, although the shrine was built only in 1889. Others represent scenes from the myth surrounding Jinmu.

The same avoidance of portraiture is observed on currency. The first currency note, designed by Chiossone, issued in 1872, bore the dragon and phoenix. The first bills to carry a portrait, issued in 1881–1883, showed the face of the legendary Empress Jingū Kōgō,[14] drawn by Chiossone, who made her look European (Nihon Kahei Shōkyōdō Kumiai [1967] 2003: 172–73; Ōhashi 1957: 18–19; Bonanza Henshūbu 1984: 151–54). She appeared on stamps in 1908, 1914, 1924, and 1937 (Nihon Yūbinkitte Shōkyōdō Kumiai 2003: esp. 165–67). In 1887, the government decreed that every bill must bear the sixteen-petal chrysanthemum, the imperial emblem, and one or another of seven approved legendary and historic figures, but no emperor.[15]

AUDITORY NON-EXTERNALIZATION

In sharp contrast to King George VI with his "king's speech," and unlike Hitler and other European dictators, the emperors of Japan had never publicly addressed the people. In 1872 Emperor Meiji read a decree to a small group of people when the first railroad opened. In 1921 Crown Prince Hirohito, *before* he became Emperor Shōwa, read an ordinance in front of 34,000 people gathered in Hibiya Park. During the time of Emperor Shōwa, the government added a number of public rituals supposedly meant for students, women, and the colonized—those previously excluded from his audience. However, the emperor never uttered a word (Hara 2002: 137–41).

When the radio became the major medium for the propagation of the imperial ideology, instead of his majesty's voice, the Japanese heard shouts of *banzai* by the people and announcements about the emperors by the state. In other words, the marching, waving of the rising-sun flags, and shouting of *banzai* were predicates for the absent emperor and the imperial system.

The non-externalization of the images and words of the emperor originated with the ancient ontology. Orikuchi Shinobu (Orikuchi [1937] 1976: 134–35; [1943] 1976; [1924] 1983; [1927] 1983) explains that a belief in the soul of words, *kotodama*, emerged shortly before the Nara period and became prevalent around the time of the *Man'yōshū*.[16] The power of *kotodama* is revealed with the utterance of words—the act called *kotoage* (word lifting), an incantation to invoke the deities and seek divine help. This releases the soul of the words. The *kotoage* must be done only when it is most appropriate, lest the power of the released soul bring calamity. H. Mack Horton (2012) exhaustively combs through the poems in the *Man'yōshū* and finds those in which *kotodama* (8 poems) and *kotoage* (10 poems) appear.

The belief in *kotodama* and *kotoage* is ultimately embedded in the ontology that Nishida Kitarō characterizes as "to see the form in the formless and to hear the voice in the inaudible" (Nishida 1965a: 6). He explains:

> Our directly immediate world, that is, the world in which the true "I" resides, is neither the world of objects nor the world of consciousness. We live in the world of action, broadly defined, or the world of expressions. We are historical persons in concrete terms. (Nishida 1965b: 265–66)

Although Nishida (1965a: 6) claims that this ontology is unique to Asia, as opposed to the West, Horton (2012: 272) reminds us how Ernst Cassirer, Walter J. Ong, and Roy Andrew Miller point to very similar beliefs in other cultures. In fact, Cassirer's statement that "Word and name do not designate and signify, they are an act. But the mythical-magical power of language is truly manifested in articulated sound" (Cassirer 1955: 40) is almost identical to Nishida's statement quoted above.

It is easy to dismiss the belief in the soul of words as an ancient shibboleth that has been long forgotten, but to the extent that the logic of the predicate still strongly governs the daily discourse of contemporary Japanese, which avoids pronouns, we might entertain the idea that spoken words are still to be treated with care, and therefore oratory, political or otherwise, has not been well developed in Japan. The absence of visual images of and political speech by the emperors should be seen in this context.

The People's Attitude toward the Emperor(s)

There has been a great deal of variation in the people's views of the emperor. For example, Kyoto was the seat of the emperors from 794 until 1868, and the old Imperial Palace still stands there. The accession ceremonies for all three modern emperors, Meiji, Taishō, and Shōwa, were held at the palace there, even after the capital was moved to Tokyo. Only the ceremony for the current emperor, Heisei, was held in Tokyo. People, especially those whose ancestors lived in Kyoto for generations, seem to be favorably aware of the emperors and the imperial system. Elsewhere, the political and intellectual elite who were close to the government, and their descendants, also have had a real sense of the emperors and the imperial system. For many other Japanese, the emperors have been remote figures, particularly because they were in the shadow of the warlords for centuries. But the Meiji "restoration" was such a big event that it aroused curiosity. A fisherman from Amakusa in Kyūshū, born in 1861, reported around the time of the Seinan conflict of 1877 that women in his village talked about what the emperor must look like and thought he must be like an aristocrat with a golden crown who appears in kyōgen (Irokawa [1970] 1997: 289, quoting from Tsurumi Shunsuke). "The Meiji people," as they, especially those in the Tokyo and Yokohama areas, identified themselves, were fond of Emperor Meiji and talked about his love of women of all ages.[17]

During the early Meiji, there was some proximity between the emperor and the people. At the beginning, some people were not in awe of the emperor. Suzuki Masayuki (1993: 21) quotes from the newspaper *Tōkyō Nichinichi Shinbun* that during an imperial tour women nursed their babies at the roadside and farmers sat on the ground, resting with their legs stretched out. During the grand ceremony for the opening of the railroad in 1872, E. W. Griffith observed with astonishment: "Four businessmen in ordinary clothes conversed with the Mikado [emperor] while standing, rather than in a prostrate position" (cited in Haga 2002: 114). Some in Tokyo must have had the idea that the emperor was powerless, as in an early woodblock print in which he is depicted as a little baby, whom the oligarchs, depicted in dignified outfits, are telling, "Stay there" (Minami 1967: 118), echoing the oligarchs' phrase for the emperor as "the crystal ball in the palm."

After the initial period of Meiji, the government imposed strict control over the people's attitude and behavior toward the emperor, as indicated by the aforementioned 1880 law prohibiting irreverence. It instructed the people to behave with utmost respect toward him, with their head down or in a prostrate position, which made it impossible for them to look at the emperor while he passed by (Inose [1986] 1988: 469; Suzuki 1993: 20). Ordinances like this to control the people's behavior and attitude toward the emperor made him a remote figure.

However, people's interest in and curiosity about how the emperor looked continued. The newly introduced photography promised commercial benefits, leading to the underground distribution of images of the emperor (Inose [1986] 1988: 476). Even the "honorable photos" of the emperor and the empress by Chiossone must have been circulated as postcards.[18] A well-known socialist, Kinoshita Naoe, observed the emperor's procession in Nagano Prefecture in 1880 as an elementary school student. A large number of people gathered. But, just as the emperor was passing by, the teacher told them to bow. The crowd, who could not see the emperor, then scrambled to pick up the gravel over which his carriage had run, believing that it would ensure the safety of their families and an abundant harvest (Inose [1986] 1988: 469–70). This episode seems to indicate that the people were indeed excited about the emperor and eager to have a glimpse of his face. Instead, they had to settle for gravel, which guaranteed only the safety of the family and the harvest— the role of the emperor before Meiji. In other words, as far as the people were concerned, the emperor remained invisible, or even more so than ever.

Most important, this incident clearly testifies that the emperor remained a magico-religious figure, even a shaman, who possessed the power to solicit supernatural power to guarantee all that ensured the people's welfare, including rice agriculture. But, his new role as the head of the state or the commander-in-chief was far from the people's thoughts.

There is no question that for the Japanese the emperor has always been an ordinary human being. As the government made no secret about the declining health of Emperor Taishō, the story began to circulate that he had rolled up an official document handed to him by his minister and used it as a telescope, whereupon the ministers replaced him with the crown prince (later the Shōwa emperor) for official duties. Even today, the Japanese refer to someone who is slow as Emperor Taishō. This would have been blasphemous had the emperor himself been considered sacred. Comments like this were not politically motivated nor circulated by liberals who opposed the emperor system; rather, they succinctly expressed the attitude of ordinary Japanese that emperors are human beings who become quasi-sacred by acquiring a special, though not almighty, power. In the only existing film of the funeral in 1926 for the Taishō emperor, housed at the Albert Kahn Museum in Paris, people are lined up for the procession, but no one is in a prostrate position and all wear ordinary clothes and watch the carriage go by seemingly without awe and even without sadness.

Political Implications of the Emperor as a Zero Signifier

The Meiji state was not consistent in its presentation/representation of the emperor. Nonetheless, in the official representation, he remained a zero signifier. From the perspective of the polity, this begs an intriguing question of the political leader's effectiveness or its absence. The following account from the World War II era offers some insight into this question.

Arishima Takeo, a well-known novelist, recalled the day during World War II when he entered the military, which he called a prison. He kept questioning in his mind what was the nation (*kokka*) and identified it as *mu* (nothingness). He declared that it was this nothingness whose orders he was forced to follow (cited in Maruyama [1961] 1993: 105). In other words, for the people, including soldiers, there was no commanding figure like Hitler, only the imageless and inaudible emperor. In his diary entry for March 4, 1942, one of the *tokkōtai* pilots, Sasaki Hachirō (Ohnuki-Tierney 2006a: 63–64), wrote about a small spider that crawled on his book as he sat reading on the banks of the Tama River. Out of mischief, he put his cigarette in front of, near, and above it, as the spider kept fleeing from the heat. Not understanding where the heat came from, after a while the spider curled up its legs and stopped moving, even though it was not burnt. Sasaki realized that the Japanese were just like the spider, unable to understand what was going on and seeking a way out of the impossible situation caused by the war, represented by the small space of the page of the book.

In 1946, Maruyama (1946: 2) famously used the metaphor of innumerable layers of an *invisible* net over the people, that is, the ideology of Japan's ultranationalism. Elsewhere Maruyama ([1961] 1993: 126–29) elaborated on the importance of image creation and the power of the image in our conceptualization of, for example, who Nehru was and what he stood for, although he did not link this observation to the invisible and inaudible emperor. Irokawa states: "As a spiritual structure, the emperor system is a huge, invisible dark box. The Japanese, both the intellectuals and the masses, unknowingly entered this box in which one cannot see the four corners, and met their death without being able to learn why they had to go through such tribulations" (Irokawa [1970] 1997: 281). Irokawa's dark box is Marx's camera obscura, which creates optical inversion, that is, ideological distortion.

Through extensive interviews with the Japanese who lived during World War II, Cook and Cook (1992: 16) found that even though the Japanese in general presumably fought "for the emperor," very few mentioned the emperor when they explained their experience. That the Japanese were forced to fight for "nothingness," the "dark box," or the "layers of an invisible net," had important implications even for the aftermath of the war. The Germans were able to come to terms with their wartime behavior by locating their guilt in Hitler and the Nazis, even though many admit their collective responsibility, especially for anti-Semitism. For the Japanese, it was far more difficult to identify and isolate the guilty. Tōjō Hideki was removed from the office of prime minister *before* the war ended, without bloodshed. But it was the American occupational forces, not the Japanese themselves, who decided the emperor was not guilty of war crimes and retained the emperor system. Enormous and lasting controversy ensued over the war responsibility of the Shōwa emperor as well as the retention of the emperor system, although it abated with the passing of the years and the death of the emperor.

Conclusion

After centuries during which the warlords had been the warrior-cum-political head of the country and the emperor had held symbolic power over the growth of rice, the Meiji constitution of 1889 defined the emperor in terms of the non-externalizable imperial soul and endowed him with divinity. Yet, within the same constitution, he was nominally assigned a human role as a politician and military commander, which nonetheless gave him no actual power. The government ordered people to revere the emperor as divine when Japanese religiosity precludes the concept of a supreme being. In the absence of any realistic visual image of the emperor, whether the "honorable photo" offered for veneration was a fake or not was of little importance. The photo was not really seen by the people at any rate. We can interpret the refusal by the oligarchs to have the emperor fully seen or heard by the people as in fact "part of the construction and maintenance of his ontological difference on the part of prewar Japanese social discourse" (Orbaugh 2007: 407). That is, the state removed all the means necessary for the emperor to be a political leader and retained his religious identity as a *kami* (deity) in the pantheon, or, in fact a shaman, adding his role as a military leader only in name.

The Meiji oligarchs wished to establish and strengthen the emperor system by including its structure in the Constitution of Imperial Japan, even against the counsel of their foreign advisors. However, only the symbols of the emperor *system* were externalized as visual images and through celebratory ceremonies. The presentation of the individual emperor did not suit their political agenda. Whereas the state made a strenuous effort to prevent the externalization of the emperor's "body natural," that is, the individual emperor, it strove to build up the "body politic," the emperor system. The creation of the myth that the emperor system had existed for the past 2,600 years was central in this project.

The imperial system was represented by symbols: for example, the sixteen-petal chrysanthemum (the imperial emblem), the phoenix (a symbol of the emperor, adopted from China), and various other objects representing the beginning of the emperor system 2,600 years earlier. Other symbols, such as the rising sun, Mount Fuji, and cherry blossoms, had long represented Japan as a whole.

The official construction and presentation of the emperor and the emperor system notwithstanding, the state continued to reveal its true understanding of the emperor as human—the view shared by the people. This became transparent in the statement issued in regard to the health of Emperor Taishō. As for the people, they too continued to regard him as a human, but with a special power to ensure people's welfare—health and a good harvest—just as the emperor had done as a shaman in ancient Japan.

The Meiji state was trapped in a cultural tradition, while facing an urgent need to modernize and counter the threat of the West. It attempted to strengthen Japan by resurrecting the imaginary ancient emperor system and identifying the emperor as the imperial soul, making him even harder to externalize. Yet his formal role as commander-in-chief, a shadow military/political leader, prevented the emergence of real political and military leaders. The oligarchs constructed the utterly archaic emperor system at a time when the wheels of modernization were turning rapidly worldwide but especially in Japan, which did manage to modernize and militarize itself with remarkable success.

The fatal trap between tradition and modernization is succinctly symbolized in Japan's military failure. Although Japan produced Zero fighter planes early in the war and knew that the war would be fought in the air, it expended enormous financial and psychological energy in building the battleship *Yamato*, precisely because the Japanese navy destroyed the Russian battleships during the Russo-Japanese War, thereby becoming the first Asian nation to defeat a Western nation. This pride of the Japanese navy sank to the bottom of the sea, together with more than three thousand men trapped in it, without achieving a single military success (Suzuki [1987] 1995). In a statement on wars in general, Steven Weinberg (2009) points out that they have been fought with major strategic errors and anachronistic war machinery, and people continue to live with "military illusions," such as wrongly assigning power to nuclear weapons that cannot be used for strategic purposes, but only for destroying cities and large numbers of people. Japan during the military period offers a superb example of such an illusion.

SEVEN

(Non-)Externalization of Religious and Political Authority/Power

A Cross-Cultural Perspective

This last chapter of the book is a counterpoint to the preceding chapter on the Japanese emperor as a visual and auditory zero signifier. This chapter focuses on the problem of religious and political authority and power and their relationship to the perceptual, especially visual and auditory externalization in a broader theoretical and ethnographic/historical context.[1] Put concretely, is externalization necessary for political leaders to exercise power? Is it also required by religious leaders? The ultimate goal is to probe the relationship between externalization or its absence in creating communicative opacity.

I begin with a brief discussion of religions and proceed to European monarchs and dictators for comparisons. Since the focus of this chapter is externalization and its absence in religions and politics, I narrowly focus on the issue of images and speeches, and their absence, in relation to the externalization of political and religious authority and power.

There has been a long tradition of representing the imperceptible, such as love, the soul, and the mind, with externalized symbols. Alessandro Nova's question, "Can one figuratively represent what one does not see?" (Nova 2011: 195), led him to many examples of artistic representations of the wind, starting with Sandro Botticelli's *The Birth of Venus*, in which the effects of the wind are portrayed through the clothes blowing in the breeze. Philippe Descola (2010) shows a vast range of modes of visual externalization across cultures. For example, a combination of a human face, expressing the subjectivity common to most beings, with an animal face, marking its identity as a species, represents the inner being of animals among the Yupiit of Alaska (Descola 2010: 61). In pointillist paintings by the aborigines of the central desert of Australia, totemic beings in Dreamtime are represented only by the imprints they left in the landscape during their journey (Descola 2010: 139). Similarly, in his *After the Fact* Geertz stresses that we get to know facts, meanings, and patterns after they have occurred, just as an Indian sage declares that "An elephant *was* here" only after the elephant has left (Geertz 1995: 167).

I wish to further explore the issue of externalization by examining how religious and political authority and power are externalized or not externalized.

Religious Authority/Power and Its (Non-)Representations

Throughout history and in various societies, from Rome to medieval Japan, religious leaders sought and acquired political power.[2] Conversely, the most powerful political leaders have sought religious power to buttress and/or enhance their political position, which alone did not accrue enough power from their perspective. Some political leaders have attempted their own apotheosis, seeking to elevate themselves to the status of a deity—a phenomenon labeled "divine kingship" in anthropology. Originally developed by James G. Frazer ([1890, 1911–1915] 1963: 15), this concept was elaborated by A. M. Hocart ([1927] 1969; [1936] 1970) and remains a perennial interest, with neo-Frazerians, neo-Hocartians, and neo-Dumontians all contributing to the debate.[3] Frazer focused on political leaders who were also priests and in some cases were considered gods. His examples include many societies, past and present: the "early Babylonian kings . . . claimed to be gods in their lifetime"; "the kings of Egypt were deified in their lifetime" and were "identified with the great sun-god Ra"; Egyptians believed that "every pharaoh was the embodiment of the god Horus" (Frazer [1890, 1911–1915] 1963: 417–19). Nina Tumarkin (1997: 1) points out that the apotheosis of political leaders originated in Egypt and was brought to the Hellenistic world by Alexander the Great. In 79 CE, the Roman emperor Vespasian proclaimed on his deathbed that he was becoming a god. Likewise, Simon Price considers that the apotheosis of Roman emperors holds the key to understanding their power; the deification of Julius Caesar was a crucial development, providing a partial model for later imperial deification (Price 1987: 56, 71, respectively). All these deified political leaders were spectacularly externalized, though often posthumously.[4]

The problem of externalization of religious figures and powers has long been the subject of academic debate. Birgit Meyer and Dick Houtman (2012: 8) call for not simply moving from "dematerialization to rematerialization" but engaging in a "reflexive endeavor that rescripts the meaning of materiality itself." Meyer (2008) calls attention to the enormous emphasis placed on the power of pictures in contemporary popular Christian aesthetics in southern Ghana.

Let me first point out that non-externalization is a deliberate act of the negation of externalization and thus it is the other side of the coin of externalization, rather than its absence. Martin Jay ([1993] 1994: 21–82) observes that Christianity had a long "visionary tradition" that stressed the importance of "an unmediated vision of the divine without the interference of textuality." "Idolatrous ocularcentrism" dominated medieval Christianity, elevating vision to the "noblest of the senses." Following her abiding interest in the meaning of corporeality, in *Christian Materiality*, Caroline Walker Bynum (2011) points to the importance of images of relics in late medieval Europe.

The Reformation was in part a struggle against visuality. John Calvin expressed "virulent hostility" to visual representations and urged a "return to the literal word of Scripture." The "iconophobic impulse of the Reformation" intensified in England and reached its peak when the Puritans smashed images of all kinds and rejected elaborate rituals (Jay [1993] 1994: 42–43), which Jay ([1993] 1994: 211–62) identifies as "the disenchantment of the eye," suggesting a decline of the power of visuality. For Bruno Latour (2002: 1–3), the basic issue of "iconoclash" was that "we are digging for the origin of an absolute—not a relative—distinction between truth and falsity, between a pure world, absolutely emptied of human-made intermediaries and a disgusting world composed of impure but fascinating human-made mediators. 'If only, some say, we could do *without* any image. How so much better, purer, faster our access to God, Nature, to Truth, to Science could be.'" The very fact of the *struggle* over relics, statues of Jesus, the Virgin Mary, and various saints as well as controversies over "sacrament" all reveal how central the visual representation of religious power has been to Christian beliefs and practices.

Nonetheless, scholars have often noted that the most powerful divinity recedes into the void and may not be externalized. In his meticulously researched book on the history of the eternal in art, François Bœspflug (2008) details the history of what was and was not permissible under the church's authority to depict in art, God being "transcendant et irreprésentable," one or all of the Three Persons of Godhead. Most striking about Christianity in all its variants is that God has remained beyond the ocular sphere. Jesus, Mary, and the saints are made visible and mediate between humans and the invisible God. As James Billington puts it:

> Since the Trinity was a mystery beyond man's power to visualize, it was represented only in its symbolic or anticipatory form of the three angels' appearance to Sarah and Abraham in the Old Testament. God the Father was never depicted, for no man had ever seen Him face to face. The Holy Spirit was also not represented in early iconography; and when the symbol of a white dove later entered from the West, pigeons came to be regarded as forbidden food and objects of reverence. (Billington [1966] 1970: 30)

Expressions such as "God's voice" or "a call from God" remain figurative. They are utterances without sound, suggesting that auditory non-externalization has also been important in conceptualizing God.

The strong negative reactions in Germany to the invention of the daguerreotype demonstrate the importance of the taboo against externalization of God. The *Leipziger Stadtanzeiger* (Leipzig City Advertiser) strongly expressed its opposition to this "black art from France": "To try to capture fleeing mirror images . . . is not just an impossible undertaking . . . ; the very wish to do such a thing is blasphemous. Man is made in the image of God, and God's image cannot be captured by any machine of human devising" (quoted in Benjamin [1931] 1998: 241). Walter Benjamin calls this view a "ludicrous stereotype" and refers to the *Leipziger Stadtanzeiger* as a chauvinistic rag.

In modern times, the Catholic Church of Mussolini's Italy and the Russian Orthodox Church of Lenin and Stalin's USSR continued to regard sacramental objects as of utmost importance. In Germany, Protestants had abolished statues and other forms of religious externalization, though the image of Christ was not altogether banished. And a third of the population was Catholic during the Nazi regime—the period of my study of the objectification of political power.

In Judaism, God was at first a friend, ruler, and commander-in-chief, and his mighty acts were seen and acclaimed. He then receded "into the vague and magnetic invisibility of an imageless existence, of a voice, if that, from the still silence of a euphemism," and the name written in the Hebrew text became "utterly forbidden to pronounce," according to Richard Jacobson (1978: 138; cf. de Certeau [1975] 1988: 339–42). Any visual representation became a violation of the Second Commandment's prohibition of making graven images. Worshippers are allowed to speak of God only by alluding to the unpronounceable, ineffable "name." The theological explanation is that "God is greater than anything one can imagine" and *ayin*, the concept of "nothingness," implies "the God beyond God, the power that is closer and further than what we call 'God'" and symbolizes "the fullness of being that transcends being itself" (Matt ([1990] 1995: 67, 93, respectively). Jacobson explains that "the plenitude of Absence replaced the (imaginary?) memory of a divine Presence, when God was replaced by Text" and that the "history of the Holy of Holies is a history of an accretion of absence" (Jacobson 1978: 138, 146).

Non-externalization of God in Judaism is neither innate nor a natural development that occurred over time. Instead, as Jacobson shows, it was the result of a series of historical changes. First, the division between priest and prophet was established; then prophecy came to an end because its intermittency and uncertainty made it less effective than the fixed and certain written word (Jacobson 1978: 140). The written text changed sometime between the completion of the books of Kings (c. 560 BCE) and Chronicles (c. 300 BCE), from a single book, which scholars call "Urdeuteronomium," to five books, the Pentateuch (Jacobson 1978: 140). The first lethal blow to prophecy took place right after the promulgation of Deuteronomy in the Pentateuch as the book of the Law of Moses (Jacobson 1978: 140). R. J. Zwi Werblowsky offers valuable insight into the matter of a receding God:

> The war against magic [was] waged, in certain religions, by prophets and theologians bent on purifying what they considered the pure gold of religions from what they considered the dross of superstition. It was not so much the atheists who denounced religion for its anthropological language, imagery, and conceptual apparatus. It was the theological philosophers who struggled with this problem to the point of denying to god all positive attributes, questioning the appropriateness of even such terms as "being" and "existence" (since these concepts too are derived from our human experience), seeking possible solutions in a *theologia negativa* or even in mystical idiom in which Absolute Being is equated with Absolute Nothingness (or Emptiness) and god is the Great Nothing. (Werblowsky 1985: 5)

Indeed, the development was historical, with theological philosophers acting as agents in a real historical context when they were forced to further articulate their religion in encounters with "pagans." Following Yehezkel Kauffmann, S. J. Tambiah (1990: 6) explains the monotheistic worship of YHWH: "YHWH was Israel's 'living God' as opposed to the pagan gods who were worshipped in the form of images, constructed out of wood and stone by man."

Islam, which spread widely from Arabia after the seventh century, was stricter than Christianity about the enforcement of the ban on images, both sacred and secular (Goody 1993: 101). Through all the historical changes it has undergone (Graham 1983: 54–55), Islam has remained characterized by the affirmation of the "One God" and by its "aniconic character," with a "Spartan austerity" in its "symbolic economy" (Graham 1983: 70, 69; see also Goody 1993: 101–19; Noyes 2013: 59–92, 165–78). In other words, God is represented by neither an auditory nor a visual signifier, but by a zero signifier, although Silvia Naef (1996, 2004) points to the multiplication of images during the modern period.

The taboo against externalization of a powerful deity is not confined to monotheistic religions, but is found in many other religions as well. For example, although iconographic representations of Hindu deities, *avatar*, are well known, A. David Napier calls attention to the representations of the void: "The empty frame, standing for all that is possible and impossible, represents for certain Hindus the Goddess as Supreme Void, a void that is specified by the frame that marks it out" (1992: xv). In the caption for a photo of *The Goddess as Void*, a bronze found in Rajasthan c. 1900, Napier writes: "an anthropomorphic frame defines the symbolic context in which the totality of the image is represented by its absence" (1992: xiv). The frame has the hands, ears, and head and becomes the predicate of the void within.

The supreme deity as a zero signifier is not confined to the so-called great religions. The Ainu of southern Sakhalin have a taboo against externalization of the sacred. The most powerful deity is the bear, whose home is the mountains. The bear allows the Ainu to capture it, making a "gift of self" in order to provide the people with its meat, their most cherished food. The ritual starts with a hunter capturing a bear cub, either in a den he dares to enter or when the mother and cubs come out of the den in early spring. After raising the cub, called the deity-grandchild, for a year and a half, the community holds a ritual during which they feast on the bear meat. Although it has been interpreted only in religious terms, it is the most important political ritual of the Ainu, as pointed out by Bronisław Piłsudski (1915). People from other settlements are invited, and the host shows his political power through the display of offerings to the Bear Deity. The bear is sent back to the mountains, releasing the soul from the body so that it can travel to its home, with presents from the Ainu—return gifts for the meat the Bear Deity offered. The head and skin are taken to a sacred place in the mountains by the elders (Ohnuki-Tierney 1974: 90–96; 1981a: 76, 84–85; Piłsudski 1915), following the Ainu taboo against externalized representations of the deity.

Given the taboo against the externalization of important deities, the use of bearskins or making carved bears is strictly prohibited (Ohnuki-Tierney 1974: 36–38).[5] The taboo against auditory externalization allows the Ainu to address the bear only as *kamui* (a general term for "deity") or "grandfather" in their prayers and "grandchild" in reference to the bear they raise from a cub (Ohnuki-Tierney 1981a: 83; Piłsudski 1915), although they can refer to it as Iso Kamui (the bear deity). Likewise, the extreme sacredness of the two most powerful sea deities, Čepehte Kamuy and Čōhaykuh, requires that no one—especially women, who are barred from fishing at all times—utter their name above a whisper. When referring to either of the deities, remarks must be prefaced by the address "the deity-elder offshore" (*Poporo un kamuy henke utah*) (Ohnuki-Tierney 1974: 101–2). This practice extends to powerful elders, for whom Ainu use teknonymy, a form of address whereby male elders are referred to as someone's grandfather without using his name.

Political Leaders and Their Externalization: Images and Speeches

As Jean-Jacques Rousseau ([1762, 1755] 1967: 10) long ago pointed out, "The strongest man is never strong enough to be always master, unless he transforms his power into right, and obedience into duty." Duty must be converted into willing participation in the ruler's scheme. In this process, various representations of power are deployed: symbols, monuments, and rituals, including parades. Monarchs as political leaders strove for the externalization of their power. This has been even more important for modern political leaders, without divine power and body politic to fortify their position.

For an understanding of the externalization of political authority and power, the following institutional distinctions are useful. First, the well-known analytical tool of the "king's two bodies" by Ernst H. Kantorowicz ([1957] 1981) provides a useful heuristic device. In his scheme, the "Body natural" of an individual monarch or emperor is distinct from the "Body politic," the monarchical institution, for example, which transcends individual monarchs whose authority and power are terminated upon their death, abdication, or usurpation. The body politic guarantees the institution's legitimacy and continuation, regardless of the passing of individual monarchs and emperors. Second, a similar distinction must be made between the state, a regime, and a ruler. Young (1994: 41) puts this incisively: "The ruler's position is inherently precarious; one may assassinate a ruler, but not a state or even a regime." As a consequence, the ruler must strive to maintain his/her power through the externalization/display of it. We will see that this applies also to monarchs, even with their institutional backing.

MONARCHS

In medieval Europe, kings and queens were a conduit for divine power in the world, as is documented in the magisterial work on medieval political theology by Ernst Kantorowicz. He quotes John of Paris: "The royal power is from God" ([1957] 1981: 330). Since "dieu fait les rois" (God makes kings), the king receives special power; for example, English and French monarchs from the early Middle Ages were given the divine power of healing (Bloch [1961] 1989). Joseph-Marie de Maistre, whom Isaiah Berlin ([1959] 1992: 96) characterizes as "ultra-modern" instead of a "fanatical monarchist" as in the standard portrait of him, suggests that each form of sovereignty is "the immediate result of the will of the Creator" (Dieu qui est l'auteur de la souveraineté) (de Maistre [1870] 1996: 57; Latin in de Maistre 1821, quoted in Berlin [1959] 1992: 118). Sovereigns manifested the sacred power from God in various ways, but they were strictly secular political leaders whose power had to be acquired and protected from enemies and rivals through war, leading to the warrior-king tradition, epitomized in the Wars of the Roses (1455–1487) between the House of Lancaster and the House of York.

Some historians of Spain point out the non-divine nature of Spanish monarchs. John Elliott emphasizes that Spanish monarchs in the Middle Ages did not possess powers of healing bestowed by God. There had been no coronation ceremony in Castile since 1379, and at the end of the sixteenth century the kings in Spain had "no official throne, no scepter, no crown" (Elliott 1985: 148–50). T. F. Ruiz (1985: 128–33), in his article "Unsacred Monarchy," emphasizes that Alfonso XI (1312–1350) declared that kings do not have the power to heal and that the law—both Visigothic *Fuero juzgo* and the Roman-inspired *Partidas*—opposed the idea of sacral kingship. Indeed, Visigothic law opened kingship to anyone of Gothic blood and good character. Ruiz underscores the warrior-king tradition in the Spanish monarchy and concludes that "the crudest and ultimate manifestation of individual power" is in "personal acts of *violence*" (1985: 132, emphasis added).

The complexity of religion and polity in reference to externalization is strikingly shown in the British coronation ceremony during which the next king/queen is anointed by the Archbishop of Canterbury with consecrated oil. This segment of the ceremony is considered sacred and, concealed with a canopy, not to be seen by the public or photographed, let alone televised. It is the crucial moment when religious power confers political power and transforms the "candidate" into the sovereign of the United Kingdom. There is a parallel in the Japanese emperor's accession ceremony—the very moment when the new emperor-to-be receives the imperial soul from the previous, deceased emperor is kept invisible in a secret and solitary ritual (Ohnuki-Tierney 2002b; 2005).

A sharp distinction between the British monarch and the Japanese emperor is that the British monarch, once he or she is transformed into a political figure, his/her image has been of crucial importance to the public, especially since the advent of photography—in portraits and on stamps, coins, bills, and so on. In contrast, the Japanese emperor has remained either completely or partly invisible.

Nonetheless, it seems safe to conclude that European monarchies shared several salient features in common. Although supported by their institutional body, European monarchs had to externalize their power for their political purposes, since they were chosen by God but never were God himself. They were by necessity warrior-kings. Some, such as Philip IV of Spain or Louis XIV of France, introduced below, strove for the visual externalization of themselves with as much intensity as dictators in later history.

MODERN DICTATORS

In contrast to monarchs, dictators in modern times have had no recourse to institutional authority. Nor do they receive divine power from their god, let alone being divine themselves. Yet they have sought and acquired enormous power in politics and beyond. They have had to individually seize power and maintain it, for which blatant externalization is a prerequisite. Thus, in regard to the externalization of power, there is no difference between political leaders with an institutional tradition and those without; monarchs as well as dictators must strive for an intense display of power, with their assumption, wrongly, that their messages are understood by their subjects.

Before the Bolshevik Revolution, the tsar was the "living icon of God, just as the whole Orthodox Empire" was the "icon of the heavenly world" (Billington [1966] 1970: 35). After the revolution, a "political religion" was established around the figure of Lenin following his death. Pictures of Lenin in the "red corner" of public spaces replaced icons of Christ and the Virgin (Billington [1966] 1970: 36), demonstrating the effectiveness of the adoption of Christian symbolism by the Communist regime. Lenin was portrayed as a martyr to the cause of the proletariat and his death likened to Christ's sacrifice for the redemption of humanity. At Lenin's funeral, palm branches, symbolizing Christ's resurrection, filled the Hall of Columns and eulogies invoked Christ (Tumarkin 1997: 84, 139, 167). This tradition was not only kept but intensified by Stalin, who became a familiar part of public life in the Soviet Union during the late 1930s (Bonnell 1997: 157–58).

In Nazi Germany, Hitler's official stance was a complete divorce from religion. Two-thirds of the Germans were Protestant, espousing a text-based faith that opposed visual representations of the sacred in statues and icons. Yet, as George Mosse richly describes it, the "political cult" of Nazi Germany made extensive use of "public festivals" in which German pietism was fused with Christian love and brotherhood. Christian liturgy was combined with Nazi political rituals (Mosse 1975: 74–81; see also Gajek 1990: 3). Equating Hitler with Germany made him the father of the *Volk* and, by extension, God the Father. The Nazis regularly used Christology to elevate Hitler, most spectacularly in the Nuremburg rallies. As effectively shown at the beginning of the film *The Triumph of the Will*, Hitler descends from heaven through clouds. A well-known poster, likely from the 1930s, depicts Hitler with an eagle hovering over him and the light of heaven in the background, which clearly alludes to Christ being baptized by John the Baptist as a dove descends. Written at the bottom is "Es lebe Deutschland!" (Bytwerk 2007a: no. 10).

In Italy, Mussolini emphasized that Christ was his protector and God looked after his actions (Falasca-Zamponi 1997: 65). He even proposed to decorate his planned palace with an enormous bas-relief of Pius XI, with himself kneeling before the Virgin, while creating "the liturgy of collective harmony" (Gentile 1996: 126, 80, respectively).

These examples led to scholarly debates about whether this phenomenon should be understood as some sort of religion. Following the concept of "civil religion," proposed by Jean-Jacques Rousseau ([1762, 1755] 1967: 136–47), the label "political religion" has been used by many scholars, while others prefer "secular religion" and "civic religion" (Billington [1966] 1970: 35–37; Gentile 1996; Kolakowski 2006; Linz 2000; Service 2007), in an attempt to view the phenomenon as a replacement for the traditional established religions in response to modernity and secularization. For Stanley Payne (2005: 163), it is the "politicization of traditional religions" rather than "political religion." These dictators' political uses of religions and the regimes' attempts at apotheosis of the leaders were intended to muster more power than the polity usually confers. Hocart's well-known statement is apposite here: "In turning from the chaos of beliefs and acts to absolutism, modern Europe is merely repeating the experience of imperial Rome, which welcomed back the firm divinity of emperors as better than the quicksands of party politics" (Hocart [1936] 1970: 101). According to Geertz ([1977] 1983: 143), "a world wholly demystified is a world wholly depoliticized. . . . The 'political theology' . . . of the twentieth century has not been written, though there have been glancing efforts here and there. But it exists. . . . The extraordinary has not gone out of modern politics, however much of the banal may have entered; power not only still intoxicates, it still exalts."

Political Speeches   Auditory externalization of power in the form of political leaders' speeches became especially important when modern technology allowed for their dissemination by radio, movies, records, and, much later, television. Hitler's oratory resounds even today in the ears of those who lived through the Nazi period, as loudly as the goose-stepping of the Reichswehr and Wehrmacht. In his diaries, Joseph Goebbels, the propaganda minister, uses the phrase "The Führer Hitler as an Orator" (1973). The purpose of the German government's distribution of the radio called the "people's receiver" was to broadcast Hitler's speeches, rather than the declared reason. Mussolini delivered speeches from the balcony of Palazzo Venezia to large audiences assembled in the piazza (Falasca-Zamponi 1997: 84–85, 97). Both dictators used oratory as a crucial means to reach people and imprint their power and ideology in the public mind.

Visual Images   In a study of political leaders from antiquity to Bill Clinton, Sergio Bertelli writes: "In strongly autocratic societies, leadership requires the visibility and physical presence of a prophet. In order to appear clearly, his charisma requires particular signs typical of himself that make him immediately and physically identifiable" (2001: xvi–xvii). The most expedient way to externalize the ruler's power is to use his/her own image. A long roster of leaders who deployed ostentatious reproductions of their image likely starts with Ramses II (1279–1213 BCE) of Egypt, with four seated statues at Abu Simbel objectifying the pharaoh's power. The first practice of placing the ruler's head on coins is usually attributed to Darius I (522–486 BCE) of Persia, followed by the Persian satrap Mazaeus (331–328 BCE), although Albert Bosworth (1996: 59) points to the repeated use of this practice under Alexander of Macedon (356–323 BCE; see also Smith 1989: 38). Michael H. Crawford (1996: 360) traces its origin to Julius Caesar (100–44 BCE).[6]

The images of deceased heads of the state are often used on currency. For example, Lenin and Mao appeared posthumously on Russian and Chinese bills respectively, just as the images of only presidents long gone appear on the bills and stamps of the United States. In these cases, the images represent a form of veneration of past great leaders, who are considered to symbolize the greatness of the state. On the other hand, in other instances images of the living head of state appear, as with the British, who place the images of their reigning kings and queens on their currency and stamps. The images of the leader may be accompanied by a symbol of the monarchy, such as a crown, or of the regime, such as a swastika.

Even before the birth of mass media, some monarchs strove to propagandize their power. Holy Roman emperor Maximilian I (1459–1519) deployed a carefully crafted and controlled public persona in both text and image (Silver 2008), as did Philip IV (r. 1621–1665) of Spain (Burke [1992] 1999: 180–81). Elliott (1958: 171) contends that the propaganda executed by Olivares for Philip IV was the model that Louis XIV (1658–1715) adopted and developed, although conventional wisdom has it that it was Louis XIV who established the protocol for glorifying the political power of the ruler in grand ceremonies. According to Peter Burke ([1992] 1999: 15–37), tapestries, medals, and printed texts, rituals, buildings, state portraits, and freestanding statues were means of impression management that Louis XIV promoted with extraordinary intensity. Three hundred portraits and seven hundred different engravings of the king survive. Twenty statues of the king on horseback were commissioned for public squares in Paris.

As detailed in the preceding chapter, the Bolshevik Revolution gave a jump-start to the modern political propaganda machinery that was fully deployed by succeeding regimes. The use of the leader's image in propaganda started after the death of Lenin, who did not seek public adoration. Posthumously Lenin became the central figure in the cult of *Vozhd*, the great leader of the proletariat. The Italian fascists used *Il Duce*, and the Nazis' *Führer* (leader) followed the model of *Vozhd* (Smith 1989: 122). Lenin's head appeared on 500- and 1,000-ruble notes, and both Lenin and Stalin appeared on stamps (Smith 1989: 194) and in a large number of visual arts (Plamper 2001). Postage stamps and currency were not major media for the Soviets, however.

Despite Hitler's denunciation of the cult of personality, a large number of "Hitler-head stamps" appeared, with various photos of Hitler's face in different poses, some with a cap and others without, in different colors and denominations. After the Nazis seized power, a new Hitler stamp was issued each year on April 20 to commemorate his birthday (Welch 2007: Scott B271) (see Figure 17). In order to represent him as the "father of the people," a stamp with Hitler receiving a bouquet from a little girl was issued in 1940 (Welch 2007: Scott #170). Stamps were an important venue for propaganda, with 334 different themes represented in stamps issued from April 12, 1933, to April 10, 1945 (Lauritzen 1988: 62). Designs symbolized, for example: modernity (the Volkswagen; autobahns; planes; industrial workers); agriculture (wheat stalks with ripe grains on both sides of the Roman eagle and agricultural workers); and primordiality (the Alps; the Roman eagle to claim Roman ancestry). Germany relied much less on posters than the Soviets did, and no statue of Hitler was erected. The dominant motifs on coins and currency were the swastika and the Roman eagle, rather than Hitler himself.

In fascist Italy, a blatant visualization of Mussolini is described by Simonetta Falasca-Zamponi: "Publicity made visible what used to be invisible; it also created an audience. In this process Mussolini attracted more attention. Visibility, appearance, and performance magnified Mussolini's personality and interest in his person grew." Il Duce made abundant use of postcards, in which he "appeared in different attire, postures, contexts and situations" (Falasca-Zamponi 1997: 49). He even flaunted his bare chest in a skiing pose without skis on his feet (Falasca-Zamponi 1997: 74). Maria Di Bella (2004: 42–43) tells us how Il Duce transformed himself into a marble statue which was then conveyed to the people through massive drawings and paintings.

The externalization of the leader's power through representations of his image continued after World War II. In addition to the well-known examples of the People's Republic of China and North Korea, practitioners include Jean-Bédel Bokassa, the "Emperor of the Central African Republic" from 1976 to 1979, and Saparmurat Niyazov, the first president of Turkmenistan, often dubbed by the foreign media a "totalitarian and repressive dictator." Obsessed with the objectification of his power, Niyazov erected an infamous gold-plated statue of himself atop the Neutrality Arch; the statue rotates 360 degrees every 24 hours so as to always face the sun.

Political Rituals   Rituals and symbols have been seen as the stuff of politics and a dramatic aspect of polity from the time of Cleopatra to contemporary political rituals in most societies. If Louis XIV placed enormous emphasis on court ceremonies, Maximilien Robespierre placed an even greater emphasis on spectacles. His Festival of the Supreme Being at the Tuileries, which surpassed the ritual grandeur of Louis XIV's spectacles, was a true political ritual to be performed and seen by the people and was coordinated with ceremonies performed all over France. François Furet considers Robespierre the first to adopt the grand ceremony of modern "political religion" ([1988] 1996: 148). There were monarchs in other countries who also held grand ceremonies. Aside from Philip IV mentioned above, Charles II (r. 1649–1685), who reigned over Scotland, Ireland, and England, was obsessed with ceremonies (Keay 2008).

The monarchical model of spectacles has been followed by many modern leaders. A striking parallel among modern dictators—including Lenin, Stalin, Hitler, Mussolini, Franco, Mao Zedong, and Kim Il-sung—is that each strove to externalize his power through political rituals as well as images and speeches, as discussed above, with ferocious intensity and the full use of modern technology.

Rituals as a form of representation of political power have received a great deal of scholarly attention. Their presumed function of promoting solidarity or maintaining and enhancing a social structure has been a main interest of many thinkers, from Machiavelli and Rousseau to Durkheim, as well as many anthropologists today, although the argument is complex, as discussed in detail by David Kertzer (1988; 1996). Kertzer argues that "symbolism is the stuff of which nations are made," and "ritual is an integral part of politics in modern industrial societies" (1988: 6, 3). Kertzer (1988: 87) locates enormous power in ritual: "Far from simply projecting the political order onto the symbolic plane, ritual propagates a particular view of the political order." Some scholars argue that the power of symbols and rituals lies in their emotive appeal. Victor Turner (e.g., 1969: 42–43) contended that the "evocative power" of symbols is what moves people to action, and that the "strong emotional stimuli" of ritual make it "a mechanism that periodically converts the obligatory into the desirable" (1967: 30).

In her study of the "Italian fascist self," Mabel Berezin concludes that "rituals are vehicles of solidarity—communities of feeling—in an ideological project" and "served as public dramatizations of the merging of the public/private self that characterized nonliberal ideology in an age of large nation–states" (Berezin 1997: 246). According to Lisa Wedeen, Hafiz al-Asad of Syria (in office February 22, 1971–June 10, 2000) was obsessed with parades and political symbols, including his own image. She suggests that the symbolic dimension of his domination helped "reduce the need to rely on sheer repression as a mechanism of control" (1999: 26, 156). In other words, symbols and rituals softened repression, thereby effectively enhancing Hafiz al-Asad's power.

Some scholars are skeptical of the presumption that symbols and rituals invariably play a positive role. John Elliott contends that in Spain, "the new propaganda resources of the seventeenth-century state," including paintings, a new palace, preachers, playwrights, and theater, "were perfectly capable of being counterproductive, and of damaging the very cause they were intended to promote" (1985: 146, 158–59, 168–70). He cautions that the display of political authority is not a surefire strategy for the maintenance of political power.

While studies of ritual often fail to ask if/how a given ritual "functioned" to achieve its aim or failed to do so, Kertzer (1996), using a ethno-historical analysis of the Italian Communist Party, offers a highly theoretical analysis of how symbols fail to sustain political efficacy or succeed by being replaced by new symbols or a redefinition of the old. Another example of an anthropological study of how ritual failed is by Martha Kaplan (2001). Kaplan discusses how "an unusual ritual" involved in the opening of a monument to a shipwreck failed to unite Fijians and Indo-Fijians in a nation-building enterprise. The monument commemorates the Fijians who swam out to rescue drowning Indians aboard the *Syria*—a "coolie" ship carrying laborers to Fijian plantations—wrecked on a reef in 1884. The ritual of building the "nation," uniting the Fijians and Indo-Fijians, failed since "the power of Fijian chiefs and colonial British authorities depended on a narrative of indigenous loyalty and aristocratic chiefly right" enacted in Fijian chiefly and colonial British rituals (Kaplan 2001: 125).

Although political performances are a means for the exercise or display of political power, their impact is difficult to determine. Symbolic communication is seldom transparent. Before the advent of mass media, not everyone had the same degree of access to ritual, even in societies with a small population (Burke [1992] 1999). The grandeur of monarchical rituals at Versailles for instance, was witnessed only by those close to the court, physically and politically—an extremely small portion of the French population.

Spatial constraints rapidly disappeared with the development of mass media, which brought forth "time space compression"—an "overwhelming sense of *compression*" of the spatial and temporal worlds, which began with the Enlightenment but reached its height with postmodernity (Harvey 1990: 240). Radio and films, and now television and cyber technology, have enabled political leaders to reach people through technological apparatus. Visual and auditory political rituals and symbols have become one big and most powerful medium of political *propaganda*. Nevertheless, the messages sent through symbols and rituals as well as via mass media are seldom understood either as intended or in the same way among the recipients. From the perspective of political leaders and the state, the message may be clear but it does not guarantee that people will understand it as they intended. This poses a great danger in political spaces, often leading to sacrifices on the part of the people precisely because they are not cognizant of the message. In order to fully understand how ideologies are disseminated and even seemingly embraced by people under authoritarianism, fascism, colonialism, and other political regimes, we must closely examine communicative opacity, that is, miscommunication and noncommunication, be it in the context of interactions of individuals, rituals, or mass media propaganda.

In 1928, Benjamin ([1928] 1986: 85) pointed to the magnitude of advertising's impact: "Today the most real, the mercantile gaze into the heart of things is the advertisement. It abolishes the space where contemplation moved and all but *hits us between the eyes* with things." He concludes: "What, in the end, makes advertisements so superior to criticism? Not what the moving red neon sign says—but *the fiery pool reflecting it in the asphalt*" (Benjamin [1928] 1986: 85–86, emphases added). By being "hit between the eyes," Benjamin meant that people do not respond to what the moving red neon sign actually says; the advertisement removes the opportunity for comprehension and contemplation of the message. In the "Age of Mechanical Reproduction," Benjamin ([1936] 1968: 223) points out that the mimetic faculty no longer required authenticity and aura, but the "desire of the contemporary masses to bring things 'closer' spatially and humanly."

Bronislaw Malinowski, an unlikely figure in this context, reminded us of this by noting similarities between the advertisements of cosmetics by

Helena Rubinstein and Elizabeth Arden and Trobriand Islanders' beauty magic. In his view:

> The great leaders such as Hitler or Mussolini have achieved their influence primarily by the power of speech, coupled with power of action. . . . The modern socialistic state . . . has developed the powers of advertisement to an extraordinary extent. Political propaganda, as it is called, has become a gigantic advertising agency, in which merely verbal statements are destined to hypnotise foreigner and citizen alike into belief that something really great has been achieved. (Malinowski [1935] 1965: 237–38)

Michael Taussig (1993: 279) criticizes the parallel Malinowski drew and refers to Benjamin: "It is not a question of the universals of rhetoric, as Malinowski would have it, but of the rebirth of mythic force in and by modernity creating fire, with neon and pools on urban asphalt." Taussig (1993: 30) writes: "Lusting to exploit the optical unconscious to the full, advertising here expands, unhinges, and fixes reality which, enlarged and racy, hitting us between the eyes, implodes to engulf the shimmer of the perceiving self."

In my view, in order for political rituals and symbols to become propaganda, three historical developments are prerequisites—all products of modernization. First, the "nationalization of the masses" (Mosse 1975) must have been accomplished. Even Robespierre's Festival of the Supreme Being was a far cry from Hitler's propaganda, which reached the *Volk* everywhere, who had been nationalized as "Germans" through the use of modern technological accomplishments such as planes, trains, radios, and automobiles. Second, society must have developed the technology that enables mass production. Third, there must be mass media, which have had a revolutionary impact on politics everywhere in the world.

It is astounding that Lenin, Stalin, Hitler, and Mussolini understood the importance of modern mass media for visual display and sound bites, and made effective use of them so that the masses would, as they hoped, become hypnotized and intoxicated by visual and auditory propaganda. In reference to Gaetano Gabriele D'Annuzio (Gaetano Rapagnetta), a talented poet-novelist who laid out all the fascist rituals for Mussolini, Mosse explains that "dramatization" was "crucial to modern mass politics" (1987: 90). Referring to Aldous Huxley's idea, Steven Heller (2008) calls the technique of selling dictators to their people "branding."

There are several problems with the neo-Durkheimian functionalist approach. First, it is synchronic—an interpretation at the time of ritual performance. It also assumes symbols and rituals function positively, without presenting evidence. There are many dots to connect between the cheers of the crowd and the real impact of a speech. No matter how powerful a political speech may be or rituals may seem, they alone do not bring about change in society; a number of historical forces must also be at work in order for them to be functionally effective.

One sure way of judging the impact of propaganda is to assess it after it has operated in society for a sufficient time. Coming out of the Braudelian *longue durée* tradition, Mona Ozouf points out in her *Festivals and the French Revolution* ([1976] 1994: 282):

> But Brumaire, which saw this astonishing system of festivals disappear, never-theless did not see the disappearance of the new values that it had sacralized. Rights, liberty, and the fatherland, which the Revolutionary festival bound together at the dawn of the modern, secular, liberal world, were not to be sepa-rated so soon. . . . How can it be said that the Revolutionary festival failed in that? It was exactly what it wanted to be: the beginning of a new era.

Ozouf's work is significant for showing a way to *historicize* our study of ritu-als (*la fête* in the French title of the book may be better translated as "rituals") and symbols and to examine symbolic structures over a long time.

In a radical departure from the neo-Durkheimian functionalism that underlies most interpretations of symbols and rituals, Clifford Geertz proposed in his *Negara* (1980) that nineteenth-century Balinese court cer-emonies were public dramatizations of the Balinese obsession with social inequality and status pride—a show for the public. The king was not "di-vine," but was a ruler who had to act on behalf of the god Siva (Geertz 1980: 104–6). He was a political actor. Yet court ceremonies, the driving force of court politics, were "not means to political ends" but "ends them-selves." Thus, turning his court and himself into "a nearer god," the king became a chess king, removed from the intricacies of power mongering. He, a sign among signs, became a pure sign (Geertz 1980: 132–33). Hence, *"Power served pomp, not pomp power"* (Geertz 1980: 13, emphasis added). This line of nonfunctional interpretation of ritual is echoed in a statement by Peter Burke ([1992] 1999: 5) in reference to Louis XIV. He considers the representations of Louis XIV to have been "commissioned to add to his glory," rather than to persuade his subjects.

The discussion and examples offered above show a general pattern wherein the externalization of the authority and power of political leaders is important for the affirmation of their power to themselves, or for the posible indoctrination of the people. The issue of externalization is more complex in religion. Much depends on the nature of the religion involved. Unlike in Buddhism and Shintoism, in some religions, such as Christianity, Islam, and Judaism, externalization has been a locus of intensive and sometimes violent controversy, with the central question being whether one is able to reach the Supreme Being without human mediation, that is, icons made by humans. Whether one rejects externalization or seeks it, such an intense focus on the question itself indicates that the supreme deity as a zero signifier has such a powerful presence that it by no means creates communicative opacity, in sharp contrast to the invisible and inaudible Japanese emperor.

Afterword

This book has been difficult to write. The theoretical questions and empirical materials it considers are so broad in scope that they challenge my limited capacity. I do not claim to have done definitive and original work on each of my subjects; my goal has been to point to issues not fully examined in our understanding of symbolic communication. I took a bold and dangerous route in using cross-cultural comparisons—Japan with Germany and other societies. Experts in other cultures and societies might well find my material too thin. However, even preliminary comparisons offer striking insights, into theoretical issues as well as Japanese culture, that would not have come through focusing only on one culture.

The major thesis of this book has been the *unawareness* of communicative opacity on the part of social actors who live under its impact. Various types of symbols, some with multiple meanings and others with a singular meaning, zero (not-externalized) signifier, and the aesthetic are all factors involved in creating communicative opacity. Having examined how innocent-looking quotidian symbols can be co-opted for political purposes, I have focused on political leaders and institutions to investigate how their religious and/or political powers may be represented. Communicative opacity, at times intentionally and at other times inadvertently created, masks changes of meaning and can prevent understanding of critical situations, which can be detrimental to individuals and society. Symbols do not operate in the confines of rituals hermetically sealed from sociopolitical currents. They are an integral and critical part of geopolitical processes, in peace or in war, with potentially momentous effects on individuals, nations, and the global community. Yet, their power is complex and often indirect. There-fore, I have pointed to the importance and urgency of understanding how symbols operate in political spaces, using quotidian objects and how their beauty often becomes transformed into the sublimity of concepts, such as patriotism, so that we appreciate the important and at times dangerous roles such seemingly innocuous symbols play in contemporary society.

In Part I, symbols of the collective self—cherry blossoms, roses, and the monkey—illustrate how polysemy and the aesthetic have contributed to communicative opacity, for example, preventing the *tokkōtai* (kamikaze) pilots and most other Japanese from recognizing that the cherry petal on the side of the death-destined airplane represented the pilot's own death, or that the propaganda refrain of "falling like a beautiful cherry petal after a short life" meant the death of each and every young soldier. When the Germans willingly offered Hitler roses, which stood for interpersonal love and solidarity among workers, they were not fully cognizant of the mean-ings of the roses or their actions, which in fact enhanced Hitler's image as the father of all Germans when deployed in the Nazis' propaganda machinery. Communicative opacity operates even with a symbol with a single meaning. "Rice as self" hides the wide disjunction between the singular representation of all Japanese and the reality of what it does not represent—non-agrarian Japanese, many marginalized—in a symbolic and aesthetic totalization in which those who are excluded do not even realize it. A singular representation achieves purity by denying the presence of heterogeneity, especially ethnicity—a common practice, as in Nazi Ger-many when impurity of the self was transferred to the Jews, Gypsies, and other "undesirable" social groups.

Parts II and III, devoted to the broader political landscape, have dis-cussed collective identities and some universal symbols such as blood, soil, and nature, as well as specific symbols in the propaganda of the Nazi and Japanese military governments, to examine how different attributes of the collective self of the Japanese and the Nazi Germans were represented, as the two nations struggled with the vertigoes of modernization against which they felt compelled to protect their identity.

In their self-representation and self-presentation, the Nazis consciously prevented a bifurcation between tradition and modernity, whereas Japan put far more emphasis on tradition. Since modernization was conterminous with Westernization, the Japanese state was forced to create *the* Japanese tradition. It refashioned the imperial system through the Constitution of

Imperial Japan adopted in 1889 and intensely promoted the idea that the imperial system had been in existence for 2,600 years.

The comparative framework of this book serves as a springboard for contemplating the complex dimensions of religious and political power. In analyzing the issue of externalization, several axes have been useful: 1) religious versus political power; 2) the "king's two bodies" (Kantorowicz [1957] 1981), that is, the institutional body versus the individual monarch/political leader's body; and 3) cultural traditions of externalization and non-externalization. Despite the wide range of beliefs and traditions referred to as "religion" and the difficulty of separating religion from the polity, conceptually and in reality, some broad generalizations can be made. Political leaders—even monarchs with an "institutional body," like Philip IV and Louis XIV—deploy externalization to acquire and enhance their power through extensive use of symbols and rituals, even though their effectiveness is not guaranteed. This suggests a parallel with the necessity for externalization of political power as practiced by European monarchs and dictators. In contrast, the most powerful religious figures are often visual and auditory zero signifiers, especially in the "great religions" that are at least nominally monotheistic. The principle also appears in some polytheistic religions in which the most sacred beings are neither seen nor to be addressed in words, as with the Japanese and Ainu deities.

The Japanese emperor's invisibility and inaudibility would not have come into such sharp relief without the contrast of blatant displays of images and important speeches of modern dictators such as Lenin, Stalin, Hitler, and Mussolini. Yet, the Japanese emperor as a zero signifier is not merely the other side of the Aristotelian binary but derives from Japanese religiosity and ontology, in which the logic of the predicate denies the presence of the subject.

The comparative approach points to some cross-cultural parallels as well. Like Japanese cherry blossoms, German roses are an example of how beauty in nature is transformed to the sublimity of the collective self in cultural and then political nationalisms—often a dangerous morphing of beautiful objects into "flowers that kill"—a point seldom noticed by Japanese and European studies of these flowers and their symbolism, despite their centrality in the respective cultures. The aesthetic disarms people even when a symbol turns lethal, as with many flowers used in political spaces.

Although the examples selected for this book are from an earlier period, the findings remain relevant today. Unfortunately, dictators continue to be part of world history. We are bombarded with political propaganda, amplified by the ever-growing mass media, by political leaders, and it is often opaque and/or misleading. Sean Mitchell's ethnography of Pax Americana in the Amazon points to "the opaque but violently omnipresent character of U.S. power" (2010: 101). Beatrice Jauregui (2010) calls the global hegemonic paradigm the "Blue in Green"—blue symbolizing the ideal pacific order of civil-legal security and green the "necessary evil" of military force. Initially, the Japanese chose the imperial system as the tradition by which to identify themselves. But then that system was used by the Allied forces to construct and fortify the stereotype of the Japanese as fervent worshippers of the emperor as God, resolved to fight for him until the last Japanese. This provided justification for dropping the two atomic bombs, on August 6 and 9, 1945. Seventy-five percent of Japan had already been carpet bombed. In Tokyo 100,000 people were killed and over 200,000 perished in Hiroshima and Nagasaki. People were killed, burnt, starved, as in Berlin, Cologne, and elsewhere (Buruma 2013). How could one believe that the Japanese remained resolute in fighting and dying for the invisible and inaudible emperor? Yet the use of that stereotype of the emperor and the Japanese to wreak destruction and win victory in war allowed for the postwar introduction of radical changes in the land tenure system that eliminated the previous economic disparity within society and its class structure and brought in its wake a new educational system and many other equalizing sociopolitical institutions.

Nevertheless, should we view massive destruction, involving killing of innumerable civilians, followed by the introduction of democracy as justified even in Japan at the time? And, should the case of Japan be considered the ur-model for the procedures to be used for any country in the world, regardless of historical and political specificities? Isn't it time to reconsider the basic assumptions of Pax Americana and the role as the world's police force assumed by the United States? The relevance and importance of what Ruth Benedict wrote at the end of her *Chrysanthemum and Sword* (1946: 314–15) cannot be overstated: "What the United States cannot do—what no outside nation could do—is to create by fiat a free, democratic Japan. It has never worked in any dominated country." She duly credited Japanese initiative for what happened in Japan after 1945. As John Kelly (2010) passionately argues, Pax Americana must be scrutinized in terms of its means and limits; it may be "justified but not just" as a method of delivering peace and democracy.

Reference Matter

Notes

All translations are mine, unless specified otherwise.

INTRODUCTION

1. For the most part, I use the term "symbol" even though this term covers "a great variety of apparently dissimilar modes of behavior" (Fernandez 1986: 30–31). The "symbols" in this book are not metaphors—a trope that singles out a similarity/analogy between an object and its referent whose denotative meanings do not belong to the same category (Basso 1981; Fernandez 1986; Ohnuki-Tierney 1990b, 1991a).

2. In political science, a technical distinction is made between the *state*, defined by certain attributes including sovereignty and territory, and the *nation*, consisting of people as a collectivity, although the two are usually used interchangeably (Young 2012: 32–43).

3. Bakhtin wrote works such as *The Dialogic Imagination* (1981) and *Rabelais and His World* (1984) in the 1930s, although political circumstances in the Soviet Union prevented their publication until the late 1960s and 1970s. Lévi-Strauss began publishing in the mid-1930s, with his influential books coming out between 1949 and 1962: *Les structures élémentaires de la parenté* in 1949, *Tristes Tropiques* in 1955, *Anthropologie structurale* in 1958, and both *Le totémisme aujourd'hui* and *La pensée sauvage* in 1962.

4.   Dulce et decorum est pro patria mori:
        mors et fugacem persequitur virum
           nec parcit imbellis iuventae
           poplitibus timidove tergo. (P. 160)

5. Althusser (1971: 182–83) is also known for the use of the term *méconnaissance*, which takes place through the individual's interpellation, "*(freely) accepts his subjection*" (1971: 174–75, italics in the original). His interpellation is a *conscious* act of an individual in a given social context.

In Lacan's framework of "incessant sliding of the signified under the signifier" (Lacan

[1966] 1977: 154), his *méconnaissance* is "misrecognition" of an image of another in the mirror that produces the self, or the "subject." It is an agental act, assigning and reading his/her own image (self), rather than accepting an "objectively" assigned meaning (Roudinesco [1993] 1997: 110–12). Derrida's deconstruction of meaning refers to "infinite implication, the indefinite referral of signifier to signifier," thereby refuting semantic closure by differing, that is, deferring to other texts (*la différance*) (Derrida [1967] 1978: 25). My concept of communicative opacity does not deny reality outside the text (signification), as in Derrida's proposition, "il n'y a pas de hors-texte" ([1967] 1976: 158, see also 163). Nor is it identical with *indeterminacy*, either in Gödel's sense (see Friedrich 1979: 121) or in the sense of deconstructionists, some of whom consider all texts to be totally indeterminate, thereby assuring full liberation from the constricting and "tyrannical" intention of the original author or text.

There are other related concepts not similar to my communicative opacity: Empson's ambiguity as a result of literary device (Empson 1963); overdetermination, originally proposed by Freud; reception theory in literature, especially in Germany; the *réel* of Lacan developed by de Certeau (de Certeau and Robin 1976). The "indeterminate" of de Certeau ([1984] 1988: 199) is not related to this technical concept.

6. I do not deny that there are other types of symbolic communication in which conscious manipulation by social agents is involved. For example, according to Kubik (1994: 250–51), the Polish state in the 1970s deliberately created and manipulated ambiguity to ensure its survival, making the official discourse opaque to the people, who therefore could not grasp what the state was doing.

7. I exclude from my discussion some arguments on art in general, such as those addressing aesthetics and its relationship to capitalism (Adorno [1970] 1997) and to "surplus energy" (*la part maudite*) (Bataille [1967] [1989] 1991), as well as its uses in violence, including wars (Marinetti 1909).

8. In Western scholarship, the discussion of sublimity often begins with Longinus, a scholar of perhaps the first century CE, who defined it as "a kind of height and conspicuous excellence," and declared that its presence in speeches and writings drives people "not to persuasion, but to ecstasy" (Longinus 1985: 8–9). That is, he emphasizes that sublimity is not a conceptual understanding but an emotive/sensory response. In addition to a seminal work by Edmund Burke ([1757] 1998: 86, 89–90, 128–29, 157–58) on the sublime and beautiful, there is a long history of scholarly work on *sublime* as an adjective and as a noun (Nova 2011: 124–26).

9. Clendinnen (2010: 14–15) interprets the Aztec flowery wars as great ceremonial performances and as "politics of competitive spectacle"—the phrase used by Clifford Geertz in reference to nineteenth-century Balinese court rituals. She cautions against an interpretation of the flowery wars as pragmatic activities, as warfare in Western societies is considered to be. Defining the aesthetic as "moral and emotional sensibilities," she finds "the aesthetic" in the flowery wars that began with a long period of training the youth and ended in public violence (2010: 23).

10. In *History of Beauty* (2005: 131–53), edited by Umberto Eco, the photo chosen for the chapter titled "The Beauty of Monsters" is a fourth-century BCE antefix in the

shape of a gorgon's head from Santa Maria Capua Vetere. Wars and killing were themes in high art from medieval times.

11. This is in contrast to English, French, German, and other languages in which there is *structural pressure* to have subjects for finite verbs, objects for transitive verbs, and the subject appear at the sentence-initial position, so much so that a sentence at times resorts to dummy subjects to retain the subject-verb pattern, as in "It is raining" (Kuno 1973: 16–17). Ellipsis in English is briefly discussed by Benveniste (1966: 163–79).

12. Although I compare Japan with Germany, it is not to lump them together under the rubric of "fascism." That term has been overly extended to a variety of regimes and remains among the vaguest of all definitions (Payne [1980] 1987). For the best-known article against the use of "fascism" to describe Japan, see Duus and Okimoto 1979; for an argument for its continued use, see Gordon 1991: 333–39.

CHAPTER ONE

1. Cherrywood is occasionally used for woodbock printmaking. Many families during the early Meiji had a charcoal heater (*hibachi*), trays, or saucers for teacups made of cherry wood (Mizukami 1982: 14). Flower petals may be floated in tea and pickled in salt, and leaves pickled in salt are used to wrap sweets.

2. This interpretation is held by such scholars as Kanzaki 1989: 77; Nishiyama 1985: 20–21; Wakamori 1975: 179–81; and Yamada 1977: 116–22. Wakamori (1975) points to other examples in which the term *kura* is used to refer to the seat of the shaman's spirit. This etymological interpretation has been criticized by some scholars as based on insufficient evidence (e.g., Saitō 1977).

3. Pictorial representations of this first appeared only in the eighteenth century (Kanzaki 1994: 16), and there is a reference to it in a late Edo almanac (Miyata 1987: 121–22).

4. For the relevant poems, see Cranston 1993: 254, 312, 327, 384, 405, 460, 479, 539, 544, 602, 607, 610, 626, 718.

5. The term *sakura* (cherry blossoms) appears 40 times (Ikeda 1987: 227–28), in addition to numerous occurrences of *hana* (flower), which also refers to cherry blossoms, thus outnumbering the references to plum blossoms, which appear 40 times (42 times, according to Kinoshita 1974).

6. See Kurano and Takeda, eds., 1958: 131–33, on the *Kojiki*; Sakamoto et al., eds., 1967: 154–55, on the *Nihongi*. Interpreting *sakuya* in her name as *sakura* (cherry blossoms), Yamada (1977: 121–22), Sakurai (1974: 25), and others consider this female deity as cherry blossoms, although Saitō ([1979] 1985: 39–42) objects to this interpretation.

7. Examples are: a nun's analogy between Genji's thoughts of a young girl and the scattering of blossoms (Seidensticker 1977b: 97; Yamagishi, ed., 1958: 204); an old man referring to an old cherry tree (Seidensticker 1977b: 97; Yamagishi, ed., 1958: 204).

8. Examples of the link to the impermanence of life are: vol. 2, no. 84 (McCullough 1985: 30; Kubota 1960 [1968]: 218–19; Takagi 1979: 58); vol. 2, no. 92 (McCullough 1985: 31; Kubota 1960 [1968]: 228–30; Takagi 1979: 18); vol. 2, no. 113 (McCullough 1985: 35; Kubota 1960 [1968]: 256–58). Examples related to death are: vol. 2, no. 71 (McCullough 1985: 27; Kubota [1960] 1968: 200–201; Takagi 1979: 134); vol. 2, no. 73 (McCullough

1985: 28; Kubota [1960] 1968: 202–3; Takagi 1979: 132); vol. 2, no. 77 (McCullough 1985: 28; Kubota [1960] 1968: 208–11; Takagi 1979: 133); vol. 2, no. 112 (McCullough 1985: 34; Kubota [1960] 1968: 255–56).

9. Examples of poems are in McCullough 1968: 82 (Arai [1939] 1965: 224); McCullough 1968: 104 (Arai [1939] 1965: 460); McCullough 1968: 125 (Arai [1939] 1965: 691); McCullough 1968: 133 (Arai [1939] 1965: 774).

10. Contemporary writer Sakaguchi Ango's well-known short story (Sakaguchi 1997) is based on the association of cherry blossoms with madness and the disclosure of one's true identity, that is, an old woman demon disguised as a beautiful young woman whose identity is revealed under cherry blossoms in full bloom.

11. Noh, founded by Kan'ami (1333–1384) as *sarugaku* during the Heian period, was developed into the most cultivated performing art during the subsequent Kamakura period by Ze'ami (1364–1443), Kan'ami's son. Upper-class warriors became its patrons. With highly sophisticated Buddhist philosophy and metaphysics at its base, it has been an important hallmark of Japan's high culture ever since (Ohnuki-Tierney 1987: 89, 169–70).

12. Identified by Okuyama Keiko of Nōgakudō (a noh theater in Tokyo) (personal communication on April 5, 1996), they are: *Kochō, Shun'nōden, Shunteika, Shundeiraku, Manzairaku, Arashiyama, Ukon, Oshio, Kurama Tengu, Kōya Monogurui, Saigyō-zakura, Sakuragawa, Shiga, Suma Genji, Sumizome-zakura, Sōshiarai Komachi, Taizan Fukun, Tadanori, Tamura, Dōjōji, Futari Shizuka, Mitsuyama, Yuya, Yoshino Shizuka,* and *Yoshino Tenjin.* (English translations are not meaningful.)

13. A permanent loss of one's self is also associated with cherry blossoms, as expressed in Ze'ami's noh play *Three Mountains* (*Mitsuyama*) (Ze'ami Motokiyo 1935b). A woman named Cherry Blossom Child wins her lover, but her rival, the moon, blows her petals away so that she will not be reborn.

14. Takigawa 1971: 141. These cherry trees were removed every year after blooming in April or May (Saitō 1979 [1985]: 17). The tradition of planting cherry trees originated with kabuki (Takigawa 1971) sometime between 1741 and 1749, when full-bloom cherry blossoms in the daytime in Nakanochō were used as a metaphor for the ephemeral gaiety of the floating world by a famous kabuki actor, Danjūrō II, in his role as Sukeroku, a favorite kabuki figure, although some claim the cherries in the stage settings were night cherry blossoms in the green bamboo fence.

15. Extensive use of artificial representations, such as those of cherry blossoms, has a long tradition. Already in the *Man'yōshū*, representations of rice plants, made of tree trunks such as willow, appear (Orikuchi [1928] 1982: 490–91; Yamada 1982: 38).

16. Cherry blossoms are the major motif in many kabuki plays, including the so-called three greatest: *Kanadehon Chūshingura, Yoshitsune Senbon Zakura,* and *Sugahara Denju Tenarai Kagami* (English translations of the titles are not meaningful). For cherry blossom viewing as famous scenes, see Toita and Yoshida 1981: 40; Watanabe 1989: 179; and Yoshida and Hattori, eds., 1991: 219. Toita (1969) considers the scenes of cherry blossom viewing in *Shin Usuyuki Monogatari* and *Kagamiyama Kokyō no Nishiki-e* to be the two most famous cherry blossom scenes in kabuki. Until the mid-Meiji period, the first scene (Cherry blossom viewing at Hasedera [*Hasedera Hanami-no-ba*]) in *Kagamiyama*

Kokyō no Nishiki (Toshikura et al., eds., 1969: 242–78) had been a critical one, enticing the audience to feel the gaiety and sensory saturation that one experiences at cherry blossom viewings. Since the mid-Meiji, this scene has often been skipped (Toita 1969: 237).

17. For example, in the famous *Sugahara Denju Tenarai Kagami* (Toita et al., eds., 1968: 139–233), three brothers are named after the plum, pine, and cherry. As the brothers quarrel, trying to hit each other with rice sacks, a cherry branch is accidentally broken off, foretelling the later death by suicide of the brother whose name bears the word for cherry tree (Sakura-maru) (Enomoto 1975: 181; Toita and Yoshida 1981: 18). In another play, *Imoseyama Onna Teikin*, a blossoming cherry tree branch floats down a stream, signaling the approaching tragedy of two lovers unable to be united (Toita and Yoshida 1981: 46).

18. Motoori's self-portrait and the poem he executed in 1790, at the age of 61, appear on the cover of the first volume of his collected works (Motoori 1968).

19. Some consider Motoori Norinaga responsible for establishing a link between cherry blossoms and the Japanese ethos of *monono aware*, the pathos of evanescence. However, in his voluminous work on *Genji* (e.g., Motoori [1790] 1968: esp. 201–42), I could not find any systematic link between cherry blossoms and the ethos of pathos. His major thesis is that *monono aware* constitutes the essence of Japanese literary and visual arts and is not a product either of the Buddhist worldview or of Confucianism (e.g., Motoori [1790] 1968: 25–26).

20. Nitobe's book became a major source for non-Japanese who wished to know the secret of how Japan, a tiny, hitherto unknown Asian country, had gained victory over Russia, a mighty Western nation, in the Russo-Japanese War. Nitobe's text exerted a major influence on Ruth Benedict's *The Chrysanthemum and the Sword*, published in 1946.

21. Tsubouchi 1900: 29, and book jacket (for the circus); 69, 73 (for horse racing). The circus also performed at Asakusa Temple (Tōkyōto Edo Tōkyō Hakubutsukan 1993: 106).

22. In a promulgation issued on October 20, 1870, the government (still called Dajōkan; in 1870 it was the highest executive organ of the government, although it has undergone various changes) specified the insignia for the navy to be a single-petal blossom, leaves, and buds around an anchor, and for the army to be a cherry blossom only in the design on the buttons on the uniform of those above the rank of second lieutenant (*shōi*) (Ōta 1980: 49, 131). In later years the army included cherry blossoms in many of its insignias. The buds are also significant because they represented young men, who were told to fall like cherry petals after a beautiful but short life.

23. The front cover of the original cloth edition in indigo has ten falling cherry petals in pink and the title in gold. The back cover has five falling cherry petals. On the spine are the title and "the editors, Yasukuni Shrine, under the supervision of the Ministry of Army and Ministry of Navy," in gold. The falling cherry petals do not appear in all copies. A copy of Volume 4 at the East Asian Collection at the Josef Regenstein Library of the University of Chicago, donated by Yamazaki Tōji, has a cover with a design of falling cherry petals. But no other volume has this design. None of the five volumes at the University of California, Berkeley, Library, donated by the Mitsui family, has the cherry petal design.

24. In 2012 the University of Tokyo and eleven other universities proposed changing the beginning of the school year to autumn in order to coordinate with academic calendars outside of Japan, thus promoting the globalization of Japanese academia, including the acceptance of foreign students—a part of the government's policy known as Global 30.

25. The first volume, *Shōgaku Kokugo Dokuhon*, volume 1, was published in 1932 and the last, volume 12, was published in 1938 (Kaigo, ed., 1964: 539). An extensive discussion of the socioeconomic and political context of the history of textbooks is in Kaigo, ed., 1964: 609–14.

26. Examples are *Hanasaka Jijii*, *Urashima Tarō*, *Momotarō*, *Usagi to Kame*, *Hatopoppo*, and *Oshōgatsu*.

27. Concerning the origin of *hanami*, Wakamori (1975: 172–73) and Saitō (1977: 41–45) reject the agrarian association of cherry blossoms and regard the flower as a symbol of kingship and urban aristocracy. Shirahata (2000: 216, 220) believes the origins of *hanami* are two: a religious ritual/banquet at the imperial court and a ritual among farmers to make offerings to the Deity of Rice Paddies, which involved feasting. See Miyake 1985: 435, on the sacredness of the tree in the ascetic mountain order called *shugendō*.

28. I use the term "warlords" rather than "shogun" because Toyotomi Hideyoshi and Tokugawa Ieyasu held the high imperial court positions of *kanpaku* and *dajōdaijin*, rather than *shōgun*, who commanded only the military.

29. It was customary for warriors (*bushō*) at the time to have a goatee (more like chin strip) and commonly those without thick facial hair used a fake goatee. Therefore it is not certain if Hideyoshi's goatee at the *hanami* was a part of his masquerade.

30. Praise for the beauty of cherry blossoms by lesser-known poets may be interpreted as an antiestablishment stance against court life in Kyoto.

31. The main hall is the Shinden (Sleeping Hall), also called Shishinden, or Nanden (South Hall), also pronounced "Nanten," and its garden is the Dantei or Nantei (Fujioka 1956: 125, 126).

32. None of the available sources in Japanese traces the history of the cherry tree in front of the palace, so some details are offered here. According to the *Kojidan* (Kuroita and Kokushi Taikei Henshūkai, eds., 1965c: 113; see also Minamoto-no-Akikane, 1965; for a translation of the *Kojidan* in contemporary Japanese, see Shimura 1980), it was originally a plum tree that was planted at the time of Emperor Kanmu's relocation of Japan's capital from Nara to Kyoto in 794. According to the *Teiō Hen'nenki* (Kuroita and Kokushi Taikei Henshūkai, eds., 1965b: 183), Emperor Saga, who held the first imperial cherry blossom viewing, also had a cherry tree planted in front of the main hall. However, other passages contradict this description. According to a later section in the *Teiō Hen'nenki* (Kuroita and Kokushi Taikei Henshūkai, eds., 1965b: 247) and the *Kojidan* (Kuroita and Kokushi Taikei Henshūkai, eds., 1965c: 113), the original plum tree planted at the time of the construction of the Imperial Palace in Kyoto died during the Jōwa period (834–848). According to the *Nihon Kiryaku* (Kuroita and Kokushi Taikei Henshūkai, eds., 1965a: 371) and the *Shoku Nihon Kōki* (Kuroita and Kokushi Taikei Henshūkai, eds., 1965a: 371), in 845, when Emperor Ninmyō held a banquet at the Shishinden, he adorned

the hair of the crown prince and his attendants with plum blossoms. In addition, both the *Nihon Kiryaku* (Kuroita and Kokushi Taikei Henshūkai, eds., 1965a: 371) and the *Shoku Nihon Kōki* (Kuroita and Kokushi Taikei Henshūkai, eds., 1966: 176, 206) refer to plum blossoms in the palace during Emperor Ninmyō's reign (833–850).

Some believe it was Emperor Ninmyō who promoted the aesthetics of cherry blossoms (Kuroita and Kokushi Taikei Henshūkai, eds., 1966: 176, 206). Yet references during his reign were primarily to plum blossoms. It was after 850 and the end of his reign when references to cherry blossoms started to appear in various records. Thus, the *Nihon Kiryaku* (Kuroita and Kokushi Taikei Henshūkai, eds., 1965a: 386, 389) refers to a beautiful cherry tree in 850 and again in 852—both at a manor of a prominent court official (*daijin*), but not at the palace itself.

Definite proof of the presence of a cherry tree in front of the Shishinden is in the *Kinpishō* by Emperor Juntoku, written between 1219 and 1222, which states that a cherry tree in front of the Shishinden withered during the Jōgan era (859–877) but was entrusted to Sakanoue no Takimori, who carefully restored the tree (Juntoku Emperor [1219–1222] 1929: 374).

The presence of a cherry tree in front of the main hall at the time of the first imperial cherry blossom viewing is dated 812 in the *Teiō Hen'nenki*. Yet, there are other records that contradict this. Another possible date is: in 845 the tree in front of the Shishinden was a plum tree. According to the *Kinpishō*, there was a cherry tree but it withered and was replaced by another cherry tree sometime between 859 and 877 (Juntoku Emperor [1219–1222] 1929: 374). One of the major sources of misreading is a pair of similar passages in the *Kojidan* (Kuroita and Kokushi Taikei Henshūkai, eds., 1965c: 113) and the *Teiō Hen'nenki* (Kuroita and Kokushi Taikei Henshūkai, eds. 1965b: 247), which describe how a plum tree was planted at the time of Emperor Kanmu's moving of the capital to Kyoto and how it withered during the Jōwa period. The description is followed by a statement that Emperor Ninmyō "planted again." Some interpret this to mean that the emperor planted a cherry tree. Yet a close reading of the text in Chinese testifies beyond doubt that what the emperor planted was another plum tree. Kubota (1990) guesses that the plum tree was replaced by a cherry tree toward the end of Emperor Ninmyō's reign in 850, whereas Nakamura (1982) places the replacement during the Seiwa period (858–876). Imae (1993) places the date between 845 and 874. The estimate of 960 by Ponsonby-Fane (1956: 63) seems to stem from a misreading of the text.

This cherry tree, however, was burned in 960 in a fire at the palace. When the palace was reconstructed in 965 (Fujioka 1956: 116), a cherry tree, originally a mountain cherry at Yoshino that had been transplanted in the garden of Prince Shigeaki, was transplanted on the left-hand side in front of the Shishinden, as recorded in the *Kojidan* (Kuroita and Kokushi Taikei Henshūkai, eds., 1965c: 113), the *Teiō Hen'nenki* (Kuroita and Kokushi Taikei Henshūkai, eds., 1965b: 247), and the *Kinpishō* (Juntoku Emperor [1219–1222] 1929: 368). See also Tsumura [1917] 1970: 82. The main section of the palace (*daidairi*), together with the plants, was destroyed by numerous fires—in the years 960, 976, 980, 982, 999, 1001, 1005, 1014, 1018, 1039, 1042, 1048, 1058, 1082, 1219, and 1227.

33. The origin of the practice is not well documented, but it appeared among aristocrats in Kyoto during the medieval period as a way of imitating or emulating court life.

34. Since 630, envoys to Tang China (*kentōshi*) had been sent to acquire knowledge of Tang civilization and the international political situation. Toward the end, a total of some five to six hundred envoys had crossed the sea to China, even though the round trip took two to three years. Sugawara-no-Michizane ordered the discontinuation of this system in 894. Reasons for the abolition included the high casualty rate during these voyages and the internal turmoil of Tang China, although Inoue (1963a [1967]: 105–6) attributes it to the loss of curiosity about the outside world on the part of the Japanese elite. The complexities of reasons behind it notwithstanding, the abolition of the envoy system was part of the picture of ninth-century Japan, whose unquestioning admiration of Tang China was going through a reassessment.

35. For *Yamato-e*, see Shinbo, ed., 1982. Another use of the cherry tree among the elite is found in the game called *kemari* (or *shūkiku*), during which about eight people in leather shoes kick a deer-hide-covered ball. For a passage in the *Nihongi*, see Sakamoto et al., eds., 1965: 254–55. Having become popular among the elite during the first half of the tenth century (Ōshima et al., eds., 1971: 703), the format of the game became well-established by the time of Emperor Goshirakawa (r. 1158–1162), with a court with four plants in each corner: cherry, willow, pine, and maple (Ōshima et al., eds., 1971: 704).

36. Composition of poems in Chinese characters (*kanbun*) remained an important cultural institution. For example, in the chapter on cherry blossom viewing (*Hana-no-en*) in *The Tale of Genji*, the viewing was immediately followed by the composition of poems in Chinese characters. According to *The Tale of Flowering Fortunes* (*Eiga Monogatari*) of the late Heian period: "The winding-water banquet, an imported pastime popular in the ninth century, involved reciting poems in Chinese and drinking from floating wine cups" (McCullough and McCullough, trans., 1980: 841, 843). During the Heian period, the Chinese practice of chrysanthemum viewing (*chōyō no sechie*) was introduced. While he viewed chrysanthemums, the emperor's body was wiped with "chrysanthemum cotton," the center part of the flower, wet with chrysanthemum dew. This annual event remained an important imperial ritual, held on September 9 of the lunar calendar, often accompanied by the recitation of poems in Chinese (Fujioka 1956: 120; Niunoya 1993: 619–23).

37. Other famous prints include those in the *Illustrated Guide to Famous Sites in Edo* (*Edo Meisho Zue*) by Hasegawa Settan, published between 1829 and 1836.

38. For example, the buildings of Kōfukuji, a famous temple in Nara, were destroyed. The five-story pagoda was sold to a person who wanted to melt it down for scrap metal (Murakami, Tsuji, and Washio, eds., 1970: 103–5, 171–72; Ōta 1979: 164; Saeki 1988: 160–62; Yamada [1941] 1993: 400).

39. Today, Japanese newspapers annually report the blooming of these cherry blossoms in the United States, often photographed against the background of the Capitol building (e.g., *Asahi Shinbun*, Jan. 11, 1998; Mar. 30, 2012). A commemorative stamp issued in 1975, when the emperor and empress visited the United States, depicts an American flag in the center with cherry blossoms clustered beneath it. The Japanese Association for Flowers (Nihon Hana no Kai), a private organization, donated 1,500 seedlings to Bulgaria for the 1,300[th] anniversary of the founding of the first Bulgarian

state; 5,000 seedlings to Versailles in France; and more seedlings to Iran and Hamburg, Germany (Kawai and Ōta 1982: 93), to Australia in 1987 (*Asahi Shinbun*, Nov. 7, 1997), to Uzbekistan in 2002 (*Asahi Shinbun*, June 12, 2002), and to Beijing in 2003 (*Japan Times*, Feb. 19, 2003). Several Japanese "sister" municipalities and private organizations pledged to plant a thousand cherry trees along the Danube River and in other sections of Vienna by the year 2000 (*Asahi Shinbun*, April 30, 1996).

40. NHK television program "Eastern Japan Great Earthquake—One-Thousand-Year-Old Cherry Tree. Live from Kasuga-chō," April 21, 2012.

41. "In contrast to spring in the human world, spring at the air force base is peaceful. I shall write again after the cherry blossoms have fallen. . . . Cherry blossoms eagerly fall after their blooming. It is a good time for me to do the same. . . . As we eagerly compete for a chosen spot to fly and [perish] like falling cherry petals, we find meaning in life" (quoted in Ebina 1983: 183, 184).

42. These male actors do not play the woman, or copy her, but "combine the signs of Woman" (Barthes [1970] 1982: 89–91).

CHAPTER TWO

1. The one by Heinrich Werner (1800–1833) became a school song for girls in Japan in 1909 (Horiuchi and Inoue, eds., 1958 [1995]: 136) and has been widely popular ever since.

2. See Löwith [1964] 1991: 16–17, for an extended discussion of Hegel's use of the rose as a metaphor for reason and Goethe's disagreement.

3. The *New York Times* reported on December 5, 1906, that he arrived via China, but on December 15 wrote that he came via Japan.

4. The caption reads: "In the year 1922, I was in Gorki. My papa worked in the Rest Home where Vladimir Il'iich was. Once when Vladimir Il'iich was preparing to go into town, I gathered a bouquet of flowers and brought them to him. Vladimir Il'iich accepted the flowers and asked me: 'Do they grow well for you in the sun?'" (Translation by Andy Spencer).

5. They include *Stalin and Molotov with Children* by V. P. Efanov (Stalinka EA000008), dated 1939. In the painting, Stalin and Molotov stroll outdoors with three children, one of whom is carried by Molotov. A boy in the front carries a bouquet of flowers. Another is *May Our Motherland Live Long and Prosper!* by P. Golub, dated 1949 (Stalinka GR000047). In this poster, Stalin, in a white uniform, and a young boy holding flowers stand in profile with a vast expansion of agricultural fields in the background.

There are others in which Stalin is depicted as father to the people. A painting by V. P. Efanov (1900–1978), *Unforgettable*, created in 1936, appears in both Stalinka (EA000002) and *Traumfabrik Kommunismus* (Groys and Hollein 2003: 146–47). The painting won the Stalin Prize for Art in 1941; it depicts a young woman giving red flowers, likely roses, to Stalin. The description in Stalinka reads:

> Congresses and Conferences of Stakhanovites and outstanding collective farm workers played an important role in the cultural mythology of the thirties. For the recipients of the honors, the meeting had a fairy-tale quality, including the chance to meet Stalin himself.

6. Another painting of people from different ethnic groups offering flowers to Stalin (Stalinka GR000026) is by V. Koretskii, dated 1950. Its title is *The Great Stalin Is the Banner of the Friendship of the Soviet Peoples!* (reproduced also in Aulich and Sylvestrová 1999: 87). The description of the poster reads: "Stalin inaugurated the Friendship of Peoples campaign in December 1935. The campaign was intended to celebrate cooperation among nations and races in the USSR." Groups of people including men, women, and children, some looking like representatives of particular ethnic groups, stand together, positioned as if listening to something or watching someone on stage. Many hold large bouquets of flowers.

CHAPTER THREE

1. I do not intend to imply that the dialogical and social definition of being human in Japanese culture translates into "groupism"—Japanese have always interacted harmoniously with each other and sacrificed themselves for the goals of the social group. This view is sometimes presented in the genre of writing known as *Nihonjinron* (theories about the Japanese).

2. These paintings include works by Iwasa Katsumochi Matabei (1578–1650) and Kusumi Morikage (1620–1690). For the relationship between the Mountain Deity and the Deity of Rice Paddies, see Yanagita, ed., 1951: 642; Ouwehand 1964.

3. Here I use the King James edition, which seems more familiar to people than the Revised Standard Version.

4. According to Nakamura's (1984) analysis of 134 tales from early historical periods, only 3 of the 42 cases of human metamorphosis into an animal involve a monkey, all as a form of punishment. For details, see Ohnuki-Tierney 1987: 32–33.

5. When the three-monkey theme—"see no evil, hear no evil, speak no evil"—was originally introduced from China, it represented three *tai* (close identifications) based on a philosophy that espoused the use of the three senses to make careful observations of the world (Iida 1973: 158).

6. Previously, this theme had had a positive meaning in Buddhism (Iida 1983; Ooms 1985).

7. It is now housed in the Freer Gallery of the Smithsonian Institution in Washington, DC.

8. In the *Shinchōki*, a biography of the feudal lord Oda Nobunaga (1534–1582) by Oze Hōan, a beggar is referred to as a monkey (Minakata 1972: 415). During the Edo period, the expression "the monkey in the kitchen" (*zensho no saru*) was commonly used to refer to beggars (Hirose 1978: 303). Minakata (1972: 407, 414–15) also cites a number of publications from the early eighteenth century in which prostitutes and various other "undesirables" are referred to as monkeys.

While not as negative as in these examples, the monkey as a scapegoat is depicted in a well-known example of *ōtsu-e*, a genre of folk paintings by anonymous artists that flourished from the late seventeenth to the early eighteenth centuries. In one of these paintings, a monkey tries to subdue a catfish, believed capable of causing an earthquake, with a slippery gourd. The immediate message is that the monkey is a fool who tries to do the impossible, to control an earthquake (Ouwehand 1964).

9. In one instance, when Emperor Gokōmei (r. 1648–1664) died of smallpox, the monkeys recovered, while in another instance, Emperor Higashiyama (r. 1688–1713) recovered from smallpox but the monkeys died from it (Minakata 1972: 378–79). The belief in the monkey as scapegoat for a human victim of disease continued. For example, around 1900 it was reported that people with eye diseases would pray at the Tennōji Shrine in the belief that the monkeys in the compound would suffer the disease, while the patients would recover (Minakata 1972: 378–79).

10. Although *kyōgen* is sometimes taken as proletarian literature, its perspectives are not proletarian, as some Marxian scholars have contended. It lampoons anyone above or below who is not clever (LaFleur 1983; Satake [1967] 1970: 110; see "saru zatō" in Nonomura and Ando 1974).

11. The play is thought to be a product of the Muromachi period (Yanagita [1920] 1982: 339). The synopsis is from Nonomura ([1953] 1968: 158–66), thought to be the most authoritative version of this play.

12. The Japanese attribute this event to the so-called Manchurian Incident of 1931, although it actually took place later, during the Japanese assault on Shanghai (Smith and Wiswell 1982: 232).

13. In later history, the monkey performance continued as entertainment on the street, in the doorway of households, and in makeshift theaters. At the height of its popularity during the Meiji and Taishō periods, there were 150 trained monkeys and an equal number of trainers (Murasaki 1980: 13–30). Most of the information about monkey performances comes from studies of Yamaguchi Prefecture in the early twentieth century. According to these studies, settlements in the southeastern part of the prefecture were the headquarters from whence the trainers journeyed all over Japan (see also Gonda 1971: 317). Since people were aware that the monkey performance was an occupation of this *hisabetsu burakumin* social group, the trainers met with discrimination simply by staging the monkey performance; they had never been an ethnic or racially distinguishable population. Some wished to eradicate any occupations that would reveal their identity; this attitude contributed to the discontinuation of the monkey performance.

14. In 1947, two brothers in Tokyo revived the monkey performance, but only briefly. The collaboration between the two did not last because of differences of opinion on two important points, reflecting a wider disagreement among the members of this social group. Some, including the younger brother, Murasaki Shūji, held that the eradication of their past was essential in achieving equality and removing prejudice, while others, like the older brother, Murasaki Tarō, felt that knowledge of their past was essential in asserting their own identity in Japanese society (Murasaki 1980: 39–43; 1983: 32; Suō Sarumawashinokai Jimukyoku, ed., 1978: 2, 17). The brothers also disagreed about the repertoire of the performance: Murasaki Shūji favored reviving the traditional monkey performance with dancing as the main feature, while Murasaki Tarō advocated adjusting to the modern audience and having the monkey perform tricks.

CHAPTER FOUR

1. According to some, this seemingly natural development from hunting and gathering to agriculture to nation-building does not necessarily translate into continuity of

the gene pool. Even today, there is no agreement on the population who carried out each type of subsistence economy, and, in particular, the relationship of the Ainu with the rest of the people on the Japanese archipelago (Ohnuki-Tierney 1974: 2–7; 1981a: 204–12).

2. The Japanese notion of *marebito* closely parallels the notion of "stranger deity" used by many peoples in the world to interpret outside forces, as originally pointed out by Simmel ([1907] 1950: 402–8) (for a detailed discussion, see Ohnuki-Tierney 1987: 79, 129, 133, 134, 148).

3. Called Ukano Kami, the soul of the rice grain is clearly identified as a female deity (Yanagita [1940] 1982) who is closely related to major deities involved in the creation of the Japanese universe. While contemporary Japanese do not believe in the soul of rice literally, this concept in part explains the special importance that rice continues to hold even in post-agricultural Japan.

4. See the "pure gift" of Mauss ([1925] 1966), "generalized exchange" of Lévi-Strauss ([1949] 1969), and "generalized reciprocity" of Sahlins ([1972] 1974: 193–94), all defined somewhat differently from the others.

5. Within a society, food is symbolically important for the definition and reproduction of class distinctions. There is artisan bread for the haves and Wonder Bread for the masses. For Bourdieu, "the body is the most indisputable materialization of class taste" (Bourdieu [1979] 1984: 190).

6. See Barthes [1970] 1982: 12–14 for an insightful but overly romantic observation on the aesthetic of Japanese food in general and rice in particular.

7. Some people continued to eat meat, but they used euphemisms, giving the names of flowers to animal flesh, such as cherry blossoms for horsemeat and peony for wild boar. See Harada 1993.

8. French cuisine became the official fare for formal entertainment at the imperial court (Harada 1993: 19) until the time of the funeral for the Shōwa emperor in 1989, when guests from all over the world were given a choice between Japanese and Western cuisine.

9. Both potatoes and sweet potatoes were introduced to Japan during the early part of the early modern period (1603–1868). The Japanese preferred sweet potatoes—because they could be eaten alone—to regular potatoes (Tsukuba [1969] 1986: 123). For a discussion of New Year's without rice cakes but with taro (*imoshōgatsu*), see Tsuboi [1982] 1984.

10. Tsukuba ([1969] 1986: 106) holds that the majority of Japanese started to eat rice during the Meiji period (1868–1912). According to Watanabe Tadayo (1989: 83) most Japanese have eaten rice as a staple food only since 1939, when a food rationing system was adopted, and 90 percent of the population during the early modern period ate some rice and 80 percent ate it three times a day. He further estimates that the remaining 20 percent of the people ate rice about half of the time and that a very small number of Japanese ate rice only occasionally. In Dore's opinion, by the 1930s, "white rice had come to be considered a part of the birthright of every Japanese" ([1958] 1973: 58–59). Other scholars claim that in northeastern Japan, most people, except warriors and upper-class merchants, ate only millet (*awa, hi'e*) until the 1960s (Ōbayashi 1973: 5–6).

1. The sentiment of belonging is often intensified among the members of diaspora groups—they may long for the homeland more than those living there. "Belonging" is often as important or even more so after death for an individual, as demonstrated by the mortuary practices among many peoples. For example, before urban renewal demolished Detroit's Chinatown, its merchant association made sure that the deceased, temporarily buried in the Detroit municipal cemetery, would be transferred every ten years to their natal villages, as inscribed on the tombstones in Chinese characters, along with other information on the person (Ohnuki-Tierney 1964).

2. Giambattista Vico (1668–1744), Johan Gottfried von Herder (1744–1803), and Isaiah Berlin (1909–1997) all saw in human history a type of nationalism based on pluralism and respect for each other's way of life, rather than one leading to bloodshed, which occurs when the encounter is hostile. Berlin uses the "bent twig" metaphor of Friedrich Schiller and sees nationalism that stems from "wounds, some form of collective humiliation" to lash back and refuse to accept the alleged inferiority, as in the case of the development of the extraordinarily aggressive *Volksgeist/Nationalgeist* of the Third Reich (Berlin [1959] 1992: 10–11, 243–51; see Hardy in Berlin [1999: 161] about this metaphor).

3. Hobsbawm ([1990] 1992: 163) also followed the historical periodicity scheme and declared in 1990 that nationalism in the late twentieth century was "no longer a major vector of historical development," although he retracted the statement in the revised edition of his book. Others do not believe modernity is a prerequisite of nationalism (Berlin [1959] 1992: 243; Schwartz 1993: 218).

Still others charge that a unilinear and universal historical scheme with nationalism as part of modernity is based on the Western notion of historical progression and is an attempt to dislodge, or "rescue," to use Duara's phrase, concepts such as nation/state, modernity, and nationalism from unilinear and unilateral social evolutionary history as conceptualized in Europe's Enlightenment (Duara 1995). Chatterjee (1993) argues that not only is nationalism not tied to so-called modernity in the Enlightenment scheme of history, but the Western paradigm of nationalism must be challenged by nationalist imaginations—in particular anticolonial nationalism—in other parts of the world. Tambiah proposes "multiple modernities": the nationalism of nation-states, as developed especially in Western Europe, and "ethnonationalism," originating separately in many parts of the world, including some parts of Europe (Tambiah 1996a: 9; Tambiah 1996b: 124; Tambiah 2000).

Since the early nineteenth century the Russians felt they belonged neither to the West nor to the East, and their society did not evolve according to the Hegelian vision of historical development—from medieval Christianity and feudalism to the Enlightenment from which the liberal state emerged (Malia 1999), leading to the Russian literati's obsession with *narodnost* (national originality), which became the *sine qua non* of Russian romanticism (Leighton 1985: 373; Terras, ed., 1985). Again, the presence of the other was pivotal to the development of cultural nationalism.

4. What I call cultural nationalism is Gellner's patriotism (Gellner 1983: 138) and predates his nationalism, which I call political nationalism. I follow Fenton's definition of "patriots": "The word 'patriot' means in this context not some flag-waving jingoist,

not someone who wishes to assert the rights of his own country over the interests of some other country, but someone who loves his country enough to wish to defend it against tyranny" (Fenton 1998: 39).

5. At the time of Horace, homogeneous (at least putatively) Romans were fighting homogeneous Parthians. But most international situations since then have been much more complex. Although rarely pointed out in the literature on patriotism, its definition as the sentiment of the members of a bounded nation must be revamped. For example, Indians and Africans (Killingray 2010) fought for the queen, that is, for the British Empire, as did Gurkhas from Nepal. Most astonishing is the example of the Takasago people—Taiwanese aborigines, who became *tokkōtai* pilots toward the end of World War II, sacrificing themselves for the Japanese emperor (Huang 2001).

6. Although the standard translation of this term by the Allied forces after the war was "Imperial General Headquarters," "Imperial" refers to the Imperial Army and Imperial Navy. Created in 1893, it was the equivalent of the Joint Chiefs of Staff.

7. As seen in the exhibition "Blood and Spirit: Bach, Mendelssohn and Their Music in the Third Reich" (May through November 8, 2009) at the Johann Sebastian Bach Museum in Eisenach, in the former East Germany.

8. Planes representing modernization, often with Stalin's image alongside, are the theme of many posters (Bonnell 1997: Figure 4.13; Stalinka EA000001, GR000013, GR000014, GR000/024, GR000041-44, GR000074, GR000094, GR000097, GR000113, GR000114, PH000139). Warships (e.g., the cruiser *Chervona Ukraina* in 1933) (Groys and Hollein, eds., 2003: 208) and tanks (1927: 209, and 1931: 189, in Groys and Hollein, eds., 2003) were painted as well. Agriculture (farmers and farms) is the theme of a number of paintings reproduced in Groys and Hollein 2003: *Reapers*, dated 1928–1929 (p. 184); *Three Women on the Road*, c. 1930 (p. 185); *Hay-makers*, first half of the 1930s (p. 186); *Collective Farms Greeting a Tank*, 1937 (p. 187); *Bread*, 1949 (p. 225). *All Union Agricultural Exhibition*, dated 1939, is reproduced in Stalinka GR000053.

9. Anderson calls the imperial nationalism of Japan a variant of "official nationalism," borrowing the term from Seton-Watson, which he defines as a "willed merger of nation and dynastic empire" (Anderson 1983 [1991]: 86, 95–99). Anderson might have wrongly assumed that the emperor system had been politically powerful in pre-Meiji Japan—a common misunderstanding. There really had been no equivalent of the Romanov dynasty in Japan (see Chapter Six).

10. A catalogue of cigarette packages was published by the Museum of Tobacco and Salt (see Tabako to Shio no Hakubutsukan, ed., 1985: 147–217). Four names came from a poem by the nativist scholar Motoori Norinaga: "If we are to ask about the spirit of the Japanese, it is mountain cherry blossoms that bloom fragrantly in the morning sun." Cherry blossoms recur as both the label and the design on these cigarette packages. These designs of cigarette packages included symbols of modernization, such as factories, and militarism, such as fighter planes. Perhaps to show their effort to modernize Japan's image, a number of the labels are in the Latin alphabet, e.g. "Cherry." Nonetheless, those of primordial Japanese identity far outweigh them, following the same pattern as stamps and currency bills.

11. "Satsuma," a brand of cigarettes, was also the name given to a warship. It refers to

the place in Kyūshū where the second most powerful *han* (feudal domain) was located in the pre-Meiji period and from which many powerful Meiji politicians came.

12. This poem was written by Ōtomo no Yakamochi (726–785), who was in charge of the imperial border guards of ancient Japan. The music was composed by Nobutoki Kiyoshi in 1937 (Ohnuki-Tierney 2002a: 76–77).

CHAPTER SIX

1. The issue of sovereignty continued to be debated for some time after the promulgation of the constitution. The major points were: 1) the locus of sovereignty—whether it should be with the emperor or with the nation; and 2) the limits on the power of imperial sovereignty. Hozumi Yatsuka and his heir, Uesugi Shinkichi, championed the view, known as "imperial sovereign authority" (*tennō shuken setsu*), that the limitless power of sovereignty should rest with the emperor. Minobe Tatsukichi was a vociferous representative of the opposing view, known as the "organ theory" (*tennō kikan setsu*), which argued that sovereignty lay with the state and the emperor was a mere organ or mechanism. The final victory for those in support of a monarchical sovereign came in 1935, when Minobe was accused of "irreverence to the emperor" (*fukeizai*) and forced to resign from the House of Peers and other official posts. A year earlier, in 1934, his publications had been banned, despite strong support for Minobe among academics, intellectuals, and even bureaucrats (Nagao [1987] 1995). The emperor's chamberlain notes in his diary that the emperor stated that he would be comfortable with the organ theory (Toriumi 1996). A comparison of the official constitution of 1889 with the drafts by foreign advisors (translated in Ohnuki-Tierney 2002a: 71–72) shows nearly identical phrasing and notions regarding the identity of the emperor, except Article 1.

2. According to Shillony (1981: 36–38), even Emperor Shōwa abided by the principle that "a monarch should sanction the decisions of the duly constituted organs of state." This interpretation remains controversial.

3. Their control was limited, however, in stark contrast to outsiders' view of both the emperor and Tōjō as supremely powerful figures. The power Tōjō exercised bore no comparison to that held by Hitler (Payne 1995: 335; Shillony 1981: 67).

4. There had been ten empresses, two of whom reigned twice, thus making the actual number eight. Except for the two, they reigned during the ancient period, between the late sixth century and the mid-eighth century (Seki 1986; Ueda 1971). Although none was comparable to powerful queens in European monarchical systems, before Meiji there had been no legal prohibition against a woman on the throne; the last one, Empress Gosakuramachi, reigned from 1762 to 1770.

5. In Japanese culture the horse was considered a sacred messenger from the deities and the color white was considered to have sacred power (Miyata 1994). Still, the image could have been modeled after conventional portraits of Western political and military leaders, such as William the Conqueror at the Battle of Hastings in 1066, Joan of Arc in fifteenth-century France, George Washington crossing the Delaware in 1776, or Napoleon at Waterloo in 1815.

6. An additional factor for misunderstandings by non-Japanese is images of the Japanese tradition of bowing—presumably toward the emperor—that frequently appear

in the mass media, at least in the United States. Bowing is one of the most frequently depicted Japanese characteristics outside Japan. The individual's thoughts behind this behavior are seldom questioned, and the action is interpreted to signify reverence. Like the Hitler salute, bowing was in most cases compulsory during the military period in Japan, and simply customary in other times. But when this behavior was interpreted to signal deep reverence and the Japanese notion of deity was interpreted as God, then the Japanese emperor became very powerful—a gross misunderstanding.

7. Barthes ([1970] 1982: 30–32) extends the hollow center notion to the imperial system and polity, with the Imperial Palace constituting an empty space in the midst of Tokyo. Using the concept of the "Place of Nothingness" (*mu no basho*), Nishida Kitarō, an influential Kyoto school philosopher, during World War II elevated the emperor above the contradiction between the political power of the government and the people (Nishida [1940] 2004).

8. Ukemochi no Kami, the deity in charge of food, was the guardian of the imperial family; only after the emperor system was well established did the Sun Goddess become the imperial ancestress.

9. They include the emperor's viewing of sumō in front of the Nanden (June 29, 861) and the Shishinden (July 24, 867), the two most important buildings in the Imperial Palace in Kyoto. In addition to the viewing of sumō and the Italian circus on April 26, 1887 (see Sensu 2009; Tierney n.d.), the first viewing of a kabuki performance by Emperor Meiji took place at the manor of the foreign minister Inoue Kaoru, now the site of the International House of Japan. Since this performing art was originally an occupation of a discriminated group, it had been taboo for the emperor to view performances.

10. Fujitani (1998: 197–229) offers a different interpretation, emphasizing the visibility of the emperor and its impact on the "crowds" at imperial pageants.

11. The painstaking research of Morita (2006) on pre-Meiji imperial ritual reveals that, although other rituals were private, some accession rituals were open to the public. The first accession ritual for which the imperial court sent out a notice to the people was in 1710 for Emperor Nakamikado, but only a limited number of tickets were issued. Although the number of people allowed to observe is not available in most cases, for the accession ritual for Emperor Momozono in 1747, there were all together three hundred people, who sat at designated places. Needless to say, they were not allowed to observe the secret *mitamashizume* ritual.

12. The practice of *mitate* in literary, visual, and performative arts uses several types of indirect representation, such as substitutes. In the artistic tradition called the "artistic representations of beautiful women" (*bijinga*), the "beautiful women" depicted in fact are men, as in the case of the monkey trainer, an occupation forbidden to women (Kobayashi 1993; Ohnuki-Tierney 1987: 102). This technique became convenient for the people under the shogunate, which in 1772 issued an ordinance prohibiting any reference to contemporary political events and officials in visual and performing arts (Kornicki 1977). The *mitate* technique enabled artists to tell the story of political events, often involving injustices committed by the government, under the guise of another occasion in a different historical period. In the performing arts, the best-known example

is the play *Chūshingura* (The Forty-seven Loyal Retainers), in which an event occurring at one time was transposed chronologically to a time several hundred years before (for a detailed analysis, see Ohnuki-Tierney 2002a: 142–50).

Censorship continued until 1884, but only nominally, and the Meiji government did not impose new regulations until 1885. Therefore, the frequent use of *mitate* in these woodblock prints in early Meiji was due not to government censorship but to artistic convention.

13. Another convention is that the reigning emperor is referred to only as Kinjō. Thus, Emperor Shōwa was referred to only as "the Emperor" or "Kinjō Tennō" while on the throne.

After the war, following the Western custom, stamps started to use the images of the crown prince and his wife. A set of stamps was issued in 1959 with the then crown prince, who is currently emperor, and another in 1993 for the current crown prince. There is a clear distinction between a crown prince, an ordinary human, and an emperor with special magico-religious powers (Ohnuki-Tierney 1991b).

14. Jingū Kōgō, who appears in the two oldest myth-histories of Japan, the *Kojiki* and the *Nihongi*, was a shaman-empress, the wife of the fourteenth emperor, Chūi, with whom she conquered the Kumaso of southern Kyūshū; acting by herself, she led the forces that conquered the Shiragi (Koreans), after which she gave birth to the fifteenth emperor, Ōjin.

15. On currency bills, they include Yamato Takeru-no-Mikoto; a semimythical prince, Prince Shōtoku; and politicians who fought for or helped various emperors (Bonanza Henshūbu 1984: 151–53, 204–9). A bill with the sixteen-petal chrysanthemum, four sets of cherry blossoms, and the rays of the rising sun over Mount Fuji was issued in 1938. It bears an inscription on the left noting the date to be the 13th year of the reign of Emperor Shōwa, and on the right, the 2,598th year from the enthronement of the legendary first emperor.

16. This belief is embedded in the notion that Japan, called *Yamato-no-kuni*, is blessed with deities and flourishes with the souls of words, as clearly expressed in the beginning of a poem by Yamanoue no Okura (Satake et al., eds., 1999: 504).

17. Until Emperor Taishō abolished it, the emperors had always practiced polygyny, and information about every emperor's mother, almost always a co-wife, was public. Co-wives were called women in "the adjacent room" (*sokushitsu*), and they came, often but not always, from upper-class families, such as the family of a former shogun or a high official at the imperial court. Emperor Meiji, who had no offspring with his wife, had six women in "adjacent rooms" with whom he had fifteen children, one of whom became Emperor Taishō.

18. I thank R. Kenji Tierney for acquiring these postcards, which bear no date of issuance.

CHAPTER SEVEN

1. There has been a debate over the relationship between magic, science, religions, and rationality (Tambiah 1990). This relationship has been an important issue in the question of modernity and modernization, which some view, erroneously in my opinion,

as a unilinear process of progress through the "disenchantment of the world"—a phrase used originally by Johan Christoph Friedrich von Schiller but made famous by Max Weber. It has been widely claimed that the West shed "magic," thereby abandoning the medieval, traversing the Enlightenment, and arriving at the modern period. Anthropological debates began with an assignment of magic to "primitives" and religion to the "civilized," i.e., Westerners—a false dichotomy that has been challenged, though it still is considered useful in some quarters (see Thomas 1971). A most memorable attack was launched by Leach ([1966] 2000), who pointed out how beliefs and practices of others are called magic, but "our" beliefs, such as virgin birth in Christianity, are considered "religious." Another problem in the study of "religion" is how the term should be defined across time and space. Asad argues that "a universal definition of religion" was made in seventeenth-century Europe (Asad 1983: 244; 1993: 40) and then privileged and widely adopted, but in fact religion is a construct—produced by power—at a particular historical place and time (1983: 252). As a minimum definition, the notion of transcendence has been variously conceptualized within Western philosophies and theologies. However, it is altogether alien to the Japanese (Ohnuki-Tierney 1991b) and many other peoples who do not practice the Abrahamic religions.

2. Although it is beyond the scope of this book, there has been a long debate in various academic disciplines over the question of what constitutes religion.

3. For a detailed discussion of the concept of divine kingship and its critique, see Ohnuki-Tierney 1993a: 58–62; 2005: 221–25. On the original formulation of "divine kingship," see also Hubert and Mauss [1898] 1964; Robertson Smith [1889] 1972. Later scholars on the topic include: Dumont (1966 [1970]); de Heusch (1985); Feeley-Harnik (1985); Geertz (1980: 124–36); Sahlins (1985); Tambiah (1976); Valeri (1985); and Vansina (1978: 207–9). Some scholars consider the Japanese emperor system as a divine kingship in Frazer's sense. Orikuchi ([1928] 1975) first proposed this interpretation; his followers include Ebersole (1989) and Yamaori (1990a; 1990b).

4. In anthropology, the model of divine kingship centered on violent death, either of a sacrificial animal or in the form of regicide, as the precondition for the rebirth of the divine king (Smith [1889] 1972: 236–43; Hubert and Mauss [1898] 1964). In recent decades, however, there have been spirited charges against this interpretation. For example, Gillian Feeley-Harnik (1985: 276) claims that divine kingship has existed mostly in the imagination of anthropologists. Benjamin C. Ray (1991: 22–53) sharply criticizes Frazer's original formulation, arguing that it was based only on the classical example of the slaying of the priest-king of Diana at Nemi near Rome but was expanded by Frazer and his followers into a universal model.

5. The Japanese government forced the Ainu to sell bearskins and carved bears as souvenirs for tourists.

6. See also Kantorowicz [1957] 1981: figures 1, 2, and 32; and Smith 1989: 46, for the Head of Constantius II, minted 337–361 CE in Alexandria.

References

The place of publication of works in Japanese is Tokyo unless otherwise noted.

Adorno, Theodor W. [1970] 1997. *Aesthetic Theory*. Minneapolis: University of Minnesota Press.

Akima Toshio. 1972. Shisha no Uta—Saimei Tennō no Kayō to Asobibe (The songs of the dead: Songs of Emperor Saimei and *Asobibe*). *Bungaku* 40(3): 97–112 (337–52).

———. 1982. The Songs of the Dead: Poetry, Drama, and Ancient Rituals of Japan. *Journal of Asian Studies* 41(3): 485–509.

Akimoto Kichirō. [713] 1958. Hitachi-no-Kuni Fudoki (Folkways in Hitachi). In *Fudoki* (Folkways). Akimoto Kichirō, ed. Pp. 33–92. Iwanami Shoten.

Althusser, Louis. 1971. *Lenin and Philosophy*. New York: Monthly Review Press.

Amino Yoshihiko. 1980. *Nihon Chūsei no Minshūzō—Heimin to Shokunin* (Portrait of the folk in medieval Japan: The common people and the "professionals"). Iwanami Shoten.

———. 1986. Ajiya to Umi no Butai o Haikei ni (Against the background of Asia and the sea). In *Asahi Hyakka: Nihon no Rekishi* (Asahi encyclopedia: Japanese history), vol. 1: 2–3. Asahi Shinbunsha.

———. 1987. Chūsei no Futan Taikei (The levy system in the medieval period). *Miura Kobunka* 41: 1–11.

———. 1989. *Ikei no Ōken* (An unorthodox kingship). Heibonsha.

———. 2000. *"Nihon" to wa Nanika* (What is so-called "Japan"?). Kōdansha.

Anderson, Benedict R. O'G. [1983] 1991. *Imagined Communities: Reflections on the Origin and Spread of Nationalism*. London: Verso.

Aoki Kōji. 1967. *Hyakushō Ikki no Nenjiteki Kenkyū* (Chronological study of peasant rebellions). Shinseisha.

Arai Mujirō. [1939] 1965. *Hyōshaku Ise Monogatari Taisei* (The *Tale of Ise* with annotations). Yukawa Kōbunsha.

Arrizabalaga y Prado, Leonardo de. 2010. *The Emperor Elagabalus: Fact of Fiction?* Cambridge: Cambridge University Press.

Asad, Talal. 1983. Anthropological Conceptions of Religion: Reflections on Geertz. *Man* 18: 237–59.

———. 1993. *Genealogies of Religion.* Baltimore: Johns Hopkins University Press.

Atkins, Jacqueline M. 2005. *Wearing Propaganda: Textiles on the Home Front in Japan, Britain, and the United States, 1931–1945.* New Haven, CT: Yale University Press.

Auerbach, Erich. [1946] 1974. *Mimesis: The Representation of Reality in Western Literature.* Princeton, NJ: Princeton University Press.

Augé, Marc. [1992] 1995. *Non-Places: Introduction to an Anthropology of Supermodernity.* London: Verso.

Aulich, James, and Marta Sylvestrová. 1999. *Political Posters in Central and Eastern Europe, 1945–95.* Manchester, UK: Manchester University Press.

Bakhtin, Mikhail M. [1965] 1984. *Rabelais and His World.* Bloomington: Indiana University Press.

Balfour, Sebastian, and Alejandro Quiroga. 2007. *The Reinvention of Spain: Nation and Identity since Democracy.* Oxford: Oxford University Press.

Barthes, Roland. [1970] 1982. *Empire of Signs.* New York: Hill and Wang.

Basso, Keith. 1981. "Wise Words" of the Western Apache: Metaphor and Semantic Theory. In *Language, Culture and Cognition: Anthropological Perspectives.* R. W. Casson, ed. Pp. 244–67. New York: Macmillan.

Bataille, Georges. [1967] [1989] 1991. *The Accursed Share.* New York: Zone Books.

Baudelaire, Charles. [1855] 2001. *The Painter of Modern Life and Other Essays.* London: Phaidon.

———. [1857] [1869] 1991. *The Flowers of Evil and Paris Spleen: Poems by Charles Baudelaire.* William H. Crosby, trans. Brockport, NY: BOA Editions.

———. [1869] 1949. *Journaux intimes: Fusées Mon coeur mis à nu Carnet.* Édition critique établie par Jacques Crépet et Georges Blin. Paris: Librairie José Corti. English trans., *My Heart Laid Bare and Other Prose Writings* [1949] 1951, edited with introduction by Peter Quennell, trans. by Norman Cameron. New York: Vanguard.

Beasley, W. G. [1989] 1996. Meiji Political Institutions. In *The Cambridge History of Japan.* Vol. 5, *The Nineteenth Century.* Marius B. Jansen, ed. Pp. 618–73. Cambridge: Cambridge University Press.

Beidelman, T. O. 1980. The Moral Imagination of the Kaguru: Some Thoughts on Trickster, Translation and Comparative Analysis. *American Ethnologist* 7(1): 27–42.

Benedict, Ruth. 1946. *The Chrysanthemum and the Sword: Patterns of Japanese Culture.* New York: New American Library.

Benjamin, Walter. [1928] 1986. One-Way Street. In *Reflections.* Peter Demetz, ed. Pp. 61–94. New York: Schoken Books.

———. [1931] 1998. A Small History of Photography. *One-Way Street and Other Writings.* In *Reflections.* Peter Demetz, ed. Pp. 240–57. London: Verso.

———. [1936] 1968. The Work of Art in the Age of Mechanical Reproduction. In *Illuminations.* Hannah Arendt, ed. Pp. 217–51. New York: Schoken Books.

————. [1950] 1968. *Theses on the Philosophy of History*. In *Illuminations*. Hannah Arendt, ed. Pp. 253–64. New York: Schoken Books.

Benveniste, Émile. 1966. *Problems in General Linguistics*. Miami, OH: University of Miami Press.

Berezin, Mabel. 1997. *Making the Fascist Self: The Political Culture of Interwar Italy*. Ithaca, NY: Cornell University Press.

Berlin, Isaiah. [1958] 1969. Two Concepts of Liberty. In *Four Essays on Liberty*, pp. 118–72. Oxford: Oxford University Press.

————. [1959] 1992. *The Crooked Timber of Humanity*. New York: Random House.

————. 1999. *The Roots of Romanticism*. Henry Hardy, ed. Princeton, NJ: Princeton University Press.

Berque, Augustin. 1984. The Sense of Nature and Its Relation to Space in Japan. In *Interpreting Japanese Society*. J. Hendry and J. Webber, eds. *Journal of the Anthropological Society of Oxford* 15(2): 100–110.

————. 1990. *Nihon no Fūkei, Seiyō no Keikan, Soshite Zōkei no Jidai* (Comparative history of landscape in East Asia and Europe [Le Paysage au Japon, en Europe, et à l'ère du paysagement]). Shinoda Katsuhide, trans. Kōdansha.

Bertelli, Sergio. 2001. *The King's Body*. Burr Litchfield, trans. College Park: Pennsylvania State University Press. Original Italian, *Il corpo del re: Sacralità del potere nell' Europa medievale e moderna*. 1990. Florence: Gruppo Editoriale Florentino.

Billington, James H. [1966] 1970. *The Icon and the Axe: An Interpretative History of Russian Culture*. New York: Random House.

Blacker, Carmen. 1975. *The Catalpa Bow: A Study of Shamanistic Practices in Japan*. London: George Allen & Unwin.

Bloch, Marc. [1961] 1989. *The Royal Touch: Sacred Monarchy and Scrofula in England and France*. J. E. Anderson, trans. London: Dorset Press.

Bœspflug, François. 2008. *Dieu et ses images: Une histoire de l'Éternel dans l'art*. Montrouge: Bayard Éditions.

Bonanza Henshūbu. 1984. *Nihon Kindai Shihei Sōran* (Overview of Japanese paper currency). Bonanza.

Bonnell, Victoria. 1997. *The Iconography of Power: Soviet Political Posters under Lenin and Stalin*. Berkeley: University of California Press.

Borneman, John. 2005a. Preface. In *Death of the Father: An Anthropology of the End of Political Authority*. John Borneman, ed. Pp. vi–x. New York: Berghahn.

————. 2005b. *Gottvater, Landesvater, Familienvater*: Identification and Authority in Germany. In *Death of the Father: An Anthropology of the End of Political Authority*. John Borneman, ed. Pp. 63–103. New York: Berghahn.

Bosworth, Albert Brian. 1996. Alexander III. In *The Oxford Classical Dictionary*. 3rd ed. Simon Hornblower and Antony Spawforth, eds. Pp. 57–59. Oxford: Oxford University Press.

Bourdieu, Pierre. [1979] 1984. *Distinction: A Social Critique of the Judgement of Taste*. Cambridge, MA: Harvard University Press.

————. 1990. *In Other Words: Essays Towards a Reflexive Sociology*. Stanford, CA: Stanford University Press.

———. 1991. *Language and Symbolic Power*. Cambridge: Polity Press.

Bourdieu, Pierre, and Alain Darbel. [1969] 1990. *The Love of Art: European Museums and Their Public*. Stanford, CA: Stanford University Press.

Bourdieu, Pierre, and Jean-Claude Passeron. 1977. *Reproduction in Education, Society and Culture*. Thousand Oaks, CA: Sage Publications.

Bourdieu, Pierre, and Loïc J. D. Wacquant. 1992. *An Invitation to Reflexive Sociology*. Chicago: University of Chicago Press.

Boyer, Dominic. 2005. *Spirit and System: Media, Intellectuals, and the Dialectic in Modern German Culture*. Chicago: University of Chicago Press.

Braudel, Fernand. [1958] 1980. *On History*. Chicago: University of Chicago Press.

Brettell, Richard R., and Caroline B. Brettell. 1983. *Painters and Peasants in the Nineteenth Century*. New York: Rizzoli.

Brubaker, Rogers, and Frederick Cooper. 2000. Beyond "Identity." *Theory and Society* 29: 1–47.

Burke, Edmund. [1757] 1998. A Philosophical Enquiry into the Origin of our Ideas of the Sublime and Beautiful. In *A Philosophical Enquiry into the Origin of our Ideas of the Sublime and Beautiful and Other Pre-Revolutionary Writings*, pp. 49–199. London: Penguin.

Burke, Kenneth. [1945] 1969. *A Grammar of Motives*. Berkeley: University of California Press.

Burke, Peter. [1992] 1999. *The Fabrication of Louis XIV*. New Haven, CT: Yale University Press.

Buruma, Ian. 2013. *Year Zero: A History of 1945*. London: Penguin.

Bynum, Caroline Walker. 2011. *Christian Materiality: An Essay on Religion in Late Medieval Europe*. New York: Zone Books.

Bytwerk, Randall L. 2004. *Bending Spines: The Propagandas of Nazi Germany and the German Democratic Republic*. East Lansing: Michigan State University Press.

———. 2007a. Nazi Era Posters: 1933–1939. www.bytwerk.com/gpa/posters2.htm.

———. 2007b. Nazi Era Posters: 1939–1945. www.bytwerk.com/gpa/posters3.htm.

Calder, Kent E. 1988. *Crisis and Compensation: Public Policy and Political Stability in Japan, 1949–1986*. Princeton, NJ: Princeton University Press.

Cassirer, Ernst. 1955. *The Philosophy of Symbolic Forms*. Vol. 2. New Haven, CT: Yale University Press.

Chabal, Patrick, and Jean-Pascal Daloz. 2006. *Culture Troubles: Politics and the Interpretation of Meaning*. Chicago: University of Chicago Press.

Chamberlain, Lesley. 2014. Sacrificing Beauty. *Times Literary Supplement*, April 18: 14–15.

Chatterjee, Partha. 1993. *The Nation and Its Fragments*. Princeton, NJ: Princeton University Press.

Chevalier, Jean, and Alain Gheerbrant. [1969] 1996. *A Dictionary of Symbols*. London: Penguin.

Clendinnen, Inga. 2010. *The Cost of Courage in Aztec Society*. Cambridge: Cambridge University Press.

Cook, Haruko Taya, and Theodore Cook. 1992. *Japan at War: An Oral History*. New York: New Press.

Cooper, J. C. 1978. *An Illustrated Encyclopaedia of Traditional Symbols*. London: Thames and Hudson.

Cowen, Painton. 2005. *The Rose Window: Splendour and Symbol*. London: Thames and Hudson.

Cranston, Edwin A. 1993. *A Waka Anthrology*. Vol. 1. Stanford, CA: Stanford University Press.

Crawford, Michael H. 1996. Coinage, Roman. *The Oxford Classical Dictionary*. 3rd ed. Simon Hornblower and Antony Spawforth, eds. Pp. 358–61. Oxford: Oxford University Press.

Davis, Natalie Zemon. [1965] 1975. *Society and Culture in Early Modern France*. Stanford, CA: Stanford University Press.

de Certeau, Michel. [1975] 1988. *The Writing of History*. New York: Columbia University Press.

———. [1984] 1988. *The Practice of Everyday Life*. Berkeley: University of California Press.

de Certeau, Michel, and Régine Robin. 1976. Le Discours historique et le réel. *Dialectiques* 14: 41–62.

de Heusch, Luc. 1985. *Sacrifice in Africa*. Bloomington: Indiana University Press.

de Lorris, Guillaume, and Jean de Meun. 1982–1984. *Le Roman de la Rose*. 2nd ed. Paris: Libraire Honoré Champion.

de Maistre, Joseph. [1870] 1996. *Against Rousseau: "On the State of Nature" and "On the Sovereignty of the People."* Richard A Lebrun, trans. and ed. Montreal: McGill-Queen's University Press.

Derrida, Jacques. [1967] 1976. *Of Grammatology*. Gayatri Chakravorty Spivak, trans. Baltimore: Johns Hopkins University Press.

———. [1967] 1978. *Writing and Difference*. Alan Bass, trans. London: Routledge & Kegan Paul.

Descola, Philippe. 2010. *La Fabrique des images: Vision du monde et formes de la Représatation*. Paris: Somogy & Musée du quai Branly.

Di Bella, Maria Pia. 2004. From Future to Past: A Duce's Trajectory. In *Death of the Father: An Anthropology of the End of Political Authority*. John Borneman, ed. Pp. 33–62. New York: Berghahn.

Dickinson, Frederick. 2009. *Taishō Tennō* (The Taishō emperor). Minerva.

Dijksterhuis, E. J. [1950] 1986. *The Mechanization of the World Picture: Pythagoras to Newton*. Princeton, NJ: Princeton University Press.

Dore, Ronald P. [1958] 1973. *Shinohata: A Portrait of a Japanese Village*. New York: Pantheon.

Duara, Prasenjit. 1995. *Rescuing History from the Nation*. Chicago: University of Chicago Press.

Dumbach, Annette, and Jud Newborn. 2006. *Sophie Scholl and the White Rose*. Oxford: One World.

Dumont, Louis. [1966] 1970. *Homo Hierarchicus*. Chicago: University of Chicago Press.

Durán, Fray Diego. 1964. *The Aztecs: The History of the Indies of New Spain*. London: Cassell.

Duus, Peter. 1988. Socialism, Liberalism, and Marxism, 1901–1931. In *The Cambridge History of Japan*. Vol. 6, *The Twentieth Century*. Peter Duus, ed. Pp. 654–710. Cambridge: Cambridge University Press.

Duus, Peter, and Daniel Okimoto. 1979. Fascism and the History of Prewar Japan: The Failure of a Concept. *Journal of Asian Studies* 39(1): 65–76.

Eagleton, Terry. [1983] 2001. *Literary Theory*. Minneapolis: University of Minnesota Press.

———. [1990] 1991. *The Ideology of the Aesthetic*. Cambridge, MA: Basil Blackwell.

Earhart, David C. 2008. *Certain Victory: Images of World War II in Japanese Media*. Armonk, NY: M.E. Sharp.

Ebersole, Gary L. 1989. *Ritual Poetry and the Politics of Death in Early Japan*. Princeton, NJ: Princeton University Press.

Ebina Kenzō. 1977. *Kaigun Yobi-Gakusei* (The navy student reserve). Tosho Shuppansha.

———. 1983. *Taiheiyō Sensō ni Shisu—Kaigun Hikō Yobi Shōkō no Sei to Shi* (To die in the Pacific War: The life and death of navy aviation reserve officers). Nishida Shoten.

Ebon, Martin. 1987. *The Soviet Propaganda Machine*. New York: McGraw-Hill.

Eco, Umberto, ed. 2005. *History of Beauty*. New York: Rizzoli.

Eisenstadt, S. N. 1996. *Japanese Civilization: A Comparative View*. Chicago: University of Chicago Press.

Eksteins, Modris. 1989. *Rites of Spring: The Great War and the Birth of the Modern Age*. New York: Doubleday.

Elison, George. 1981. Hideyoshi, the Bountiful Minister. In *Warlords, Artists and Commoners: Japan in the Sixteenth Century*. George Elison and Bardwell L. Smith, eds. Pp. 222–44. Honolulu: University of Press of Hawaii.

Elliott, John H. 1985. Power and Propaganda in the Spain of Philip IV. In *Rites of Power: Symbolism, Ritual and Politics since the Middle Ages*. Sean Wilentz, ed. Pp. 145–73. Philadelphia: University of Pennsylvania Press.

Empson, William. 1963. *Seven Types of Ambiguity*. 3rd ed. London: Chatto and Windus.

Emura Eiichi, ed. [1989] 1996. *Kenpō Kōsō* (Drafts of the constitution). Vol. 9 of *Nihon Kindai Shisō Taikei* (Compendium of modern Japanese thought). Iwanami Shoten.

Enomoto Yukio. 1975. San Dai Kessaku no Seiritsu (The development of three masterpieces). In *San Dai Kabuki* (Three kabuki masterpieces). Gunji Masakatsu, ed. Pp. 171–95. Mainichi Shinbunsha.

Erdheim, Mario. 1972. *Prestige und Kulturwandel: Eine Studie zum Verhältnis subjektiver und objektiver Faktoren des kulturellen Wandels zur Klassengesellschaft bei den Azteken*. Wiesbaden: Focus-Verlag.

Evans, Richard J. 2005. *The Third Reich in Power, 1933–1939*. London: Penguin.

Falasca-Zamponi, Simonetta. 1997. *Fascist Spectacle: The Aesthetics of Power in Mussolini's Italy*. Berkeley: University of California Press.

Feeley-Harnik, Gillian. 1985. Issues in Divine Kingship. *Annual Review of Anthropology* 14: 273–313.

Fenton, James. 1998. Keats the Radical. Review of *John Keats and the Culture of Dissent* by Nicholas Roe. *New York Review of Books* 15(8): 39–41.

Fernandez, James. 1980. Reflections on Looking into Mirrors. *Semiotica* 30(1/2): 27–39.

————. 1986. *Persuasions and Performances: The Play of Tropes in Culture.* Bloomington: Indiana University Press.

Field, Norma. 1987. *The Splendor of Longing in the "Tale of Genji."* Princeton, NJ: Princeton University Press. Repr., University of Michigan Press, 2001.

Flaubert, Gustave. 1884. *Madame Bovary.* Paris: G. Charpentier.

————. [1950] 1968. *Madame Bovary.* English trans. New York: Penguin.

Flett, Keith. 2002. May Day: Festival for the Workers. *Socialist Review,* no. 263 (May): 24–25.

Foucault, Michel. [1975] 1995. *Discipline and Punish.* New York: Random House.

Frazer, James George. [1890] [1911–1915]. 1963. *The New Golden Bough: A Study in Magic and Religion.* 3rd ed. Part 1. *The Magic Art and the Evolution of Kings.* Vol. 1. London: Macmillan.

Friedrich, Paul. 1979. *Language, Context, and the Imagination.* Stanford, CA: Stanford University Press.

Fujii Jōji. 2011. *Tennō to Tenkabito* (Emperors and warlords). Kōdansha.

Fujii Shōichi. [1984] 1996. Kigen Nisen Ryoppyakunen Hōshukuten (The celebration of the accession of the Jinmu emperor 2,600 years ago). In *Kokushi Daijiten* (Dictionary of national history), vol. 4: 55–56. Yoshikawa Kōbunkan.

Fujioka Michio. 1956. *Kyōto Gosho* (The Kyoto imperial palace). Shōkokusha.

Fujitani, Takashi. 1998. *Splendid Monarchy: Power and Pageantry in Modern Japan.* Berkeley: University of California Press.

Fukuyama Toshio. [1985] 1997. Kōreiden (Shrine for the imperial soul). In *Kokushi Daijiten* (Dictionary of national history), vol. 5: 561. Yoshikawa Kōbunkan.

Furet, François. [1988] 1996. *The French Revolution, 1770–1814.* Oxford: Blackwell.

Gajek, Esther. 1990. Christmas under the Third Reich. *Anthropology Today* 6(4): 3–9.

Geertz, Clifford. 1973. *The Interpretation of Cultures.* New York: Basic Books.

————. [1977] 1983. *Local Knowledge.* New York: Basic Books.

————. 1980. *Negara: The Theatre State in Nineteenth-Century Bali.* Princeton, NJ: Princeton University Press.

————. 1995. *After the Fact: Two Countries, Four Decades, One Anthropologist.* Cambridge, MA: Harvard University Press.

Gellner, Ernest. 1983. *Nations and Nationalism.* Ithaca, NY: Cornell University Press.

Gentile, Emilio. 1996. *The Sacrization of Politics in Fascist Italy.* Cambridge, MA: Harvard University Press.

Geschiere, Peter. 2009. *The Perils of Belonging: Authochthony, Citizenship, and Exclusion in Africa and Europe.* Chicago: University of Chicago Press.

Giddens, Anthony. 1979. *Central Problems in Social Theory: Action, Structure, and Contradiction in Social Analysis.* London: Macmillan.

Gluck, Carol. 1985. *Japan's Modern Myths.* Princeton, NJ: Princeton University Press.

Goebbels, Joseph. 1973. The Führer Hitler as an Orator. In *The Propaganda of Adolf Hitler.* Hermann Goering et al., eds. Pp. 27–34. English edition by J. R. Manning. Phoenix, AZ: O'Sullivan, Woodside.

Goering, Hermann, and eleven other ministers of the Third Reich. [1936] 1973. *The Propaganda of Adolf Hitler.* Originally published in 1936 as *Adolf Hitler, Bilder aus dem Leben des Führers*. English edition by J. R. Manning. Phoenix, AZ: O'Sullivan, Woodside.

Gonda Yasunosuke. 1971. Sarumawashi (The monkey performance). In *Ryūmin* (The non-settlers). Hayashi Hideo, ed. Pp. 317–18. Shinjinbutsu Ōraisha.

Goody, Jack. 1993. *The Culture of Flowers*. Cambridge: Cambridge University Press.

Gordon, Andrew. 1991. *Labor and Imperial Democracy in Prewar Japan*. Berkeley: University of California Press.

Gotō Shigeki. 1975. *Tōkaidō Gojū-San Tsugi* (Fifty-three stations along the Tōkaidō). Shūeisha.

Graham, William A. 1983. Islam in the Mirror of Ritual. In *Islam's Understanding of Itself*. Richard G. Hovannisian and Speros Vryonis, Jr., eds. Pp. 53–71. Malibu, CA: Gustave E. Von Grunebaum Undena Publications.

Griffin, Jasper. 2004. The Myth of the Olympics. *New York Review of Books*, Oct. 21: 19–21.

Groys, Boris, and Max Hollein, eds. 2003. *Traumfabrik Kommunismus: Die Visuelle Kultur der Stalinzeit* (Dream factory communism: The visual culture of the Stalin era). Catalogue of exhibition at Schirn Kunsthalle Frankfurt, Sept. 24, 2003–Jan. 4, 2004. Schirn Kunsthalle Frankfurt.

Gunji Masakatsu et al., eds. 1970. *Meisaku Kabuki Zenshū* (A collection of kabuki masterpieces). Vol. 19. Sōgen Shinsha.

Habermas, Jürgen. 1984. *The Theory of Communicative Action: Reason and the Rationalization of Society*. Vol. 1. Thomas A. McCarthy, trans. Boston: Beacon.

Haga Shōji. 2002. Tennō to Junkō (The emperor and his tours). In *Tennō to Ōken o Kangaeru* (On the emperor and kingship), pp. 111–34. Vol. 10 of *Ō o Meguru Shisen* (The gaze in reference to the emperor). Amino Yoshihiko et al., eds. Iwanami Shoten.

Hall, Edward T. [1966] 1969. *The Hidden Dimension*. New York: Doubleday.

Hall, John A., ed. 1998. *The State of the Nation*. Cambridge: Cambridge University Press.

Handler, Richard. 1988. *Nationalism and the Politics of Culture in Quebec*. Madison: University of Wisconsin Press.

Hara Takeshi. 2002. "Kokutai" no Shikakuka—Taishō Shōwa Shoki ni okeru Tennōsei no Saihen (Visualization of the "national body": The reorganization of the imperial system during the Taishō and the beginning of Shōwa). In *Tennō to Ōken o Kangaeru* (On the emperor and kingship), pp. 135–59. Vol. 10 of *Ō o Meguru Shisen* (The gaze in reference to the emperor). Amino Yoshihiko et al., eds. Iwanami Shoten.

Harada Nobuo. 1993. *Rekishi no Naka no Kome to Niku—Shokumotsu to Tennō Sabetsu* (Rice and meat in history: Food, emperor, and discrimination). Heibonsha.

Harada Tomohiko. 1978a. Buraku no Zenshi (The early history of the buraku). In *Buraku Mondai Yōsetsu* (Outline of buraku problems). Buraku Kaihō Kenkyūsho, ed. Pp. 16–23. Buraku Kaihō Kenkyūsho.

———. 1978b. Kinsei Hōken Shakai to Buraku Keisei (The feudal society of the early modern period and the formation of the buraku). In *Buraku Mondai Yōsetsu*. Buraku Kaihō Kenkyūsho, ed. Pp. 24–33. Buraku Kaihō Kenkyūsho.

Harootunian, Harry. 1988. *Things Seen and Unseen: Discourse and Ideology in Tokugawa Nativism*. Chicago: University of Chicago Press.

Hart-Davis, Duff. 1986. *Hitler's Games: The 1936 Olympics*. New York: Harper and Row.

Haruyama Takematsu. 1953. *Nihon Chūsei Kaigashi* (History of paintings in medieval Japan). Asahi Shinbunsha.

Harvey, David. 1990. *The Condition of Postmodernity: An Enquiry into the Origins of Cultural Change*. London: Blackwell.

Hassig, Ross. 1988. *Aztec Warfare: Imperial Expansion and Political Control*. Norman: University of Oklahoma Press.

Hattori Shōgo. 1991. Kamikaze Tokkōtai no Kōgeki (Attacks by kamikaze special attack forces). *Rekishi to Tabi* (Rinji Zōkangō 50): 342–45.

Hayashi Mikiya. [1986] 1994. Shōtoku Taishizō (Portraits of Shōtoku Taishi). *Kokushi Daijiten* (Dictionary of national history), vol. 7: 577. Yoshikawa Kōbunkan.

Hayashi Ya'ei. 1982. Kinsei Saibaishi (Horticulture in the early modern period). *Nihon Jishin* 23: 53–55.

Hayashiya Tatsusaburō. 1981. Chūsei Geinō no Shakaiteki Kiban (The social foundation of arts during the medieval period). In *Yōkyoku Kyōgen* (Yōkyoku and kyōgen). Nihon Bungaku Kenkyū Shiryō Kankōkai, ed. Pp. 201–9. Yūseidō Shuppan.

Heller, Steven. 2008. *Iron Fists: Branding the 20th-Century Totalitarian States*. London: Phaidon.

Hicks, Michael. 2012. *The Wars of Roses*. New Haven, CT: Yale University Press.

Hirose Shizumu. 1978. *Nihonzaru o Meguru Animaru Roa no Kenkyū* (Research on the animal lore of Japanese macaques). In *Shakai Bunka Jinruigaku* (Sociocultural anthropology). Katō Taian, Nakao Sasuke, and Umesao Tadao, eds. Pp. 287–334. Chūōkōronsha.

Hobsbawm, Eric. 1984. *Worlds of Labour*. London: Weidenfeld and Nicolson.

———. [1990] 1992. *Nations and Nationalism since 1780*. Cambridge: Cambridge University Press.

Hocart, A. M. [1927] 1969. *Kingship*. Oxford: Oxford University Press.

———. [1936] 1970. *Kings and Councilors: An Essay in the Comparative Anatomy of Human Society*. Chicago: University of Chicago Press.

Hoffmann, Heinrich. 1935. *Hitler baut Großdeutschland. Im Triumph von Königsberg nach Wien*. Berlin: Zeitgeschichte-Verlag.

———. 1938. *Hitler holt die Saar heim*. Foreword by Josef Bürckel. Berlin: Zeitgeschichte-Verlag.

———. 1939. *Ein Volk ehrt seinen Führer. Der 20. April 1939 im Bild*. Berlin: Zeitgeschichte-Verlag.

Horace [Quintus Horatius Flaccus]. [23 BCE] 1999. *Odes and Epodes*. C. E. Bennett, trans. Loeb Classical Library 33. Cambridge, MA: Harvard University Press.

Horiuchi Keizō and Inoue Takeshi, eds. [1958] 1995. *Nihon Shōkashū* (Collection of Japanese songs). Iwanami Shoten.

Hornblower, Simon, and Antony Spawforth, eds. 1996. *The Oxford Classical Dictionary*. Oxford: Oxford University Press.

Horton, H. Mack. 2012. *Traversing the Frontier: The "Man'yōshū" Account of a Japanese Mission to Silla in 736–737*. Cambridge, MA: Harvard University Press.

Hubert, Henri, and Marcel Mauss. [1898] 1964. *Sacrifice: Its Nature and Function.* Chicago: University of Chicago Press.

Huang, Chih-huei. 2001. The *Yamatodamashi* of the Takasago Volunteers of Taiwan. In *Globalizing Japan: Ethnography of the Japanese Presence in Asia, Europe and America.* Harumi Befu and Syvlie Guichard-Anguis, eds. Pp. 222–50. London: Routledge.

Hyers, Conrad. 1973. *Zen and the Comic Spirit.* Philadelphia: Westminster.

Iida Michio. 1973. *Saru Yomoyama Banashi—Saru to Nihon no Minzoku* (Tales about monkeys: The monkey and Japanese folkways). Hyōgensha.

———. 1983. *Mizaru Kikazaru Iwazaru—Sekai Sanzaru Genryūkō* (No see, No hear, No say: The sources of the three monkeys in various cultures of the world). Sanseidō.

Ikeda Kikan. 1987. *Genji Monogatari Jiten* (Dictionary of the *Tale of Genji*). Tōkyōdō Shuppan.

Imae Hiromichi. 1993. Sakon no Sakura Ukon no Tachibana (Cherry blossoms on the left and the mandarin orange on the right [of the Imperial Palace]). In *Nihonshi Daijiten* (Dictionary of Japanese history), vol. 3: 614. Shimonaka Hiroshi, ed. Heibonsha.

Inada Kōji and Ōshima Tatehiko. 1977. *Nihon Mukashibanashi Jiten* (Dictionary of Japanese folktales). Kōbundō.

Inada Masatsugu. 1960. *Meiji Kenpō Seiritsushi (Jō)* (History of the development of the Meiji constitution [Vol. 1]). Yūhikaku.

Inose Naoki. [1986] 1988. *Mikado no Shōzō* (Portraits of the emperor). Shōgakukan.

Inoue Hisashi. 1988. Kome no Hanashi (5)—Amerika no Kome (Discussion of rice (5): American rice). *Days Japan* 1(6): 103.

Inoue Kiyoshi. [1953] 1967. *Tennōsei* (The emperor system). Daigaku Shuppankai.

———. [1963a, 1963b] 1967. *Nihon no Rekishi* (History of Japan). Vol. 1 *(Jō)* (1963a), Vol. 2 *(Chū)* (1963b). Iwanami Shoten.

Irokawa Daikichi. [1970] 1997. *Meiji no Bunka* (The culture of Meiji Japan). Iwanami Shoten.

———. 1990. *Jiyūminken no Chikasui* (The underground water of the freedom and people's rights movement). Iwanami Shoten.

———. 1995. *The Age of Hirohito: In Search of Modern Japan.* Mikiso Hane and John K. Urda, trans. New York: Free Press.

Ishibashi Fushiha. 1914. Minzokugaku no Hōmen yori Mitaru Kagami (Anthropological interpretations of mirrors). *Jinruigaku Zasshi* 29(6): 223–27.

Ishii Ryōsuke. 1963. *Zoku Edo Jidai Manpitsu* (Essays on the Edo period), vol. 2 [1961]. Inoue Shoten.

Isozaki Arata. 1995. Ise. In *Ise Jingū* (Ise shrine). Ishimoto Yasuhiro, Isozaki Arata, and Inagaki Eizō, eds. Pp. 7–31. Iwanami Shoten.

Itō Shirō. 2011. *Matsuo Taisha no Shin'ei* (The images of the deities at the Matsuo Shrine). Matsuo Taisha.

Jacobson, Richard. 1978. Absence, Authority, and the Text. *Glyph* 3: 137–47.

Jameson, Fredric. [1991] 1993. *Postmodernism, or The Cultural Logic of Late Capitalism.* Durham, NC: Duke University Press.

———. 1992. *Signatures of the Visible.* London: Routledge.

Jauregui, Beatrice. 2010. Categories of Conflict and Coercion: The Blue in Green and the Other. In *Anthropology and Global Counterinsurgency*. J. D. Kelly, B. Jauregui, S. Mitchell, and J. Walton, eds. Pp. 17–22. Chicago: University of Chicago Press.

Jay, Martin. [1993] 1994. *Downcast Eyes: The Denigration of Vision in Twentieth-Century French Thought*. Berkeley: University of California Press.

Juntoku Emperor. [1219–1222] 1929. Kinpishō (Record of the affairs at the imperial palace). In *Gunsho Ruijū* (Collection of writings on related topics), vol. 26: 367–418. Hanawa Hoki'ichi, ed. Gunsho Ruijū Kanseikai.

Kageyama Haruki. 1978. *Shinzō* (Images of deities). Hōsei Daigaku Shuppankyoku.

Kaigo Tokiomi, ed. 1964. *Kokugo 6* (The national language [Vol. 6]). *Nihon Kyōkasho Taikei* (Outline of Japanese textbooks). Vol. 9, *Kindaihen* (Modern period). Kōdansha.

Kamo Momoki, Kaigun Daijin Kanbō, and Rikugun Daijin Kanbō, eds. 1933–1935. *Yasukuni Jinja Chūkonshi* (History of the loyal souls at the Yasukuni Shrine). Vol. 1 (1935), Vol. 2 (1934), Vol. 3 (1934), Vol. 4 (1935), Vol. 5 (1933). Yasukuni Jinja Shamusho.

Kant, Immanuel. [1790] 2000. *The Critique of Judgment*. Amherst, NY: Prometheus Books.

———. [1793] 2001. Second Book, Analytic of the Sublime. In *Basic Writings of Kant*. Allen W. Wood, ed. Pp. 306–8. New York: Random House.

Kantorowicz, Ernst H. [1957] 1981. *The King's Two Bodies*. Princeton, NJ: Princeton University Press.

Kanzaki Noritake. 1989. Monomiyusan no Minzoku: Sakariba eno Tenkai (The custom of viewing and playing in the mountains: Incipient development of entertainment districts). In *Nihonjin to Asobi* (The Japanese and their recreational activities). *Gendai Nihon Bunka ni okeru Dentō to Hen'yō 6* (Traditon and change in Japanese modern culture). Moriya Takeshi, ed. Pp. 76–91. Domesu Shuppan.

———. 1994. Hitobito wa Naze Yama ni Asondanoka (Why did people play in the mountains?). *Mahora* 1: 8–20.

Kaplan, Martha. 2001. Blood on the Grass and Dogs Will Speak. In *Represented Communities: Fiji and World Decolonialization*. John D. Kelly and Martha Kaplan. Pp. 121–42. Chicago: University of Chicago Press.

Kashiwagi Hiroshi. 2005. Design and War: Kimono as "Parlor Performance" Propaganda. In *Wearing Propaganda: Textiles on the Home Front in Japan, Britain, and the United States, 1931–1945*. Jacqueline M. Atkins, ed. New Haven, CT: Yale University Press.

Kata Kōji. 1994. Kamishibai (Paper theater). In *Taishūbunka Jiten* (Dictionary of popular culture). Ishikawa Hiroyoshi et al., eds. P. 156. Kōbundō.

Kawai Hayao. 1982. *Chūkū Kōzō Nihon no Shinsō* (The void in the center, the deep structure of Japanese thought). Chūōkōronsha.

Kawai Ryōichi and Ōta Yōai. 1982. Nihonjin no Kokoro no Furusato: Sakura (The primordial space for the Japanese soul: Cherry blossoms). *Nihon Jishin* 23: 89–93.

Kawamura Minato. 1998. *Manshū Tetsudō Maboroshi Ryokō* (Dream travel by the Manchurian Railroad). Nesuko.

Kawasaki Fusagorō. 1967. *Edo Fūbutsushi: Shijitsu ni Miru Shomin Seikatsu* (The folk customs of Edo: The lives of the folk in historical records). Tōgensha.

Kawasoe Taketane. 1980. *Kojiki no Sekai* (The world of the *Kojiki*). Kyōikusha.

Keay, Anna. 2008. *The Magnificent Monarch: Charles II and the Ceremonies of Power.* London: Continuum.

Keene, Donald. 2002. *Emperor of Japan: Meiji and His World, 1852–1912.* New York: Columbia University Press.

Kelly, John D. 2010. Seeing Red: Mao Fetishism, Pax Americana, and the Moral Economy of War. In *Anthropology and Global Counterinsurgency.* J. D. Kelly, B. Jauregui, S. Mitchell, and J. Walton, eds. Pp. 67–83. Chicago: University of Chicago Press.

Kelly, John D., and Martha Kaplan. 2001. Nation and Decolonization. In *Represented Communities: Fiji and World Decolonization.* Pp. 1–29. Chicago: University of Chicago Press.

Kenez, Peter. 1985. *The Birth of the Propaganda State: Soviet Methods of Mass Mobilization, 1917–1929.* Cambridge: Cambridge University Press.

Kertzer, David I. 1988. *Ritual, Politics, and Power.* New Haven, CT: Yale University Press.

———. 1996. *Politics and Symbols: The Italian Communist Party and the Fall of Communism.* New Haven, CT: Yale University Press.

Killingray, David. 2010. *Fighting for Britain: African Soldiers in the Second World War.* Woodbridge, Suffolk: James Currey.

Kinoshita Masao. 1974. *Genji Monogatari Yōgo Sakuin* (Index for terms in the *Tale of Genji*). 2 vols. Kokusho Kankōkai.

Kisaka Jun'ichirō. [1987] 1996. Taisei Yokusankai (The Imperial Rule Assistance Association). In *Kokushi Daijiten* (Dictionary of national history), vol. 8: 790–91. Yoshikawa Kōbunkan.

Kitagawa, Joseph M. 1990. Some Reflections on Japanese Religion and Its Relationship to the Imperial System. *Japanese Journal of Religious Studies* 17(2–3): 129–78.

Kobayashi Tadashi. 1993. Mitate-e in the Art of the Ukiyo-e Artist Suzuki Harunobu. In *The Floating World Revisited.* Donald Jenkins, ed. Pp. 85–91. Portland, OR: Portland Art Museum and University of Hawaii Press.

Kobayashi Tatsuo. 2008. *Jōmon no Shikō* (Jōmon ontology). Chikuma Shobō.

Kōdansha Sōgō Hensankyoku, ed. 1997. *Nichiroku Nijūseiki* (A daily record of the twentieth century). Vol. 1 (21). Kōdansha.

Kojima Noriyuki and Arai Eizō, eds. 1989. *Kokin Wakashū.* Iwanami Shoten.

Kokuritsu Rekishi Minzoku Hakubutsukan, ed. 1987. *Nihon no Rekishi to Bunka* (Japanese history and culture). Daiichi Hōki Shuppan.

Kolakowski, Leszek. 2006. *Main Currents of Marxism: The Founders, the Golden Age, the Breakdown.* P. S. Falla, trans. New York: Norton.

Komatsu Kazuhiko. 2008. *Kami ni natta Nihonjin* (Japanese who became deities). NHK Publishers.

Kornicki, Peter F. 1977. Nishiki no Ura: An Instance of Censorship and the Structure of a Sharebon. *Monumenta Nipponica* 32(2): 153–88.

Koshar, Rudy. 1998. *Germany's Transient Pasts: Preservation and National Memory in the Twentieth Century.* Chapel Hill: University of North Carolina Press.

Koyama Hiroshi. 1960. *Kyōgenshū* (*Jō*) (A collection of kyogen [Vol. 1]). Iwanami Shoten.

Koyanagi Teruichi. 1972. *Tabemono to Nihon Bunka* (Food and Japanese culture). Hyōgensha.

Krebs, Christopher B. 2011. *A Most Dangerous Book: Tacitus's "Germania" from the Roman Empire to the Third Reich*. New York: Norton.

Krivoguz, Igor. 1989. *The Second International, 1889–1914*. Moscow: Progress Publishers.

Kubik, Jan. 1994. *The Power of Symbols against the Symbols of Power: The Rise of Solidarity and the Fall of State Socialism in Poland*. College Park: Pennsylvania State University Press.

Kubota Jun. 1990. Nanden no Sakura (Cherry Blossoms in the South Garden [of the Imperial Palace]). *Bungaku* 1(1): 34–48.

Kubota Utsubo. 1960 [1968]. *Kokin Wakashū Hyōshaku (Jō)*(An interpretation of the *Kokin Wakashū* [Vol. 1]). Tōkyōdō Shuppan.

Kumakura Isao. 2007. *Kobori Enshū Chayū-roku* (Record of the friends of Kobori Enshū through the tea ceremony). Chūōkōronsha.

Kunaichō. [1933] 1972. *Meiji Tennōki* (Record of Emperor Meiji). Vol. 7. Yoshikawa Kōbunkan. Originally compiled by Kunaichō Rinji Teishitsu Henshūkyoku.

Kuno, Susumu. 1973. *The Structure of the Japanese Language*. Cambridge, MA: MIT Press.

Kurano Kenji and Takeda Yūkichi, eds. 1958. *Kojiki Norito* (The *Kojiki* and the *Norito*). Iwanami Shoten.

Kurihara Hirota. 1953. *Ningen Meiji Tennō* (Emperor Meiji as a human being). Surugadai Shobō.

Kuroda Toshio. 1972. Chūsei no Mibunsei to Hisen Kannen (Social stratification during the early medieval period and the concept of baseness). *Buraku Mondai Kenkyū* 33: 23–57.

Kuroita Katsumi and Kokushi Taikei Henshūkai, eds. 1965a. *Nihon Kiryaku* (Zenpen) (Chronicle of Japanese history, vol. 1). In *Kokushi Taikei* (Outline of national history), vol. 10: 1–546. Yoshikawa Kōbunkan.

———. 1965b. *Teiō Hen'nenki* (Chronicle of imperial reigns). In *Kokushi Taikei*, vol. 12: 1–456. Yoshikawa Kōbunkan.

———. 1965c. *Kojidan* (Stories of ancient times). In *Kokushi Taikei*, vol. 18: 1–132. Yoshikawa Kōbunkan.

———. 1966. *Shoku Nihon Kōki* (Sequence for later history of Japan). In *Kokushi Taikei*, vol. 3: 1–246. Yoshikawa Kōbunkan.

Kushner, Barak. 2006. *The Thought War: Japanese Imperial Propaganda*. Honolulu: University of Hawaii Press.

Kyōto-shi, ed. 1975. *Kyōto no Kindai* (Kyōto during the modern period). Vol. 8 of *Kyōto no Rekishi* (History of Kyoto). Gakugei Shorin.

———. 1981. *Shigai Seigyō* (Streets and livelihood). Vol. 4 of *Shiryō Kyōto no Rekishi* (Archival history of Kyoto). Heibonsha.

Kyōto Kokuritsu Hakubutsukan. 2012. *Ōchōbunka no Hana* (The efflorecence of Heian court culture). National Museum of Kyoto.

Lacan, Jacques. [1966] 1977. *Écrits: A Selection*. Alan Sheridan, trans. New York: Norton.

LaFleur, William R. 1983. *The Karma of Words: Buddhism and the Literary Arts in Medieval Japan*. Berkeley: University of California Press.

Lane, Christel. 1981. *The Rites of Rulers: Ritual in Industrial Society—The Soviet Case*. Cambridge: Cambridge University Press.

Latour, Bruno. 2002. What Is Iconoclash? Or Is There a World Beyond the Image Wars? In *Iconoclash*. Bruno Latour and Peter Weibel, eds. Pp. 1–41. Cambridge, MA: MIT Press.

Lauritzen, Frederick. 1988. Propaganda Art in the Postage Stamps of the Third Reich. *Journal of Decorative and Propaganda Arts* 10 (Autumn): 62–79.

Leach, Edmund. [1954] 1965. *Political Systems of Highland Burma*. New York: Beacon Press.

———. [1966] 2000. Virgin Birth. In *The Essential Edmund Leach*, vol. 2: 102–19. Stephen Hugh-Jones and James Laidlaw, eds. New Haven, CT: Yale University Press.

———. 1976. *Culture and Communication: The Logic by Which Symbols Are Connected*. Cambridge: Cambridge University Press.

Leighton, Lauren G. 1985. Romanticism. In *Handbook of Russian Literature*. Victor Terras, ed. Pp. 372–76. New Haven, CT: Yale University Press.

Lévi-Strauss, Claude. [1949] 1969. *The Elementary Structures of Kinship*. Boston: Beacon Press.

Linz, Juan J. 2000. *Totalitarian and Authoritarian Regimes*. Boulder, CO: Lynne Rienner.

Longinus. 1985. *On the Sublime*. J. A. Arieti and J. M. Crossett, trans. New York: Edwin Mellen Press.

Löwith, Karl. [1964] 1991. *From Hegel to Nietzsche: The Revolution in Nineteenth-Century Thought*. David E. Green, trans. New York: Columbia University Press.

Lyotard, Jean-François. [1979] 1989. *The Postmodern Condition: A Report on Knowledge*. Minneapolis: University of Minnesota Press.

Malia, Martin. 1999. *Russia under Western Eyes: From the Bronze Horseman to the Lenin Mausoleum*. Cambridge, MA: Harvard University Press.

Malinowski, Bronislaw. [1935] 1965. *The Language of Magic and Gardening*. Vol. 2 of *Coral Gardens and Their Magic*. Bloomington: Indiana University Press.

Mallarmé, Stéphane. 1945. *Œuvres complètes*. Paris: Gallimard.

Marinetti, F. T. 1909. Le Futurisme. *Le Figaro*, Feb. 20.

Maruyama Masao. 1946. Chōkokkashugi no Riron to Shinri (The theory and psychology behind ultranationalism). *Sekai* (May): 2–15.

———. [1961] 1993. *Nihon no Shisō* (Japanese thought structure). Iwanami Shoten.

Marx, Karl. [1867] 1992. *Capital*, vol. 1. Frederick Engels, ed. New York: International Publishers.

Marx, Karl, and Frederick Engels. [1852] 1989. Manifesto of the Communist Party. In *Basic Writings on Politics and Philosophy: Karl Marx and Friedrich Engels*. Lewis S. Feuer, ed. Pp. 1–41. New York: Doubleday.

Matsuda Makoto. 2007. *Takaki Kanehiro no Igaku* (Takaki Kanehiro's medical science). Tokyo Jikei University Medical School.

Matsumae Takeshi. 1960. *Nihon Shinwa no Shin Kenkyū* (New research on Japanese mythology). Ōfūsha.

———. 1977. *Nihon no Kamigami* (Japanese deities). Chūōkōronsha.

Matsumoto Shinpachirō. 1981. Kyōgen no Omokage (Images in kyōgen). In *Yōkyoku Kyōgen* (Yōkyoku and kyōgen). Nihon Bungaku Kenkyū Shiryō Kankōkai, ed. Pp. 190–200. Yūseidō Shuppan.

Matsumura Takeo. 1948. *Girei Oyobi Shinwa no Kenkyū* (Research on ritual and myth). Baifūkan.

———. 1954. *Nihon Shinwa no Kenkyū* (Research on Japanese myths). Vol. 1. Baifūkan.

Matsuoka Shinpei. 1991. *Utage no Shintai* (The body of the feast). Iwanami Shoten.

Matsuyama Yoshio. 1941. Nanshin Dōbutsushi—Uma, Saru Kaiko (Notes on animals in southern Shinshū: Horses, monkeys, and silk worms). *Dōbutsu Bungaku* 81: 23–29.

Matt, Daniel C. [1990] 1995. Ayin: The Concept of Nothingness in Jewish Mysticism. In *Essential Papers on Kabbalah*. Lawrence Fine, ed. Pp. 67–108. New York: New York University Press.

Mauss, Marcel. [1925] 1966. *The Gift: Forms and Functions of Exchange in Archaic Societies*. London: Cohen & West.

———. 1938. Une catégorie de l'esprit humain: la notion de personne, celle de "moi." *Journal of the Royal Anthropological Institute of Great Britain and Ireland* 68: 263–81.

McCullough, Helen Craig, trans. 1968. *Tales of Ise*. University of Tokyo Press.

———. 1985. *Kokin Wakashū: The First Imperial Anthropology of Japanese Poetry*. Stanford, CA: Stanford University Press.

McCullough, William H., and Helen Craig McCullough, trans. 1980. *A Tale of Flowering Fortunes* (trans. of *Eiga Monogatari*). Vol. 2. Stanford, CA: Stanford University Press.

Meyer, Birgit. 2008. Powerful Pictures: Popular Christian Aesthetics in Southern Ghana. *Journal of the American Academy of Religion* 76(1): 82–110.

Meyer, Birgit, and Dick Houtman. 2012. Introduction: Material Religion—How Things Matter. In *Things: Religion and the Question of Materiality*. Pp. 1–23. New York: Fordham University Press.

Minakata Kumakusu. 1972. *Minakata Kumakusu Zenshū* (Complete works of Minakata Kumakusu). Vol. 1 [1971]. Heibonsha.

Minamoto-no-Akikane. 1965. *Kojidan* (Stories of ancient times). Kuroita Katsumi and Kokushi Taikei Henshūkai, eds. *Kokushi Taikei* (Outline of national history), vol. 18: 1–132. Yoshikawa Kōbunkan.

Minami Hiroshi. 1967. Shakai Shinrigaku no Me (Perspectives from social psychology). In *Kataritsugu Sengoshi* (Postwar dialogue), no. 4. Tsurumi Shunsuke, ed. Pp. 111–19. Shisō no Kagakusha.

Minear, Richard H. [1999] 2001. *Dr. Seuss Goes to War: The World War II Editorial Cartoons of Theodor Seuss Geisel*. New York: New Press.

Mintz, Sidney W. 1985. *Sweetness and Power: The Place of Sugar in Modern History*. New York: Viking.

Mitani, Taichirō. 1988. The Establishment of Party Cabinets, 1898–1932. *The Cambridge History of Japan*. Vol. 6, *The Twentieth Century*. Peter Duus, ed. Pp. 55–96. Cambridge: Cambridge University Press.

Mitchell, Sean T. 2010. Paranoid Styles of Nationalism after the Cold War: Notes from an Invasion of the Amazon. In *Anthropology and Global Counterinsurgency*. J. D. Kelly, B. Jauregui, S. Mitchell, and J. Walton, eds. Pp. 89–103. Chicago: University of Chicago Press.

Mitsukoshi Kabushikigaisha. 2005. *Mitsukoshi Hyakunen no Kiroku* (Records of one hundred years of the Mitsukoshi Department Store). Mitsukoshi Honten.

Miyachi Masato. [1988] 1996. Shūkyōkankei Hōrei Ichiran (List of ordinances related to religion). *Shūkyō to Kokka* (Religion and the state). Yasumaru Yoshio and Miyachi Masato, eds. Pp. 433–88. Vol. 5 of *Nihon Kindai Shisō Taikei* (Compendium of modern Japanese thought). Iwanami Shoten.

Miyaji Denzaburō. 1973. Shōwa Sanzaru (Three monkeys of the Shōwa period). *Monkī* 17(2): 12.

Miyajima Shin'ichi. 1994. *Shōzōga* (Portraits). Yoshikawa Kōbunkan.

———. 1996. *Shōzōga no Shisen* (On portraits). Yoshikawa Kōbunkan.

Miyake Hitoshi. 1985. *Shugendō Shisō no Kenkyū* (Research on the mountain ascetic religion). Shunjūsha.

Miyamoto Tsuneichi. 1981. Nihonjin no Shushoku (The staple food of the Japanese.) In *Shoku no Bunka Shinpojūmu '81—Higashi Ajiya no Shoku no Bunka* (Symposium on the culture of food: The dietary culture of East Asia). Heibonsha.

Miyata Noboru. 1975. *Kinsei no Hayarigami* (Popular deities during the early modern period). Hyōronsha.

———. 1987. *Hime no Minzokugaku* (The folklore of princesses). Seidosha.

———. 1989. Nihon Ōken no Minzokuteki Kiso (The ethnographic basis of Japanese kingship). *Shikyō* 18: 25–30.

———. 1992. *Hiyorimi: Nihon Ōkenron no Kokoromi* (Weather forecasting: An attempt at interpreting the Japanese king's power). Heibonsha.

———. 1993. *Yama to Sato no Shinkō* (Belief in the mountains and the villages). Yoshikawa Kōbunkan.

———. 1994. *Shiro no Fōkuroa* (Folklore of the color white). Heibonsha.

Mizukami Tsutomu. 1982. Oizakura ni Haru naki Kuni (The country with spring for old cherry trees). *Nihon Jishin* 23 (Mar.): 10–16.

Moore, Sally Falk. 1986. *Social Facts and Fabrications: "Customary" Law on Kilimanjaro, 1880–1980.* Cambridge: Cambridge University Press.

———. 1987. Explaining the Present: Theoretical Dimensions in Processual Ethnography. *American Ethnologist* 14: 727–36.

Morita Toyoko. 2006. Kinsei Minshū, Tennō Sokuishiki Haiken—Yūraku Toshiteno Sokui Girei Kenbutsu (English title: Imperial enthronements as tourist attractions). *Nihon Kenkyū* 32: 181–203.

Morris, Ivan. 1964 [1979]. *The World of the Shining Prince: Court Life in Ancient Japan.* London: Penguin.

Mosse, George L. 1975. *The Nationalization of the Masses: Political Symbolism and Mass Movements in Germany from the Napoleonic Wars through the Third Reich.* Ithaca, NY: Cornell University Press.

———. 1987. *Masses and Man: Nationalist and Fascist Perceptions of Reality.* Detroit: Wayne State University Press.

———. 1990. *Fallen Soldiers.* Oxford University Press.

Motoori Norinaga. [1790] 1968. *Motoori Norinaga Zenshū* (The complete works of Motoori Norinaga). Vol. 1. Ōno Susumu, ed. Chikuma Shobō.

Murakami Senjō, Tsuji Zennosuke, and Washio Junkei, eds. 1970. *Meiji Ishin Shinbutsu*

Bunri Shiryō (Records on the separation between buddhas and deities at the time of the Meiji Restoration). Vol. 2. Meicho Shuppan.

Murakami Shigeyoshi. 1977. *Tennō no Saishi* (Imperial rituals). Iwanami Shoten.

Murasaki Yoshimasa. 1980. *Sarumawashi Fukkatsu* (The revival of monkey performances). Kyoto: Buraku Mondai Kenkyūsho Shuppanbu.

Naef, Silvia. 1996. *A la recherche d'une modernité arabe: L'évolution des arts plastiques en Egypte, au Liban et en Irak.* Geneva: Éditions Slatkine.

———. 2004. *Y a-t-il "une question de l'image" en Islam?* Paris: Téraèdre.

Nagao Ryūichi. [1987] 1995. Dainihon Teikoku Kenpō (The constitution of imperial Japan). *Kokushi Daijiten* (Dictionary of national history), vol. 8: 840–44. Yoshikawa Kōbunkan.

Naitō Yōsuke. 2004. *Kitte to Sensō: Mou Hitotsu no Shōwashi* (Postal stamps and the war: Another Shōwa history). Shinchōsha.

Nakamura Hiroshi. 1982. *Sakura no Gogen* (The etymology of cherry blossoms). *Nihon Jishin* 23: 59–61.

Nakamura Teiri. 1984. *Nihonjin no Dōbutsukan—Henshintan no Rekishi* (Japanese views of animals: The history of tales about metamorphoses). Kaimeisha.

Nakanishi Susumu. 1995. *Hana no Katachi: Nihonjin to Sakura* (The forms of the flower: Japanese and cherry blossoms). Vol. 1 (*Jō*), *Koten*, Vol. 2 (*Ge*), *Kindai*. Kadokawa Shoten.

Nakayama Tarō. 1976. Mizukagami Tenjin (Mizukagami Tenjin). *Nihon Minzokugaku* (Japanese folklore) 1: 181–88. Yamato Shobō.

Nanba Kōji. 1998. *Uchiteshi Yamamu* (Do not fall until you shoot all your enemies). Kōdansha.

Napier, A. David. 1992. *Foreign Bodies: Performance, Art, and Symbolic Anthropology.* Berkeley: University of California Press.

Narazaki Muneshige, ed. 1981. *Utamaro.* Vol. 6 of *Nikuhitsu Ukiyo-e* (Ukiyo-e paintings). Shūeisha.

National Park Service, U.S. Department of the Interior. 2009. Cherry Blossom Festival: History of the Cherry Trees. www:nps.gov/cherry/. National Park Service, U.S. Department of the Interior. Accessed April 3.

Natsume Sōseki. [1907] 1984. Kōfu (The miners). In *Sōseki Zenshū* (Complete works of Sōseki). Vol. 3. Iwanami Shoten.

Newby, Howard. 1979. *Green and Pleasant Land?* London: Hutchinson.

Nihon Hōsō Kyōkai, ed. 1988. *Nihon no Bi: Sakura* (The beauty of Japan: Cherry blossoms). NHK Shuppan.

Nihon Kahei Shōkyōdō Kumiai. [1967] 2003. *Nihon Kahei Katarogu* (Catalogue of Japanese bills). Nihon Kahei Shōkyōdō Kumiai.

Nihon Ukiyo-e Kyōkai, ed. 1968. *Edo Meisho* (Famous Places of Edo). Yamada Shoin.

Nihon Yūbinkitte Shōkyōdō Kumiai. 2003. *Nihon Yūbinkitte Katarogu* (Catalogue of Japanese postal stamps). Nihon Yūbinkitte Shōkyōdō Kumiai.

Nishida Kitarō. [1940] 2004. *Nishida Kitarō Zenshū* (Complete works of Nishida Kitarō). Vol. 9. Iwanami Shoten.

———. 1965a. *Nishida Kitarō Zenshū,* vol. 4. Iwanami Shoten.

————. 1965b. *Nishida Kitarō Zenshū*, vol. 6. Iwanami Shoten.

Nishiyama Matsunosuke. 1985. *Hana to Nihon Bunka* (Flowers and Japanese culture). *Nishiyama Matsunosuke Chosaku-shū* (Collected works of Nishiyama Matsunosuke). Vol. 8. Yoshikawa Kōbunkan.

Nishizawa Sō. 1990. *Nihon Kindai Kayōshi (Ge)* (History of popular songs in modern Japan [Vol. 2]). Ōfūsha.

Nitobe Inazō. 1899 [1912]. *Bushidō: The Soul of Japan*. Teibi Publishing.

————. 1933 [1969]. Bushidō to Shōnindō (The way of warriors and the way of merchants). In *Nitobe Inazō Zenshū* (Complete works of Nitobe Inazō), vol. 6: 324–36. Kyōbunkan.

Niunoya Tetsuichi. 1993. *Nihon Chūsei no Mibun to Shakai* (Status and society in medieval Japan). Hanawa Shobō.

Nōda Tayoko. 1943. *Mura no Josei* (Women of the village). Mikuni Shobō.

Noguchi Michihiko. 1978. Chūsei no Shomin Seikatsu to Hisabetsumin no Dōkō (The life of the common people and the discriminated people movement during the medieval period). In *Buraku Mondai Gaisetsu* (Introduction to buraku problems). Buraku Mondai Kenkyōjo, ed. Pp. 86–99. Osaka: Kaihō Shuppansha.

Noguchi Takehiko. 1982. Utsurou Hana (Flowers losing their color). *Nihon Jishin* 23: 77–80.

Nonomura Kaizō, ed. [1953] 1968. *Kyōgenshū (Jō)* (Collection of kyōgen [Vol. 1]). Asahi Shinbunsha.

Nonomura Kaizō and Andō Tsunejirō, eds. 1974. *Kyōgen Shūsei* (A collection of kyōgen). Nōgaku Shorin.

Normile, Dennis. 1997. Yangtze Seen as Earliest Rice Site. *Science* 275: 309.

Nova, Alessandro. 2011. *The Book of the Wind: The Representation of the Invisible*. Montreal: McGill-Queen's University Press.

Noyes, James. 2013. *The Politics of Iconoclasm*. London: I.B. Tauris.

Ōbayashi Tarō. 1973. *Inasaku no Shinwa* (The myth of rice cultivation). Kōbundō.

Ōbayashi Tarō et al. 1983. *Sanmin to Ama* (Mountain people and sea people). Shōggakan.

Oda Kōji. 1968. Kinsei Daidō Geinin Shiryō—Sarumawashi no Fukei (Data on roadside performing artists during the early modern period: The history of monkey trainers). *Geinō* 10(6) (1968): 34–42.

————. 1980. Suō ni okeru Sarumawashi (Monkey performance at Suō). In *Suō Sarumawashi Kinkyū Chōsa Hōkokusho* (Report on an urgent investigation of monkey performances at Suō). Yamaguchiken Kyōiku Iinkai Bunkaka, ed. Pp. 3–29. Yamaguchi: Yamaguchiken Kyōiku Iinkai.

Ōhashi Yoshiharu. 1957. *Ishin Ikō Nihon Shihei Taikei Zukan* (Illustrated outline of Japanese currency since the Meiji Restoration). Bankoku Kahei Kenkyūkai.

Ohnuki-Tierney, Emiko. 1964. *The Detroit Chinese—A Study of Socio-Cultural Changes in the Detroit Chinese Community from 1872 through 1963*. Manuscript bound and housed at Detroit Public Library and UCLA Library.

————. 1974. *The Ainu of the Northwest Coast of Southern Sakhalin*. New York: Holt, Rinehart and Winston.

————. 1981a. *Illness and Healing among the Sakhalin Ainu: A Symbolic Interpretation.* New York: Cambridge University Press.

————. 1981b. Phases in Human Perception/Conception/Symbolization Process—Cognitive Anthropology and Symbolic Classification. *American Ethnologist* 8(3): 451–67.

————. 1984. *Illness and Culture in Contemporary Japan.* Cambridge: Cambridge University Press.

————. 1987. *The Monkey as Mirror: Symbolic Transformations in Japanese History and Ritual.* Princeton, NJ: Princeton University Press.

————, ed. 1990a. *Culture Through Time: Anthropological Approaches.* Stanford, CA: Stanford University Press.

————. 1990b. Monkey as Metaphor? Transformations of a Polytropic Symbol in Japanese Culture. *Man* (N.S.) 25: 399–416.

————. 1991a. Embedding and Transforming Polytrope: The Monkey as Self in Japanese Culture. In *Beyond Metaphor: Trope Theory in Anthropology.* J. W. Fernandez, ed. Pp. 159–89. Stanford, CA: Stanford University Press.

————. 1991b. The Emperor of Japan as Deity (*Kami*): An Anthropology of the Imperial System in Historical Perspective. *Ethnology* 33(3): 1–17.

————. 1993a. *Rice as Self: Japanese Identities Through Time.* Princeton, NJ: Princeton University Press.

————. 1993b. Nature, pureté et soi primordial: La nature japonaise dans une perspective comparative. *Géographie et Cultures* 7: 75–92.

————. 1993c. Presence of the Absence: Zero Signifiers and Zero Meanings. *Semiotica* 96(3/4): 301–8.

————. 1994a. The Power of Absence: Zero Signifiers and Their Transgressions. *L'Homme* 130 (April–June), 34(2): 59–76.

————. 1994b. Brain Death and Organ Transplantation: Cultural Bases of Medical Technology. *Current Anthropology* 35(3): 233–54.

————. 1995. Structure, Event and Historical Metaphor: Rice and Identities in Japanese History. *Journal of the Royal Anthropological Institute* 30(2) (June): 1–27.

————. 1997. The Reduction of Personhood to Brain and Rationality? Japanese Contestation of Medical High Technology. In *Western Medicine as Contested Knowledge.* A. Cunningham and B. Andrews, eds. Pp. 212–40. Manchester, UK: Manchester University Press.

————. 1998. A Conceptual Model for the Historical Relationship between the Self, and the Internal and External Others: The Agrarian Japanese, the Ainu, and the Special Status People. In *Making Majorities.* Dru Gladney, ed. Pp. 31–51 (text), 287–94 (notes), 309–13 (references). Stanford, CA: Stanford University Press.

————. 2001. Historicization of the Culture Concept. *History and Anthropology* 12(3): 213–54.

————. 2002a. *Kamikaze, Cherry Blossoms, and Nationalisms: The Militarization of Aesthetics in Japanese History.* Chicago: University of Chicago Press.

————. 2002b. Ōnamesai to Ōken (The imperial accession ritual and kingship). In *Tennō to Ōken o Kangaeru* (On the emperor and kingship), pp. 41–67. Vol. 5 of *Ōken to Girei* (Kingship and ritual). Amino Yoshihiko et al., eds. Iwanami Shoten.

————. 2005. Japanese Monarchy in Historical and Comparative Perspective. In *The Character of Kingship*. Declan Quigley, ed. Pp. 209–32. Oxford: Berg Publishers.

————. 2006a. *Kamikaze Diaries: Reflections of Japanese Student Soldiers*. Chicago: University of Chicago Press.

————. 2006b. Against "Hybridity": Culture as Historical Process. In *Dismantling the East-West Dichotomy: Essays in Honor of Jan van Bremen*. Joy Hendry and Dixon Wong, eds. Pp. 11–16. New York: Routledge.

Okada Yoneo. [1985] 1997. *Kōreisai* (Ritual for the imperial soul). In *Kokushi Taikei* (Outline of national history), vol. 5: 561. Yoshikawa Kōbunkan.

Ōkurashō Insatsukyoku Kinenkan, ed. 1997. *Zuroku Oyatoi Gaikokujin Kiyossone— Botsugo 100 nenten* (Exhibit on Chiossone, the hired foreigner, 100 years after his death). Ōkurashō Insatsukyoku Kinenkan.

Omodaka Hisataka. [1961] 1983. *Man'yōshū Chūshaku* (Interpretation and annotation of the *Man'yōshū*). Vol. 8. Chūōkōronsha.

————. [1967] 1984. *Man'yōshū Chūshaku* (Interpretation and annotation of the *Man'yōshū*). Vol. 18. Chūōkōronsha.

Ōmori Tokuko. [1984] 1996. Kindō (Kinder). In *Kokushi Daijiten* (Dictionary of national history), vol. 4: 621. Yoshikawa Kōbunkan.

Ono Sawako. 1992. *Edo no Hanami* (Cherry blossom viewing in Edo). Tsukiji Shokan.

Ono Takeo. 1983. *Yūjo to Kuruwa no Zushi* (Illustrated history of the "play women" and their quarters). Tenbōsha.

Ooms, Herman. 1985. *Tokugawa Ideology*. Princeton, NJ: Princeton University Press.

Orbaugh, Sharalyn. 2005. Kamishibai as Entertainment and Propaganda. *Transactions of the Asiatic Society of Japan*, 4th series, vol. 19: 21–58.

————. 2007. *Japanese Fiction of the Allied Occupation: Vision, Embodiment, Identity*. Brill's Japanese Studies Library 26. Leiden: Brill.

Orikuchi Shinobu. [1918] 1982. Aigo no Waka (Waka, the beloved child). In *Orikuchi Shinobu Zenshū* (The complete works of Orikuchi Shinobu), vol. 2: 310–35. Chūōkōronsha.

————. [1924] 1982. Shinoda Tsuma no Hanashi (The wife at Shinoda). In *Orikuchi Shinobu Zenshū*, vol. 2: 267–309. Chūōkōronsha.

————. [1924] 1983. Jugen no Tenkai (The development of spells). In *Orikuchi Shinobu Zenshū*, vol. 1: 76–93. Chūōkōronsha.

————. [1927] 1983. Jugen kara Jushi e (From spells to celebratory words). In *Orikuchi Shinobu Zenshū*, vol. 1: 124–67. Chūōkōronsha.

————. [1928] 1975. Ōnamesai no Hongi (The meaning of the *Ōnamesai*). In *Orikuchi Shinobu Zenshū*, vol. 3: 174–240. Chūōkōronsha.

————. [1928] 1982. Hana no Hanashi (About flowers). In *Orikuchi Shinobu Zenshū*, vol. 2: 467–93. Chūōkōronsha.

————. [1932] 1976. Man'yōshū Kōgi (Lecture on the *Man'yōshū*). *Orikuchi Shinobu Zenshū* 9: 106–305. Chūōkōronsha.

————. [1937] 1976. Kokugo to Minzokugaku (The Japanese language and the study of folklore). In *Orikuchi Shinobu Zenshū*, vol. 19: 127–88. Chūōkōronsha.

————. [1943] 1976. Kotodama Shinkō (Belief in the soul of words). In *Orikuchi Shinobu Zenshū*, vol. 20: 245–52. Chūōkōronsha.

Ōshima Kiyoshi. 1984. *Shokuryō to Nōgyō o Kangaeru* (Thoughts on food and agriculture). Iwanami Shoten.

Ōshima Takehiko et al., eds. 1971. *Nihon o Shiru Jiten* (Dictionary for knowledge on Japan). Shakai Shisōsha.

Ōta Hirotarō. 1979. *Nanto Shichidaiji no Rekishi to Nenpyō* (History and chronology of the Seven Great Temples at Nanto). Iwanami Shoten.

Ōta Rin'ichirō. 1980. *Nihon no Gunpuku* (Japanese army uniforms). Kokusho Kankōkai.

Ōtsuka Nobukazu. 2013. *Kao o kangaeru* (On the face). Shūeisha.

Ouwehand, Cornelius. 1964. *Namazu-e and Their Themes: An Interpretive Approach to Some Aspects of Japanese Folk Religions*. Leiden: Brill.

Ozawa Hiroshi. 1987. Minshū Shūkyō no Shinsō (The deep structure of folk religion). In *Nihon no Shakaishi* (Social history of Japan). Vol. 8, *Seikatsu Kankaku to Shakai* (Daily life and society). Asao Naohiro et al., eds. Pp. 296–332. Iwanami Shoten.

Ozawa Shōichi. 1978. Sarumawashi Fukkatsu. In *Suō Sarumawashi* (Monkey performances at Suō). Suō Sarumawashinokai Jimukyoku, ed. Pp. 4–5. Hikari City, Yamaguchi Prefecture: Sarumawashinokai.

Ozouf, Mona. [1976] 1994. *Festivals and the French Revolution*. Cambridge, MA: Harvard University Press.

Payne, Stanley. [1980] 1987. *Fascism: Comparison and Definition*. Madison: University of Wisconsin Press.

————. 1995. *A History of Fascism, 1914–1945*. Madison: University of Wisconsin Press.

————. 2005. On the Heuristic Value of the Concept of Political Religion and Its Application. *Totalitarian Movements and Political Religions* 6(2): 163–74.

Pecheur, Julie. 2002/2003. French Citizenship. *Correspondence: An International Review of Culture and Society* 10: 7–9.

Philippi, Donald L., trans. 1969. *Kojiki*. Princeton, NJ: Princeton University Press/ University of Tokyo Press.

Piłsudski, Bronisław. 1915. Na medvezh'em prazdnike aĭnov o. Sakhalina. *Živaja Starina* 23(1–2) (1914): 67–162.

Plamper, Jan. 2001. *The Stalin Cult in the Visual Arts: 1929–1953*. Berkeley: University of California Press.

Plato. [1935] 2000. *Republic*, Books 6–10. Paul Shorey, trans. Loeb Classical Library 276. Cambridge, MA: Harvard University Press.

Pollack, David. 1986. *The Fracture of Meaning: Japan's Synthesis of China from the Eighth through the Eighteenth Centuries*. Princeton, NJ: Princeton University Press.

Ponsonby-Fane, R. A. B. 1956. *Kyoto*. Ponsonby Memorial Society.

Potter, Pamela. 2006. What Is "Nazi Music"? *Musical Quarterly* 88: 428–55.

Price, Simon. 1987. From Noble Funerals to Divine Cult: The Consecration of Roman Emperors. In *Rituals of Royalty: Power and Ceremonial in Traditional Societies*. David Cannadine and Simon Price, eds. Pp. 56–105. Cambridge: Cambridge University Press.

Proctor, Robert N. 1999. *The Nazi War on Cancer*. Princeton, NJ: Princeton University Press.

Putzar, Edward D. 1963. The Tale of Monkey Genji, *Sarugenji-zōshi*. *Monumenta Nipponica* 1–4: 286–312.

Quinn, Malcolm. 1994. *The Swastika: Constructing the Symbol*. London: Routledge.

Radzinsky [Radzinskii], Edvard. 1996. *Stalin: The First In-depth Biography Based on Explosive New Documents from Russia's Secret Archives*. H. T. Willetts, trans. New York: Doubleday.

Ray, Benjamin C. 1991. *Myth, Ritual, and Kingship in Buganda*. Oxford: Oxford University Press.

Rosenthal, Rachel. 2005. Visual Fiction: The Development of the Secular Icon in Stalinist Poster Art. *Zhe* 1 (Spring): 1–13.

Roubaud, Jacques. 1970. *Mono no aware: Le Sentiment des choses cent quarante-trois poèmes empruntés au japonais*. Paris: Gallimard.

Roudinesco, Elisabeth. [1993] 1997. *Jacques Lacan*. New York: Columbia University Press.

Rousseau, Jean-Jacques. [1762, 1755] 1967. *The Social Contract and Discourse on the Origin of Inequality*. New York: Simon and Schuster.

Rubin, Jay. 1984. *Injurious to Public Morals: Writers and the Meiji State*. Seattle: University of Washington Press.

Ruiz, Teofilo F. 1985. Unsacred Monarchy. In *Rites of Power: Symbolism, Ritual and Politics since the Middle Ages*. Sean Wilentz, ed. Pp. 109–44. Philadelphia: University of Pennsylvania Press.

Ruoff, Kenneth J. 2001. *The People's Emperor: Democracy and the Japanese Monarchy, 1945–1995*. Cambridge, MA: Harvard University Press.

———. 2010. *Imperial Japan at Its Zenith: The Wartime Celebration of the Empire's 2,600th Anniversary*. Ithaca, NY: Cornell University Press.

Saeki Etatsu. 1988. *Haibutsu Kishaku Hyakunen* (One hundred tears of the expulsion of Buddhism and Buddha's teaching). Miyazaki: Kōmyakusha.

Sahlins, Marshall. [1972] 1974. *Stone Age Economics*. Chicago: Aldine.

———. 1976. *Culture and Practical Reason*. Chicago: University of Chicago Press.

———. 1985. *Islands of History*. Chicago: University of Chicago Press.

Saigō Nobutsuna. [1967] 1984. *Kojiki no Sekai* (The world of the *Kojiki*). Iwanami Shoten.

Saitō Shōji. 1977. *Hana no Shisōshi* (The history of concepts associated with flowers). Kyōsei.

———. [1979] 1985. *Shokubutsu to Nihon Bunka* (Plants and Japanese culture). Yasaka Shobō.

———. 1982. Futatabi Sekai no Sakura e (Once again cherry blossoms of the world). *Nihon Jishin* 23: 25–30.

Sakaguchi Ango. 1997. *In the Forest, Under Cherries in Full Bloom*. J. Rubin, trans. In *The Oxford Book of Japanese Short Stories*. T. W. Goossen, ed. Pp. 187–205. Oxford: Oxford University Press.

Sakamoto Masayoshi. 1995. Sakura-e (The cherry blossom meeting). In *Kokushi Daijiten* (Dictionary of national history), vol. 6: 323. Yoshikawa Kōbunkan.

Sakamoto Tarō, Ienaga Saburō, Inoue Mitsusada, and Ōno Susumu, eds. 1965. *Nihonshoki* (Ge) (*Nihonshoki* [Vol. 2]). Iwanami Shoten.

————. 1967. *Nihonshoki (Jō)*. (*Nihonshoki* [Vol. 1]). Iwanami Shoten.

Sakurai Mitsuru. 1974. *Hana no Minzokugaku* (Folkloric study of flowers). Yūzankaku.

Sakurai Tokutarō. 1976. *Minkan Shinkō to Sangaku Shūkyō* (Folk beliefs and the belief in the mountains). Meicho Shuppan.

Sano Tōemon. 1998. *Sakura no Inochi Niwa no Kokoro* (The life of cherry blossoms, the soul of the garden). Sōshisha.

Sansom, George B. 1961. *A History of Japan, 1334–1615*. Stanford, CA: Stanford University Press.

Sasaki Kōmei. 1983. *Inasaku Izen* (Before rice cultivation). Nihon Hōsō Shuppan Kyōkai.

————. 1985. Ine to Nihonjin—Inasaku Bunka to Hi-Inasaku Bunka no Aida (The rice plant and the Japanese: Between rice culture and non-rice culture). In *Toro Iseki to Yayoi Bunka—Ima Toinaosu Wajin no Shakai* (The Toro site and Yayoi culture: The question of the society of the ancient Japanese). Ōtsuka Hatsushige and Mori Kōichi, eds. Pp. 36–62. Shōggakan.

————. 1991. *Nihonshi Tanjō* (The birth of Japanese history). Shūeisha.

————. 2009. *Nihon Bunka no Tayōsei: Inasaku Izen o Saikōsuru* (The multiplicity of Japanese culture: A reevaluation of Japan before rice cultivation). Shōgakkan.

Sasaki Suguru. 1984. Tennōzō no Keisei Katei (The process of the formation of the image of the emperor). In *Kokumin Bunka no Keisei* (The formation of the culture of the national subjects). Pp. 183–238. Chikuma Shobō.

————. 2001. "Goshin'ei" o Meguru Monogatari (The story behind the emperor's image). *Jinmon Kakgaku Kenkyū* (2001): 58–59.

Satake Akihiro. [1967] 1970. *Gekokujō no Bungaku* (Literature of the *Gekokujō* [The below conquering the above]). Chikuma Shobō.

Satake Akihiro et al., eds. 1999. *Man'yōshū*. Vol. 1. Iwanami Shoten.

Satō Hideo. [1985] 1997. *Goshin'ei* (Imperial images). In *Kokushi Daijiten* (Dictionary of national history), vol. 5: 794. Yoshikawa Kōbunkan.

Satō Takumi. 2004. *Genron Tōsei* (The control of freedom of expression). Chūōkoronsha.

Satomi Kishio. 1972. *Tennō-hō no Kenkyū* (Research on the laws of the emperor system). Kinseisha.

Schama, Simon. 1996. *Landscape and Memory*. New York: Vintage.

Scholl, Inge. [1970] 1983. *The White Rose: Munich, 1942–1943*. Middletown, CT: Wesleyan University Press.

Schwartz, Benjamin. 1993. Culture, Modernity, and Nationalism: Further Reflections. *Daedalus* 122(3): 207–26.

Seidensticker, Edward G., trans. 1977a. *The Tale of Genji*. Vol. 1. New York: Alfred A. Knopf.

————. 1977b. *The Tale of Genji*. Vol. 2. New York: Alfred A. Knopf.

Seki Akira. 1986. Jotei (Empresses). In *Kokushi Daijiten* (Dictionary of national history), vol. 7: 712–13. Yoshikawa Kōbunkan.

Sensu Tadashi. 2009. *Nishiki'e ga Kataru Tennō no Sugata* (Images of the emperor as told in woodblock prints). Yūshūkan.

Service, Robert. 2007. *Comrades! A World History of Communism.* Cambridge, MA: Harvard University Press.

Seward, Barbara. 1960. *The Symbolic Rose.* New York: Columbia University Press.

Seward, Desmond. 2010. *The Last White Rose.* London: Constable.

Shibundō Henshūbu. 1973. *Senryū Yoshiwara Fūzoku Ezu* (Illustrated customs at Yoshiwara as expressed in senryū poems). Shibundō.

Shillony, Ben-Ami. 1981. *Politics and Culture in Wartime Japan.* Oxford: Clarendon Press.

————. 2005. *Enigma of the Emperors: Sacred Subservience in Japanese History.* Kent, UK: Global Oriental.

Shimazono Susumu. 2010. *Kokka Shindō to Nihonjin* (National Shinto and the Japanese). Iwanami Shoten.

Shimogaito Hiroshi. 1988. *Zoku Okome to Bunka* (Rice and culture, sequel). Osaka: Zen-Ōsaka Shōhisha.

Shimonaka Yasaburō, ed. 1941. *Shintō Daijiten* (Encyclopedia of Shinto). Vol. 2. Heibonsha.

Shimura Kunihiro, trans. 1980. *Kojidan* (Stories of ancient times). Vol. 58. Kyōikusha.

Shinbo Tōru, ed. 1982. *Yamato-e no Shiki* (The four seasons of Yamato style of painting). Vol. 1 of *Kachō-ga no Sekai* (The world of paintings of flowers and birds). Gakushū Kenkyūsha.

Shirahata Yōsaburō. 2000. *Hanami to Sakura* (Cherry blossom viewing and cherry blossoms). PHP Kenkyūjo.

————. 2012. *Niwa o Yomitoku Kyōto no Koji* (Interpreting gardens: Ancient temples in Kyoto). Kyoto: Tankōsha.

Silver, Larry. 2008. *Marketing Maximillian: Visual Ideology of a Holy Roman Emperor.* Princeton, NJ: Princeton University Press.

Simmel, Georg. [1907] 1950. *The Sociology of Georg Simmel.* Glencoe, IL: The Free Press.

Smith, Henry D. II, and Amy G. Poster. [1986] 1988. *Hiroshige: One Hundred Famous Views of Edo.* New York: George Braziller.

Smith, Paul A. 1989. *On Political War.* Washington, DC: National Defense University Press.

Smith, Robert J., and Ella L. Wiswell. 1982. *The Women of Suye Mura.* Chicago: University of Chicago Press.

Smith, W. Robertson. [1889] 1972. *The Religion of the Semites.* New York: Schocken Books.

Sonobe Saburō. [1962] 1980. *Nihon Minshū Kayōshikō* (Research on the popular songs of Japan). Asahi Shinbunsha.

Sonobe Saburō and Yamazumi Masami. 1962 [1969]. *Nihon no Kodomo no Uta* (Children's songs of Japan). Iwanami Shoten.

Stalinka, Digital Library of Staliniana. University of Pittsburgh. http://images.library. pitt.edu/cgi-bin/i/image/image-idx?sid. Accessed on July 14, 2007.

Steinsaltz, Adin. 2006. *The Thirteen Petalled Rose: A Discourse on the Essence of Jewish Existence and Belief.* New York: Basic Books.

Stokes, Rose Pastor. 1919. Bread and Roses. *The Communist* (Nov. 8): 4.

Strötgen, Stefan. 2008. "I Compose the Party Rally . . . ": The Role of Music in Leni Riefenstahl's *Triumph of the Will*. *Music and Politics* 2(1): 1–14.

Sugiura Minpei. 1965. *Sengoku Ransei no Bungaku* (Literature of the turbulent world during the cyclical conquest). Iwanami Shoten.

Suō Sarumawashinokai Jimukyoku, ed. 1978. *Suō no Sarumawashi* (Monkey performances at Suō). Suō Sarumawashinokai.

Suzuki Masamune. 1991. *Yama to Kami to Hito* (Mountains, deities, and humans). Kyoto: Tankōsha.

Suzuki Masayuki. 1993. *Kōshitsu Seido* (The emperor system). Iwanami Shoten.

Suzuki Shō. [1987] 1995. Senkan (Battleship). In *Kokushi Daijiten* (Dictionary of national history), vol. 8: 389–92. Yoshikawa Kōbunkan.

Tabako to Shio no Hakubutsukan (Museum of Tobacco and Salt), ed. 1985. *Nihon no Tabako Dezain* (Designs on Japanese cigarette packages). Tabako to Shio no Hakubutsukan.

Takagi Hiroshi. 1998. Sakura to Nashonarizumu (Cherry blossoms and nationalism). In *Seiki Tenkanki no Kokusai Chitsujo to Kokumin Bunka no Keisei* (The world order and the formation of the culture of the national subjects around the turn of the century). Nishikawa Nagao and Watanabe Kōzō, eds. Pp. 1–15. Kashiwa Shobō.

Takagi Kiyoko. 1979. *Sakura Hyakushu* (One hundred poems about cherry blossoms). Tanka Shinbunsha.

Takahashi Masae. [1965] 1969. *Shōwa no Gunbatsu* (Military cliques of the Shōwa period). Chūōshinsho.

Takaki, Kanehiro. 1888. Report on the Second Experimental Feeding of Dogs in the Medical School of the Imperial Navy. *Sei-I-Kwai Medical Journal* 7: 46–57, 109–27.

———. 1905. Experiments on Dogs during 'Kak'ke Investigation. *Sei-I-Kwai Medical Journal* 24(12): 149–54.

Takasaki Masahide. 1956. "Hina" no kuni (The country of "Hina"). *Kokugakuin Zasshi* 56(5): 4–26.

Takeuchi Osamu. 1994. Norakuro. In *Taishū Bunka Jiten* (Dictionary of mass culture). Ishikawa Hiroyoshi et al., eds. P. 602. Kōbundō.

Taki Kōji. [1988] 1990. *Tennō no Shōzō* (The portrait of the emperor). Iwanami Shoten.

Takigawa Masajirō. 1971. *Yoshiwara no Shiki* (The four seasons at the Yoshiwara geisha quarters). Seiabō.

Tambiah, S. J. 1976. *World Conqueror and World Renouncer*. Cambridge: Cambridge University Press.

———. 1990. *Magic, Science, Religion and the Scope of Rationality*. Cambridge: Cambridge University Press.

———. 1996a. *Leveling Crowds: Ethnonationalist Conflicts and Collective Violence in South Asia*. Berkeley: University of California Press.

———. 1996b. The Nation-State in Crisis and the Rise of Ethnonationalism. In *The Politics of Difference*. Edwin N. Wilmsen and Patrick McAllister, eds. Pp. 124–43. Chicago: University of Chicago Press.

———. 2000. Transnational Movements, Diaspora, and Multiple Modernities. *Daedalus* 129(1): 163–94.

Tanaka, Stephan. 1993. *Japan's Orient: Rendering Pasts into History*. Berkeley: University of California Press.

Tanizaki Jun'ichirō. [1933] 1959. *In-ei Raisan* (In praise of shadows). In *Tanizaki Jun'ichirō Zenshū* (Complete works of Tanizaki Jun'ichirō), vol. 22: 2–41. Chūōkōronsha.

Taussig, Michael. 1993. *Mimesis and Alterity: A Particular History of the Senses*. New York: Routledge.

Terras, Victor. 1985. Naródnost'. In *Handbook of Russian Literature*. Victor Terras, ed. P. 293. New Haven, CT: Yale University Press.

Thomas, Keith. 1971. *Religion and the Decline of Magic*. New York: Charles Scribner's Sons.

Tierney, Kenji. n.d. *Wrestling with Tradition*. Book manuscript in preparation.

Toita Yasuji. 1969. *Kaisetsu Kagamiyama Kokyō no Nishikie* [title of a puppet play]. Toshikura Kōichi et al., eds. Vol. 13 of *Meisaku Kabuki Zenshū* (A collection of kabuki masterpieces). Sōgen Shinsha.

Toita Yasuji and Yoshida Chiaki. 1981. *Shashin Kabuki Saijiki* (Photo illustrations of the seasonal chronicle in kabuki plays). Kōdansha.

Toita Yasuji et al., eds. 1968. *Meisaku Kabuki Zenshū* (A collection of kabuki masterpieces). Vol. 2. Sōgen Shinsha.

Tōkei Kenkyūkai. 1969. Shokuryō Kanrishi Kenkyū Iinkai (Research Committee on the History of Food Policy). *Shokuryō Kanrishi Sōron* (History of food policy). Shokuryōchō (Shokuryō Kanrishi Henshūshitsu.)

Tōkyōto Edo Tōkyō Hakubutsukan. 1993. *Edo Tōkyō Hakubutsukan Sōgō An'nai* (Introduction to the Edo-Tokyo Museum). Tōkyōto Edo Tōkyō Hakubutsukan.

Toriumi Yasushi. 1996. Tennō Kikansetsu Mondai (The problem with the organ theory of the emperor). In *Kokushi Daijiten* (Dictionary of national history), vol. 9: 1004–6. Yoshikawa Kōbunkan.

Toshikura Kōichi et al., eds. 1969. *Meisaku Kabuki Zenshū* (A collection of kabuki masterpieces). Vol. 13. Sōgen Shinsha.

Tribe, Laurence H. 2008. *The Invisible Constitution*. Oxford: Oxford University Press.

Tsuboi Hirofumi. [1982] 1984. *Ine o Eranda Nihonjin* (The Japanese who chose the rice plant). Miraisha.

Tsubouchi Shōyō [Yūzō]. 1900. *Kokugo Dokuhon* (National language text). Vol. 1. Fuzanbō.

Tsukuba Tsuneharu. 1969 [1986]. *Beishoku, Nikushoku no Bunmei* (Civilizations of rice consumption and meat consumption). Nihon Hōsō Shuppansha.

Tsumura Masayoshi. [1917] 1970. *Tankai* (The ocean of stories). Kokusho Kankōkai.

Tumarkin, Nina. 1997. *Lenin Lives! The Lenin Cult in Soviet Russia*. Cambridge, MA: Harvard University Press.

Tupitsyn, Margarita. 1996. *The Soviet Photograph, 1924–1937*. New Haven, CT: Yale University Press.

Turner, Victor. 1967. *The Forest of Symbols: Aspects of Ndembu Ritual*. Ithaca, NY: Cornell University Press.

———. 1969. *The Ritual Process*. Chicago: Aldine.

———. 1975. Symbolic Studies. *Annual Review of Anthropology* 4: 145–61.

Ueda Kazuo. 1978a. Buraku no Bunpu to Jinkō (The distribution of buraku settlements and population). In *Buraku Mondai Gaisetsu* (Introduction to buraku problems). Buraku Kaihō Kenkyūsho, ed. Pp. 3–10. Osaka: Kaihō Shuppansha.

———. 1978b. Kinsei hōken shakai to mibunsei (The feudal society of the early modern period and the hierarchical system). In *Buraku Mondai Gaisetsu*. Buraku Kaihō Kenkyūsho, ed. Pp. 100–118. Osaka: Kaihō Shuppansha.

Ueda Masaaki. 1971. *Jotei: Kotdai Nihon no Hikari to Kage* (Empresses: Light and shadows in ancient Japan). Kōdansha.

Umezu Jirō. 1978. Tengu Zōshi ni tsuite (About tengu stories). In *Shinshū Nihon Emakimono Zenshū* (Newly edited collection of Japanese scroll paintings), vol. 27: 3–14. Umezu Jirō, ed. Kadokawa Shoten.

Valeri, Valerio. 1985. *Kingship and Sacrifice*. Chicago: University of Chicago Press.

van Gennep, Arnold. [1909] 1961. *The Rites of Passage*. Chicago: University of Chicago Press.

Vansina, Jan. 1978. *The Children of Woot: A History of the Kuba Peoples*. Madison: University of Wisconsin Press.

Vlastos, Stephen. 1986. *Peasant Protests and Uprisings in Tokugawa Japan*. Berkeley: University of California Press.

Wakamori Tarō. 1975. *Hana to Nihonjin* (Flowers and the Japanese). Sōgetsu Shuppan.

Warren, Nathan B. 1876. *The Holidays: Christmas, Easter, and Whitsuntide; Together with the May-Day, Midsummer and the Harvest-Home Festivals*. 3rd ed. Troy, NY: H.B. Nims.

Watabe Tadayo. 1989. Nihonjin to Inasaku Bunka (The Japanese and rice culture). *Nikkan Ugama* (103): 81–91.

Watanabe Tamotsu. 1989. *Kabuki*. Shin'yōsha.

Watsuji Tetsurō. 1959. *Rinrigaku* (Ethics). Vol. 1. Iwanami Shoten.

Weber, Max. [1930] 1992. *The Protestant Ethic and the Spirit of Capitalism*. Talcott Parsons, trans. New York: Routledge.

———. 1947. *The Theory of Social and Economic Organization*. New York: Free Press.

Wedeen, Lisa. 1999. *Ambiguities of Domination: Politics, Rhetoric, and Symbols in Contemporary Syria*. Chicago: University of Chicago Press.

Weinberg, Steven. 2009. *Lake Views: This World and the Universe*. Cambridge, MA: Belknap Press of Harvard University Press.

Welch, Colin. 2007. Stamps of the Nazi Era. www.fvdes.com/stamps/naziweb/frame_f.htm. Accessed on Sept. 22, 2007.

Werblowsky, R. J. Zwi. 1985. What's in a Name: Reflections on God, Gods, and the Divine. *Japanese Journal of Religious Studies* 12(1): 3–16.

Wheeler, J. M. 1932. *Paganism in Christian Festivals*. London: Pioneer Press.

White, Stephen. 1988. *The Bolshevik Poster*. New Haven, CT: Yale University Press.

Williams, Brackette F. 1989. A Class Act: Anthropology and the Race to Nation across Ethnic Terrain. *Annual Review of Anthropology* 18: 401–44.

Williams, Raymond. 1973. *The Country and the City*. Oxford: Oxford University Press.

Wilson, Andrew. 2005. *Ukraine's Orange Revolution*. New Haven, CT: Yale University Press.

Wolf, Eric R. 1999. *Envisioning Power*. Berkeley: University of California Press.

Yamada Munemutsu. 1977. *Hana no Bunkashi* (The cultural history of flowers). Yomiuri Shinbunsha.

———. 1982. Ōshigi (Review of the history of the symbolism of cherry blossoms). *Nihon Jishin* (23): 32–38.

Yamada Yoshio. [1941] 1993. *Ōshi* (History of the flowering cherry in Japan). Yamada Tadao, ed. Kōdansha.

Yamagishi Tokuhei, ed. 1958. *Genji Monogatari* (The *Tale of Genji*), vol. 1. Vol. 14 of *Nihon Koten Bungaku Taikei* (Compendium of Japanese classical literary works). Iwanami Shoten.

———. 1962. *Genji Monogatari* (The *Tale of Genji*), vol. 4. Vol. 17 of *Nihon Koten Bungaku Taikei*. Iwanami Shoten.

Yamaguchi, Iwao. 1987. Maintaining Japan's Self-Sufficiency in Rice. *Journal of Trade and Industry* 6(2): 40–42.

Yamaguchi Osamu. 1996. Yūbinkitte (Postal stamps). In *Kokushi Daijiten* (Dictionary of national history), vol. 14: 285. Yoshikawa Kōbunkan.

Yamaguchiken Kyōiku Iinkai Bunkaka (Cultural Section, Kyōiku Iinkai, Yamaguchi Prefecture), ed. 1980. *Suō Sarumawashi Kinkyū Chōsa Hōkokusho* (Report on an urgent investigation of the monkey performances at Suō). Board of Education, Yamaguchi Prefecture.

Yamamoto Kōji. 2002. Joron (Introduction). In *Tennō to Ōken o Kangaeru* (The emperor and his power), pp. 111–34. Vol. 10 of *Ō o Meguru Shisen* (The gaze of the emperor). Amino Yoshihiko et al., eds. Iwanami Shoten.

Yamanaka Hisashi. 1989. *Bokura Shōkokumin to Sensō Ōenka* (We, the little national subjects and songs in support of the war). Asahi Bunko.

Yamaori Tetsuo. 1990a. *Kakureta Tennōrei Keizoku no Dorama: Daijōsai no Bunka Hikaku* (A hidden drama of the succession of the imperial soul: Cross-cultural comparison of the *Daijōsai*). *Gekkan Asahi* (Feb.): 80–85.

———. 1990b. *Shi no Minzokugaku* (Folklore of death). Iwanami Shoten.

Yamazumi Masami. 1970. *Kyōkasho* (School textbooks). Iwanami Shoten.

Yanagita Kunio. [1920] 1982. "Sarumawashi no Hanashi" (About the monkey performance). In *Yanagita Kunio shū* (Collected works of Yanagita Kunio), vol. 27: 336–40. Chikuma Shobō.

———. [1930] 1982. Shidare-zakura no Mondai (About the weeping cherry). In *Yanagita Kunio shū*, vol. 22: 213–19. Chikuma Shobō.

———. [1931] 1982. Shokumotsu no Kojin Jiyū (Personal freedom regarding food). In *Yanagita Kunio shū*, vol. 24: 160–86. Chikuma Shobō.

———. [1940] 1982. Kome no Chikara (The power of rice). In *Yanagita Kunio shū*, vol. 14: 240–58. Chikuma Shobō.

———. [1947] 1982a. Shinanozakura no Hanashi (About the Shinano cherry blossoms). In *Yanagita Kunio shū*, vol. 22: 220–27. Chikuma Shobō.

———. [1947] 1982b. Sannō no saru (The mountain deity and the monkey). In *Yanagita Kunio shū*, vol. 11: 333–40. Chikuma Shobō.

———, ed. 1951. *Minzokugaku Jiten* (Ethnographic dictionary). Tōkyōdō.

————. [1955] 1982. Misaki-Kami Kō (Thoughts on animal deities). In *Yanagita Kunio shū*, vol. 30: 158–68. Chikuma Shobō.

Yasukuni Jinja. 1983, 1984. *Yasukuni Jinja Hyakunenshi* (History of the one hundred years of the Yasukuni Shrine). Vol. 1 (1983), Vol. 3 (1984). Yasukuni Jinja.

Yoshida Chiaki and Hattori Sachio, eds. 1991. *Kabuki Iroha Ezōshi* (Illustrated stories of the kabuki). Kōdansha.

Young, Crawford. 1994. *The African Colonial State in Comparative Perspective*. New Haven, CT: Yale University Press.

————. 2012. *The Postcolonial State in Africa: Fifty Years of Independence, 1960–2010*. Madison: University of Wisconsin Press.

Yui Masaomi, Fujiwara Akira, and Yoshida Yutaka, eds. [1996] 1989. *Guntai Heishi* (Armies and soldiers). *Nihon Kindai Shisō Taikei* (Compendium of modern Japanese thought), vol. 4. Iwanami Shoten.

Ze'ami Motokiyo. 1935a. *Sakuragawa* (Cherry blossom river). In *Kaichū Yōkyoku Zenshū* (Annotated collection of noh texts), vol. 3: 323–40. Nogami Toyoichirō, ed. Chūōkōronsha.

————. 1935b. *Mitsuyama* (Three mountains). In *Kaichū Yōkyoku Zenshū*, vol. 3: 309–22. Nogami Toyoichirō, ed. Chūōkōronsha.

Zimmermann, Otto, and Eugen Osswald. 1935. *Westermanns Groß-Berliner Fibel* (Westermann's primer for greater Berlin). Berlin: G. Westermann.

Index